Open Before Crisis

The Definitive Guide for CPA Firm Cyber Insurance

Joseph E. Brunsman, MSL

&

Capt. (Ret) Daniel W. Hudson, CPCU

Praise for Open Before Crisis

"Open Before Crisis is hands-down the most comprehensive and easy to read guide that every CPA Firm and frankly small business leader should read. The content goes far beyond simply a conversation about cyber insurance and provides both education and guidance to protect you, your staff, your vendors and your clients from the what-if scenario of a cybersecurity attack."

-Byron Patrick, CPA, CITP/CGMA, CCA, MCSE
Director of Presales & Solutions at Botkeeper

"Joe and Dan make what could otherwise be a dry and technical subject engaging, refreshing, and stimulating to read. Books on insurance and cybersecurity policies aren't usually classified as page turners, but once I started this book, I didn't want to put it down. For anyone working in financial services, this book is a must read, and would make a worthy addition to any professional collection."

- Dr. Sean Stein Smith, CPA, CGMA
City University of New York - Lehman College
Visiting Fellow (2019) American Institute for Economic Research

"When dealing with a complex issue like cyber-security you want someone on your team who isn't just knowledgeable, you want someone who is the expert in the area. This book proves why they and their team are not just a resource, but the only resource, to help CPA firms deal with the complex issue of cyber security threats we are faced with today. As a practitioner, you can count on the partner steps listed throughout the book so you have a list of follow up items ready for you and the 12 golden rules at the end are a must read for everyone."

-Garrett Wagner, CPA/CITP
CEO/Founder C3 Evolution Group

Publishing History

Paperback Edition 1 / October, 2019
ISBN: 978-0-578-61289-8

Disclaimer

This book was designed for general insurance guidance and considerations only.

Limit of liability/disclaimer of warranty: The publisher and the authors make no representations or warranties with regard to:
The completeness or accuracy of the contents of this work and specifically disclaim and exclude all warranties, express or implied, including without limitation, warranties of fitness for a particular purpose or usage of trade. No warranty may be created or extended by sales or promotional materials. The advice and strategies contained herein may not be suitable for every situation. This work is sold with the understanding that the publisher and authors are not engaged in rendering legal, accounting, or other professional services. If professional assistance is required or needed, the services of a competent professional should be sought. Neither the publisher nor the authors shall be liable for damages resulting herefrom. The fact that this work refers to an organization or website as a citation and/or a potential source of further information does not mean that the publisher or the authors endorse the information, the organization, the website, or the recommendations each may provide. Readers should be aware that Internet websites and website addresses listed may have changed or been deleted since this work was written. This limitation/disclaimer also specifically excludes any third-party beneficiaries.

Dedications

Without the infinite patience of my loving wife, I never would have been able to write another book. I am forever grateful that you once again held the world together so I could go off and chase my obsession late into the nights. To my two young sons: Years from now, you will find this book – and these words – dusty and buried on a bookshelf. While the contents will long since be obsolete, it is my physical reminder to you both. Do something difficult. Find a worthy obsession which will make your hours feel like minutes. As you toil long into the night, bleary-eyed, frustrated, and alone, do not relent. While common men sleep soundly in their beds content with a day complete, you will join the ranks of those crazy few who, if even just ever so slightly, made this world a slightly more tolerable one for the rest of us.

~ Joseph E. Brunsman – 3:37 a.m., 23 May 2019

I dedicate this book to my U.S. Naval Academy shipmates, to those who have served, to those that continue to serve, and to my wonderful family. Thank you all for your generous support throughout the years.

~ Daniel W. Hudson

We would both like to thank Bill Smart for his wisdom and assistance in helping us bring this book to fruition.

About the Authors

Joseph E. Brunsman

Joe is an avid truth seeker, sought-after keynote speaker, and a best-selling author. He began his life by skipping school and hanging out in the library where he read every technology and science book available. This inevitably led him to military school where he served the remainder of his sentence dodging alien hunters at New Mexico Military Institute (NMMI) in Roswell, New Mexico. Upon graduation, he enlisted in the Navy, serving three years as an Information Services Technician (IT) where he focused on database management, network security, radio communications, and satellite communications.

Upon receiving an appointment to the United States Naval Academy, he majored in Systems Engineering. He won the senior design award for creating a semi-autonomous, beer-launching fridge. That fridge is still used today to lure unsuspecting freshman into taking 20 credit hours a semester for the next three years. As a naval officer, he served as a Surface Warfare Officer where he held positions ranging from Electronic Warfare Officer to Anti-Terrorism Force Protection Officer.

After visiting over 30 countries, he left the service for the greener pastures of insurance life. Within the first eight months on his new job, he became a best-selling author by co-authoring the first book ever published on the topic of insurance for accounting firms. This has been followed up by numerous publications in magazines such as *Journal of Accountancy*, *The CPA Journal*, and *CPA Practice Advisor*.

In 2019, he completed his Master of Science in Law in Cybersecurity Law from the Francis King Carey School of Law. He is the Vice-President and Chief Content Officer of Chesapeake Professional Liability Brokers in Annapolis, MD.

When not being humored by his infinitely patient wife or playing with his two young sons, he can be found furiously researching his latest technology article or doing his best to learn Brazilian Jiu-Jitsu.

Daniel W. Hudson

A United States Naval Academy graduate with an MBA from the University of North Florida, Dan has specialized in insurance solutions for CPA firms for over 25 years. He holds both a Chartered Property Casualty Underwriter (CPCU) and an Associate in Risk Management (ARM) designations.

He is the co-author of a best-selling book on insurance as well as numerous articles in various magazines.

Dan served as a naval flight officer, flying more than 550 missions in the navy submarine hunter, P-3C Orion. He conducted worldwide, anti-submarine, littoral warfare and counter-narcotics operations. He served as the Commanding Officer of Patrol Squadron Six-Four (VP-64), earning the prestigious Battle "E." On his final tour of duty, he served as Deputy Commander of Reserve Patrol Wing, retiring as a captain.

Why We Wrote this Book
...and Why You Should Read It

For the foreseeable future, educated choices regarding cyber insurance will remain mainly with the consumer. This is because, among other reasons, the average insurance agent in the United States is 59 years old.[1] Learning this non-standardized, evolving, and complex line of insurance while in the twilight years of their careers is decidedly unpalatable. Unsurprisingly, a joint survey from the Griffith Insurance Education Foundation and The Institutes found that younger employees consider insurance, "boring," and thus young agents with the requisite technical knowledge are unlikely to be available.

While the promise of large premiums could lure current insurance agents into developing the expertise necessary to knowledgeably advise clients, there also lies another problem. Although cyber insurance is the hot, new product on the market, the premiums are comparatively minor. Globally, the cyber insurance market in 2017 was estimated to be at $4.52 billion and is expected to reach $17 billion by the year 2023.[2] By comparison, the entire United States Insurance market wrote a total of $1.2 trillion in premiums in 2017 alone.[3]

Even if the premiums available for cyber insurance rise as forecasted, the driver behind most insurance agents will continue to remain the commission payable for each policy written. Here too, the numbers will not give rise to experts in cyber insurance. Take, for example, a recent case where the restaurant chain P.F. Chang's cyber insurance policy limits were made public. Although a multi-billion-dollar-per-year business with significant exposure across untold numbers of computers and terminals, their cyber insurance policy premium was approximately $134,000.[4] The average commissions for insurance agents range from roughly 10% to 18% of the total premium. This would result in payday of $13,400 at the low end and $24,000 at the high end.

While this may appear to be a sizeable commission, remember that there are only so many multi-billion-dollar-grossing companies requiring cyber insurance insights. Businesses of that size will most assuredly have in-house general counsel to advise them on their policy choices. Most likely, it will be small- to medium-sized businesses that will lean heavily on their insurance agents to "get it right." For an insurance agent to write a cyber policy for a one-million-dollar-grossing business, the commission can come out to between $150 and $200 per policy.[5] This is not exactly a panacea of potential revenue that would spur the average insurance agent to specialize in cyber insurance. When compared to the hundreds of thousands, or millions, of dollars that a business is legally obligated to pay out following a data breach, there is a decided asymmetric barrier to the importance given to cyber insurance.

Breaches may be increasing in both frequency and severity, but the insurance market has so far responded in a novel way. Foremost, the cyber insurance market is currently "soft." This is insurance industry parlance for a highly competitive market where numerous insurers are all vying to write new policies. This often results in premiums far lower than the limited actuarial data would support. In turn, this can lower the commission an insurance agent is paid even further.

Further exacerbating the downward pressure on cyber insurance premiums is the "actuary's paradox." In all other surveyed lines of insurance, claims reported by the insured generally result in higher premiums when the policy is renewed. In cyber insurance, certain insurers rationalize that following a breach, a business will take the threat more seriously. Thus, they can be classified as a better risk in the future. As a result, a business's premium can be lower <u>after</u> a breach than before.[6] It would be hard to conceive of a sustainable auto insurer who lowered rates after a crash.

The final issue is that the law continues to evolve at a rapid pace. Any hard-won knowledge learned by an insurance broker is easily rendered irrelevant by the swiftly changing legal landscape. For example, in 2018 alone, 37 different states and territories introduced over 256 new bills or resolutions that would affect data security or cybersecurity.[7] Consider that roughly 89% of those who join the insurance industry will quit within 36 months; there is simply not enough time for the average broker to gain any level of competence in this field.[8]

As breach frequency and severity continues to rise, consumers will increasingly demand knowledgeable brokers who are able to assist them in navigating the bewildering world that is cyber insurance. Yet, the general rule within insurance law is that "absent special circumstances that might give rise to a broader duty, the default rule is that agents and brokers have no duty to advise insureds about the adequacy or appropriateness of the insurance coverage they purchase or about optional coverage that might be available."[9]

To add to the ambiguity, in most jurisdictions, the insurance company has no obligation to explain the policy to the firm. As the Supreme Court of California once paradoxically noted, "[w]hen a court is reviewing claims under an insurance policy, it must hold the insured bound by clear and conspicuous provisions in the policy even if evidence suggests that the insured did not read or understand them."[10]

Ergo, it's on you to get it right or risk potential financial ruin and professional damage to your firm.

Why We Wrote this Book

Ultimately, if firms want to maximize their chances of having the correct coverage options and avoid the most common reasons for a declination of coverage, they must first perform their own due diligence. This would include a knowledge of the threats they face, common regulatory schemes they must adhere to – including state and federal laws, and hold a basic understanding of cyber insurance policy specifics.

We wrote this book to help you with that task.

How to Use This Book

Big problems happen when cybersecurity is the responsibility of only one person in an organization. In the modern age, every member of a firm has a responsibility toward cybersecurity.

Staff needs to know what rules they're supposed to follow, <u>and why</u>. HR needs to inform the IT department who needs access to what and when. The IT department needs to coordinate with management and explain why certain projects require funding and how to prioritize those requests. The CIO needs to have buy-in with other stakeholders when approaching the CFO for budget requests. The CEO needs to understand the big picture and balance competing interests. Of course, the partner in charge of purchasing cyber insurance can benefit from this book.

Read the book from front to back. You will be surprised to learn what regulations you may fall under and how cyber insurance will – or will not – respond. Give it to your business partners and other responsible parties. Give it to your friends. Tell them all to read it front to back. Help them avoid preventable and costly mistakes.

All this may seem heretical in the modern age where we are torn from one meeting to the next, and information comes in 30-second segments. When your firm is facing a breach or inquiries from regulators, all those other distractions will seem trivial. Make sure that you are armed with as much knowledge as possible so you can make the best decisions possible.

Best case scenario: You're armed with knowledge you will thankfully never use.

Worst case scenario: You're facing the storm – a very expensive and difficult storm – without a compass.

We wish you the best.

Table of Contents

Table of Cases

Open Before Crisis
The Definitive Guide for CPA Firm Cyber Insurance

Joseph E. Brunsman, MSL

&

Capt. (Ret) Daniel W. Hudson, CPCU

Section 1: Cybersecurity Basics

Before a firm contemplates cyber insurance, it is helpful to understand their common adversaries, attack vectors, and types of malware. Beyond merely demonstrating that every firm is at risk, such knowledge will later assist the firm in purchasing the most suitable cyber insurance coverage.

Firm Adversaries

Cyber-criminals

These actors may have no personal vendetta against your firm. Their payoff comes from having ransomware injected in your firm or stealing your client's personal information, often to file fraudulent returns. It's not personal; it's business. According to a recent report by *Krebs on Security*, stolen W-2 tax forms are going for between $4 and $20 per record depending on the total wages of the affected person. Considering that even small accounting firms could have upwards of a thousand W-2's on file. That represents a payday that may eclipse what a hacker would earn in years of legitimate work in their home country – all in one single day.[11]

Employees

This is the most difficult threat to counter as they already have access to your firm. Often, employees can damage your network or release information by accident. Occasionally, they will abscond with sensitive information for blackmail purposes or purposefully cripple your network for revenge. In one case, a staff member publicly posted a high-profile client's tax information to the Internet for political purposes. That firm was acquired within a week.

Foreign States

This may seem a strange addition in that your firm is unlikely to be directly targeted by a foreign state. But, as was shown with the NotPetya virus, collateral damage is certainly a possibility. The virus was allegedly created by the Russian government to cripple Ukrainian networks. However, the virus quickly spread beyond the boundaries of Ukraine and caused an estimated $10 Billion in damages worldwide. A British manufacturer, a French construction company, and Danish shipping company were the most high-profile victims of its collateral damage.[12]

Random Attackers

This category can include random adolescents and bored adults just looking for a kick. While their motivation to specifically target your firm is questionable. These groups often unleash malicious code purely for wreaking widespread havoc. Never underestimate the power of a low-skilled but highly motivated person to cause a disproportionate amount of damage.

Hacktivists

This classification of hacker has an ax to grind. Their motivations can be political, personal, religious, purely for spite, and more. Their methods of attack can range from malware to physical intrusions. Hacktivist groups can prove to be a particularly challenging adversary due to their structure. Anonymous, a particularly well-known hacktivist group, has no structure, no governing body, and no formal membership.[13] Their targets have included the Church of Scientology, the Epilepsy Foundation of America, and Sarah Palin's personal email address[14].

Corporate/Industrial Espionage

In a hypercompetitive marketplace, never underestimate unscrupulous competitors. A quick Internet search can provide numerous stories of competitors seeking every conceivable means to learn confidential information.

Attack Vectors

There is no end to the cryptically named threats facing firms across the country. It is important to understand how those threats are generally deployed. By understanding the most common threat vectors, a business can consciously do their best to oversee the defenses against them.

Advanced Persistent Threat

This is perhaps the most dangerous threat your firm could face. A hacker is specifically targeting your firm, and they will stop at nothing. While this type of attack is often perpetrated by large groups or foreign states due to the time requirement, smaller groups and individuals can also be included. Due to the constant threat and varied techniques employed within these attacks, your firm is likely to fail in its defense at some point.

Phishing Attacks

Depending on the type, these attacks can also be referred to as "deceptive phishing," "spear phishing," and "whaling." Regardless of the name, they all boil down to a common element of social engineering. The essence of social engineering is that a hacker will attempt to deceive a person into believing that they are someone else – typically, a senior member in the firm or a client. The objective is either to steal credentials or have funds transferred to the criminal's fraudulent bank account.

Brute Force Attacks

These attacks lack sophistication and subtlety. It is all about raw computing power. Often, these attacks attempt to guess every possible permutation of a password until the hacker gains access to your system. Depending on the length and sophistication of your password requirements, this type of attack could be impossible or relatively easy. According to *BetterBuys*, a seven-character password such as, "abcdefg" would take roughly 0.29 milliseconds to crack with a brute force attack. By comparison, a 12-character password would take approximately 200 years.[15]

Cryptojacking

While a relatively new type of attack, its effects should not be understated. Cryptojacking occurs when a firm has had their computer systems or website accessed by a third party to mine for digital currency. This can not only result in additional utility costs but may also create unstable computer systems due to the large diversion of their computer resources to assist in perpetrating the crime, further hindering workers from accomplishing their daily tasks.

Firms should be aware that the prevalence of these intrusions fluctuates in tandem with the costs of various cryptocurrencies. In addition, large businesses are much more likely to be targeted for such schemes because of their concentrated computing power.[16]

Man-in-the-Middle Attacks

These types of attacks can come in two forms. The first involves being physically close to the target. In this type of attack, the hackers gain access via an improperly secured router. Once inside the victim's network, they can deploy numerous types of tools to act as an in-between for transmitted information such as banking information and log-in credentials.[17]

The second type of man-in-the-middle attack involves the use of malicious code inserted into a business' computer system via infected webpages or email attachments. Utilizing malware such as a keylogger, the hacker can then have log-in credentials and other sensitive data sent back to them at regular intervals.[18]

Push Payment Fraud Schemes

This particularly insidious fraud attempts to manipulate customers of the firm into making payments to fraudsters by impersonating the firm. Often, this is done with real-time payment methods, or by setting up fake websites that purport to be made by the firm.

Zero-Day Exploits

As the name suggests, these are vulnerabilities that are unknown to the security world until they are used on a broad scale. The ultimate danger of these attacks is that security experts have not yet created a defense to counter the threat. In other words, neither your IT professional nor any other IT professionals in the world is likely to stop this type of threat. Your best defense is your incident response plan.

It should be noted by firms that many of these threats rely on mass scanning of IP addresses. Attacks against a business can be indiscriminate and originate anywhere across the globe with little to no recourse from law enforcement or legal entities. For any firm with a connection to the Internet, there can be no belief in absolute security. A globally connected world equates to globally connected risks.

Forms of Malware

Firms will often see the following types of malware being discussed but rarely defined. As firms attempt to make a reasonable effort towards their cybersecurity, they should have a passing understanding of the most common types of malware and how they propagate themselves.

Viruses

Earning this moniker for their ability to infect other computers, viruses require human input to be spread. Their presence can often be unknown by the user. Common avenues of transmission include infected email files and USB drives.

Worms

Unlike viruses, worms do not require human input to be transmitted. Once a worm infects a computer, they use the host computer's resources to spread to other computers across the network or even the Internet. What makes this malware so dangerous is its ability to replicate without user intervention.

Famously the "Iloveyou" worm attacked and infected millions of computers across the world in a single day. After opening the email attachment, the worm would overwrite random file types and then send a copy of itself to every contact in the user's Microsoft Outlook file. This resulted in an estimated one out of every ten computers in the world being infected and resulted in upwards of $15 billion in damages.[19]

Trojans

In reference to Greek history, trojans mislead users of their actual intent. Often this is accomplished with an email attachment such as a spreadsheet or by clicking on fake advertisements. Once executed, a trojan can be used by the cybercriminal to access the user's personal information such as passwords, banking credentials, and personal information.

Ransomware

Ransomware is a sub-category of trojan that has crippled hospitals, businesses, and, most famously, the government of the city of Atlanta, Georgia in 2018.[20] It operates by encrypting files and then demanding a ransom, often in bitcoin. Initially this type of malware contained flaws that would allow specialists to find methods to break the process and recover files. As the economic windfall has beset the ransomware programmers, their incentive to create ever more effective software has increased. While traditionally the ransomware would begin immediately infecting files, reports now suggest that the ransomware is infecting backups and using higher levels of encryption to force a payment by the infected firm.

Often the most successful response to a ransomware event involves the utilization of unencrypted backups. This is one reason that firms should take a serious look at the periodicity, security, and breadth of their backup information.

Fileless

This especially pernicious form of malware does not actually contain any malicious code that requires installation on a firm's computer. All it takes is the username and password of one computer for a hacker to effectively infect the entire network. The methods used by fileless attacks utilize pre-existing operating system tools, which, in turn, pits the computer against itself. This means that detection is incredibly difficult if not impossible for even the most skilled cybersecurity personnel and most security programs. Currently, the best counter to this type of threat is a behavioral detection system.

Common avenues for such an attack can utilize PowerShell and Windows Management Instrumentation (WMI). These tools are already installed on every Windows OS computer and are frequently, and legitimately used by the firm's IT professionals for daily tasks. Though a firm could outright ban the use of PowerShell and WMI, this would render the network effectively useless as Microsoft has made these tools essential to the use of many of its products.[21]

Spyware

Though not as immediately damaging as the other forms of malware, spyware earned its name due to the ability for one person to spy on another. Some businesses are now legitimately using spyware to monitor the engagement of their employees while on the clock.

One form of spyware particularly damaging to a firm is known as a "keylogger." Often accounting firms will enter a full social security number into their tax software, which in turn redacts all but the last four numbers. Keyloggers function by logging every keystroke and often take screenshots whenever a new program is opened. In turn, this information is routinely sent back to the hacker for inspection. In such a case, an unassuming accountant would be providing not only every social security number to a hacker, but also the username and password to their tax software.

Bots

Legitimate bots are used to automatically execute specific operations. A legal example would be starting up your Internet browser every time you open your computer. Hackers naturally value this type of power and can use a bot to execute commands with no direct knowledge by the user. These bots can be used to steal sensitive data, spy on the user, or create a veritable army of computers that can be used to attack other networks via a distributed denial of service (DDoS) attack.

Rootkits

A rootkit is a program which allows remote access of a computer by a third party. Legal rootkits are frequently used by IT professionals to remotely access staff computers to assess problems or install updates. Naturally, this same remote access is prized by cybercriminals who can use this access either directly steal data or install various other forms of malware.

Bricking

Bricking occurs when a piece of hardware is rendered unusable by re-writing or overwriting the firmware of the device. In effect, this makes the device inaccessible at the most fundamental levels as the malware survives a wipe of the system and a reboot.

This term was coined with the idea that it turns the hardware into nothing more than a "brick" because it is no longer useful for any other purpose. This may be done to cover the tracks of the hacker from forensics experts.

Recently, this attack was seen in late 2018 when malware known as "VPNFilter" infected numerous routers. Not only did the malware spy on the traffic being sent through the router, but it could "brick" the device in question with a remote signal from the hacker. [22] If a firm were to be subject to such an attack, it could not only compromise data including usernames, passwords, and personal information, but it could effectively destroy the device by rendering it totally inoperable.

Partner Action Items:

- ☐ Become familiar with the adversaries, attack vectors, and delivery systems that could be used to infiltrate your firm's security system;
- ☐ Discuss with your IT professionals how they are countering such threats and if additional investment is needed;

<u>Types of Defense (Controls)</u>

For partners overseeing cybersecurity at their firm or for those
determining the budget, it is crucial that they have a basic
understanding of the most common cybersecurity defenses available.
These defenses are generally referred to as "controls" and can be
divided or combined into numerous product offerings.

Whether a firm requires any, all, or more than those listed below
will depend on the cybersecurity framework of the firm and various
regulatory requirements. In addition, each control listed below can
further be segmented into different types. For the sake of brevity, and
your sanity, they will be described in a general fashion.

- **Anti-virus and anti-malware software**: This type of
software is what will most commonly be installed on every
firm's computer. In short, it attempts to detect and remove
offending software. As threats have increased, these types of
software have evolved to protect from viruses, worms,
rootkits, keyloggers, trojans, adware, and other common
exploits.[23]

- **Backups**: These take the information you have on your
system and create a redundant copy in another location.
There are various methods that can be used to accomplish
this task including full, incremental, differential, and
mirrored backups. No matter what method is used, firms
should also be aware of the periodicity, i.e. the frequency, at
which backups are being performed. Anything less than daily
backups is likely insufficient.

- **User Permission Segmentation**: This limits the access that
any one person has to those functions required by their job.
Usually, this is accomplished after a successful user-
entitlement audit. This can assist in compliance with various

regulatory requirements as well as potentially limit how far a
malicious virus can immediately spread within a system.

- **Data Loss Prevention (DLP) software**: DLPs are used to
  detect potential breaches by monitoring covered data. It can
  then flag unauthorized use of that data or unauthorized traffic
  which contains that data. This is particularly important for
  entities which hold personally identifiable
  information/personal health information/payment card
  information (PII/PHI/PCI) as a DLP can be configured to
  identify this information.

- **Firewalls**: Broadly speaking, firewalls protect the firm's
  internal network from the Internet at large. This is generally
  done by inspecting information coming from or going to the
  firm's network using a defined set of security rules. Firewalls
  can be software, hardware, or both.

- **Intrusion Detection Systems (IDSs)**: The primary goal of an
  IDS is to provide an automated inspection of logs and events
  for intrusions or system failures. In turn, the IDS alerts
  personnel that an event may be occurring so a timely
  response can begin.[24]

- **Intrusion Prevention Systems (ISPs)**: An ISP is much like
  the aforementioned IDS but attempts to proactively prevent
  or halt intrusions. Due to their similarity, ISPs and IDSs will
  often be combined and referred to as an Intrusion Detection
  and Prevention System (IDPS). [25]

- **Security Information and Event Management Systems
  (SIEMS)**: SIEMS are software that combine Security
  Information Management (SIM) and Security Event
  Management (SEM). The goal of this control is to provide
  real-time analysis of events currently happening on a system.

They will contain alarms that are triggered either automatically or through configured inputs.[26]

- **Employee Training**: While not particularly high-tech, employee training can come in many different forms. These range from informal talks at company-wide meetings to tracked computer-based training and fake phishing emails. This control is crucial as humans are often the weakest link in any security plan.

- **Multi-Factor Authentication (MFA)**: This type of control attempts to utilize multiple factors to authenticate a user. To be useful, they must generally include something a user knows with something the user has. For example, a user knows a username and password and has their cellphone to authenticate the login request. If a user is required to input a username, password, and PIN, this all constitutes what a user knows and does not include what a user has. Therefore, this last example would not be considered MFA. [27]

- **Encryption**: The purpose of this control is to secure electronic data by rendering it unusable/unreadable to an unauthorized third party. Firms can elect to perform encryption at various architectural levels of their system and use different types of encryption.

- **Vulnerability Scanning**: By automatically scanning and probing networks, systems, and applications, third parties attempt to find flaws in security.[28]

- **Penetration Testing**: This is typically a much more involved process than vulnerability scanning as it attempts to exploit the system being assessed. [29]

- **Physical Penetration Testing**: One of the most overlooked security features; this control attempts limit the access that an unauthorized third party would have to data. This can include a vendor attempting to overcome common security features such as locks, biometrics, card readers, and physical barriers.

From the above, it should be understood that there is no one control that will guarantee a breach-free firm. Ideally, firms will employ a "defense-in-depth" strategy that encompasses multiple controls that complement and overlap each other. In turn, layers of defense should be employed so that if one control fails, ideally, the next control layer would identify the threat and respond accordingly. Depending on the insurer, the implementation of these controls should lower the firm's cyber insurance premium. In some cases, such controls may be required before insurers offer terms for cyber insurance.

Partner Action Items:

- ☐ Read NIST SP 800-12, Rev. 1, *An Introduction to Information Security*. It can be found for free at: https://nvlpubs.nist.gov/nistpubs/SpecialPublications/NIST.SP.800-12r1.pdf;
- ☐ Discuss with your IT professionals what controls they have implemented, and if those controls are sufficient for the security the firm requires;
- ☐ Determine if additional investment is needed;
- ☐ Determine if there are any preventable holes in your firm's defense-in-depth strategy. Compare to the firm's cybersecurity framework;
- ☐ Utilize this information when constructing/reviewing your firm's incident response plan.

Section 2: State-Level Requirements

Firms must have a grasp on the various state-level requirements that apply to them before and after a breach. Failing to grasp these fundamentals can result in a material misrepresentation on their insurance application leading to a potential declination of coverage or missing crucial time requirements that can lead to unnecessary fines. In addition, knowledge of these laws can impact the security practices and internal controls of protected information. In other words, you have to know what to protect before you can protect it appropriately.

<u>State Breach Notification Laws</u>

As recently as 2013, the Government Accounting Office (GAO) issued a report that recommended, with concurrence from the Department of Commerce (DOC) and the Federal Trade Commission (FTC), for Congress to develop a consumer privacy framework to increase privacy protections and thereby increase security requirements for all businesses.[30] While there have been numerous attempts to create a federal level breach notification standard, all have failed. As recently as February 2018, two House representatives circulated a draft of the Data Acquisition and Technology Accountability and Security Act. This act was intended to set federal-level requirements on breach notification requirements and data privacy.[31]

In response, 32 state attorneys general wrote a joint letter to the House strongly objecting to this proposal. Although the points of contentions were numerous, their main objections are listed below:

- A federal law would eliminate the state's enforcement actions against consumer reporting agencies and financial institutions.
- Such a law would eliminate all state-level data security and breach notification laws.
- The Act would allow entities who suffered a breach to notify consumers, "on their own judgment," which was deemed to result in a lack of transparency.
- The law appeared to be concerned with addressing large, national-level breaches of major corporations at the expense of more frequent but smaller breaches experienced by local or state-wide businesses.[32]

Even if most of the listed issues could be addressed at the federal level to the satisfaction of most states – a difficult proposition at best – there remains the Constitutional issue of preemption. Per the Supremacy Clause in Article VI of the Constitution, federal law will always prevail over state law.[33]

Therefore, if a federal law is passed, any state law addressing the same issue would become unenforceable. No matter how the proposed federal-level legislation is worded, there will be states which want more protection, and those that will want less. No matter how the statutory language is parsed, the possibility of federal-level breach law remains unlikely for the foreseeable future.

Firms must look to the state-level requirements, but this too provides its own issues. It would be common sense to assume that a firm would only need to adhere to the breach notification laws which are enacted by the state in which their firm legally resides. As a common point of confusion among firm owners, it is worth the time to understand the mechanics of breach notification law adherence.

To illustrate the point, consider a large firm whose sole office is in Washington, D.C. attempting to navigate its legal requirements following a breach. Conceivably, they would have clients who are residents of Maryland, D.C., and Virginia at a minimum. Which of the following breach notification laws will guide their breach process?

The applicable Maryland Law considers a covered entity, "[A] business* that owns or licenses computerized data that includes personal information of an individual residing in the State[.]"[34]

Under the D.C. law, a covered entity is, "Any person or entity who conducts business in the District of Columbia, and who, in the course of such business, owns or licenses computerized or other electronic data that includes personal information."[35]

Per Virginia's breach law, a covered entity is, "[A]n individual or entity that owns or licenses computerized data that includes personal information."[36]

To further emphasize how complex breach notification can become, consider the timing of notifications. Maryland requires notice, "as soon as reasonably practicable."[37] D.C. requires, "notification...made in the most expedient time possible and without unreasonable delay."[38] Virginia more simply requires notification, "without unreasonable delay."[39]

So, which state's law should be adhered to, and which residents should receive priority in notification?

Primarily, the answer depends on where the client, not the firm, resides.[40] In instances where state laws are ambiguous or conflicting, such as with dual residency in New York, it will often be up to legal counsel to advise the breached firm on what they deem as the best course of action. For nationwide firms with multiple offices across multiple states, the patchwork of state notification laws serves to further complicate the process. National firms could conceivably be required to comply with 50 different breach notification laws following an unauthorized intrusion of their computer system.

Thus, the discussions in this book will include various state's breach notification laws for the following reasons:

- Breach law requirements vary depending on the residency status of the firm's client requiring notification;
- Each state has a nuanced take on their law which is contrasted against other states for illustrative purposes;
- This book is intended to be used by firms of differing sizes in different geographical locations. Each firm will have vastly different levels of expertise, areas of practice, and access to legal knowledge;

- The laws controlling cybersecurity and breach responses change rapidly and frequently. Thus, an overreliance on one state's laws could otherwise render this book obsolete in a matter of months.

Firms should strongly consider an on-going relationship with legal counsel familiar with privacy and cybersecurity law to keep up to date with any changes that could affect them.

Protected Information

For any business to adequately understand their need for cyber insurance, they must first understand how the various states and territories – not to discount any federal and international regulatory requirements – define what information they must protect from unnecessary disclosure. Unfortunately, these definitions, and indeed the entirety of the statutes which encompass them, are being continuously and independently changed by the requisite judicial bodies. Therefore, it would be prudent for every business to continuously monitor the laws which they are subjected to with competent legal counsel.

For illustrative purposes, these definitions can be broken down into three categories: 1) Personally Identifiable Information, 2) Protected Health Information, and, 3) Ancillary Information. As this book continues, it will use the term "covered data" or, "protected information" interchangeably as a broad term to describes all three categories.

Personally Identifiable Information (PII)

Each state and territory breach notification law contain its own distinct definition of PII.

For example, California contains the following: "(1) An individual's first name or first initial and last name in combination with any one or more of the following data elements…:

1. Social Security number,
2. Driver's license number or [State] identification card number,
3. Account number or credit or debit card number, in combination with any required security code, access code, or password that would permit access to an individual's financial account."[41]

By comparison, North Carolina identifies Personal Information as meaning a "person's first name or first initial and last name in combination with any of the following information:

1. Social security or employer taxpayer identification numbers.
2. Driver's license, state identification card, or passport numbers.
3. Checking account numbers.
4. Savings account numbers.
5. Credit card numbers.
6. Debit card numbers.
7. Personal Identification (PIN) Code:
   a) as defined in G.S. 14-113.8(6), or;
   b) a user name or email address, in combination with a password or security question and answer that would permit access to an online account. (§1798.82(h))

Protected Health Information

Certain firms may also be exposed to Protected Health Information through the course of their services; thus, they should be aware that certain states consider PHI to be data covered under their breach statutes, even if the firm is not subject to HIPPA/HITECH.

Per Arkansas, their definition of covered medical data is "(D) Medical Information. * Medical information is defined as "any individually identifiable information, in electronic or physical form, regarding the individual's medical history or medical treatment or diagnosis by a health care professional." (§4-110-103(5))

Other states and territories which include health information as covered data include Alabama, Arizona, California, Colorado, Delaware, Florida, Illinois, Missouri, Montana, Nevada, New Hampshire, North Dakota, Rhode Island, Virginia, Wyoming, and Puerto Rico.[42]

Ancillary Covered Information

As noted before, each state and territory have its own unique definitions as they pertain to data covered under their breach notification law.

Returning to North Carolina's law, they also include the following elements as "personal information":

8. Digital signatures;
9. Any other numbers or information that can be used to access a person's financial resources;
10. Biometric data;
11. Fingerprints;
12. Passwords.[43]

While the probability of any firm storing this information is situationally dependent, it does point toward the need of firms to investigate applicable breach notification laws and monitor any changes therein. As technology is employed at the firm, and service areas changes, firms must pay close attention to how the dynamic landscape of breach notification law definitions will change their risk profile. This risk profile will directly impact the cyber insurance policy features and limits that a firm will require.

Partner Action Items:

☐ Understand which breach notification laws your firm must follow in the event of a breach;

☐ Take an inventory of what information your firm is collecting;

☐ Continuously monitor applicable breach notification laws for any changes;

☐ Check that your firm is adequately protecting all covered data appropriately;

☐ Communicate this data to relevant stakeholders including IT
    and staff;
☐ Update the firm's incident response plan as necessary;
☐ Determine if the firm's cyber insurance policy covers the
    unauthorized disclosure of protected information as defined
    by applicable breach notification laws.

Exempted Information

Not every piece of information requires protection, nor does every breach require notification. Most states and territories contain an exemption to data named under their law. While these definitions tend to be vaguer than those requiring protection, they all follow the same general trend. Information that is publicly available is exempt.

For example, Oklahoma is quite brief in its exception. Personal Information "does not include information that is lawfully obtained from publicly available information, or from federal, state, or local government records lawfully made available to the general public."[44]

Ohio is more detailed in their exemption, stating: Personal information "does not include "publicly available information that is lawfully made available to the general public from federal, state, or local government records, or any of the following media that are widely distributed:

i.   Any news, editorial, or advertising statement published in any bona fide newspaper, journal, or magazine, or broadcast over radio or television;

ii. Any gathering or furnishing of information or news by any bona fide reporter, correspondent, or news bureau to news media described in division (A)(7)(b)(i) of this section;

iii. Any publication designed for and distributed to members of any bona fide association or charitable or fraternal nonprofit corporation;

iv. Any type of media similar in nature to any item, entity, or activity identified in [this section]."[45]

Businesses should take note of what information is not considered covered data. Such considerations will have direct impact on their business activities, network architecture, and cybersecurity controls.

Partner Action Items:

- ☐ Understand what information is *not* mandated to be protected by applicable breach notification laws;
- ☐ Monitor those applicable states' breach notification laws for any changes;
- ☐ Communicate this data to relevant stakeholders including IT and staff;
- ☐ Update the firm's incident response plan as necessary;
- ☐ Certain circumstances may warrant or require notification for the disclosure of exempted information. Determine if the firm's cyber policy covers voluntary notification.

The Definition of a Breach

Unsurprisingly, most states generally consider a breach to be the unauthorized acquisition of defined, covered data by a third party. However, there are differences which firms should take notice of as this will have a direct impact on their internal business practices and cyber insurance needs.

Vermont, for example, defines a security breach as, "unauthorized acquisition of **electronic data** or a reasonable belief of an unauthorized acquisition of electronic data that compromises the security, confidentiality, or integrity of a consumer's personally identifiable information maintained by the data collector."[46]

Ergo, if a completed tax return, with an unredacted social security number for a Vermont resident was stolen from the desk of a staff member, such an action would not necessarily trigger the need for a breach notification.

Firms should also note which states place requirements on both digital and paper records. They are Alaska, Hawaii, Indiana, Iowa, Massachusetts, North Carolina, Washington State, and Wisconsin, at the time of publication.[47] Whether or not this requirement is implicit or implied depends upon the state's specific statute.

For example, North Carolina defines a covered entity within their statute as, "Any business that owns or licenses personal information of residents of North Carolina or any business that conducts business in North Carolina that owns or licenses personal information in any form (**whether computerized, paper, or otherwise**) …"[48]

In contrast, the Washington State does not specifically mention paper records, but rather implies such a standard by defining a breach as the "unauthorized acquisition of data that compromises the security, confidentiality, or integrity of personal information maintained by the person or business."[49]

The question then arises, how should accounting firms deal with paper documents containing personal information? Actions brought by the FTC regarding paper documents provide useful instruction.

In the Matter of CVS Caremark Corporation, C-2459 (2009), the FTC brought action against CVS, a nationwide pharmacy chain. The FTC began its investigation after news reports alleged that CVS pharmacies were throwing away customer information which included social security numbers, credit card numbers, driver's license numbers, and personal health data.[50]

According to the complaint, CVS failed to:

- Implement reasonable disposal procedures for personal information;
- Adequately train their employees;
- Use measures which would reasonably assess in-store compliance with CVS's own disposal procedures;
- Employ a process to discover and correct risks associated with the personal information of its customers.[51]

CVS Caremark ultimately agreed to a settlement order. That settlement required CVS to establish an information security plan to protect the sensitive information of consumers and employees. Every two years, for the next 20 years, CVS is required to receive an audit showing compliance with applicable security measures. Additionally, CVS is required to maintain "standard record-keeping and reporting provisions to allow the FTC to monitor compliance."[52]

From this case, firms should understand that data security extends beyond the keyboard and into the physical realm. Regardless of each state's unique breach definition, every piece of information containing sensitive client data should be treated with reasonable care to avoid inadvertent disclosure. Furthermore, data security procedures involving physical records should be routinely assessed and updated as necessary.

Partner Action Items:

- ☐ Understand if the firm is required to provide breach notification for paper documents as well as for digital documents per applicable breach notification law definitions;
- ☐ Determine if the firm's cyber insurance policy would respond to the loss of paper documents;
- ☐ Communicate this data to relevant stakeholders including IT and staff;
- ☐ Implement continued training on the proper storage and disposal procedures of paper and digital documents;
- ☐ Consider implementing an "absent desk – clean desk" policy;
- ☐ Communicate this data to relevant stakeholders including IT and staff;
- ☐ Update the firm's incident response plan and document retention policy, as necessary.

Exceptions

Most states have included a provision in their breach notification laws which excludes the "good faith" acquisition of covered information if that information is being used by an employee of the firm for legitimate purposes.

For example, New York includes the following exception: "Good-faith acquisition of personal information by an employee or agent of the business for the purposes of the business is not a breach of the security of the system, provided that the private information is not used or subject to unauthorized disclosure."[53]

These types of breach notification exclusions provide safety for a firm if an employee, in good faith, accesses the wrong file while searching for other material. For example, a staff member is searching the file folders for a previous year's tax return and opens the wrong, "Smith" file. Immediately, they realize that this is the wrong Smith, and they continue with their search – no harm, no foul. No notification or investigation is likely required.

Further exceptions to investigation and notifications occur with many state's statutes containing a risk of harm analysis. Such analysis may be implied, as in the case of New York's law, or specifically stated.

New Jersey contains such a stated provision: "Disclosure of a breach of security to a customer shall not be required under this section if the business or public entity establishes that misuse of the information is not reasonably possible."[54] While they are not specific on how a business can reasonably come to this conclusion, it is advisable that firms consult legal counsel and, at a minimum, document the event for future reference.

Certain states such as Florida have a more strict interpretation by stating a "notice to the affected individuals is not required if, after an appropriate investigation and consultation with relevant federal, state, or local law enforcement agencies, the covered entity reasonably determines that the breach has not and will not likely result in identity theft or any other financial harm to the individuals whose personal information has been accessed."[55]

Further, there must be written documentation and preservation of the actions taken by the firm in regard to this analysis. "Such a determination must be documented in writing and maintained for at least 5 years. The covered entity shall provide the written determination to the department within 30 days after the determination."[56]

A common accounting firm example would be a tax organizer sent to the wrong address of a Florida resident. While the organizer may include full socials and other sensitive information, the receiving entity noticed that the name on the envelope was incorrect and has not opened the packet. The receiving entity immediately notified the firm and returned the packet. In this instance, a firm could reasonably argue that because the third party had access to another's social security number, there is no risk of harm because the packet was not opened, and it was returned.

Partner Action Items:

- ☐ Understand if good faith acquisition is exempted in the applicable breach notification laws;
- ☐ Understand if a risk of harm analysis is allowed in applicable breach notification laws;
- ☐ Communicate this data to relevant stakeholders including IT and staff;
- ☐ Consider a review and update of the firm's computer use policy and user permission segmentations;
- ☐ Update the firm's incident response plan as necessary.

Data Encryption Safe Harbors

There is further guidance for firms within most state breach notification laws that are attempting to make a reasonable attempt at cybersecurity. As of publication, all states have adopted definitions which exempt encrypted data from requiring notification. Often this is found within the definition of a breach.

For example, South Carolina defines a breach as the "unauthorized access to and acquisition of computerized data **that was not rendered unusable through encryption, redaction, or other methods** that compromises the security, confidentiality, or integrity of personal identifying information maintained by the person, when illegal use of the information has occurred or is reasonably likely to occur or use of the information creates a material risk of harm to a resident."[57]

If a firm was to lose an encrypted laptop containing the social security numbers of only South Carolina residents, such as loss would not classify as a breach and would not require notification.

It should be noted that Tennessee is currently the sole state with a minor exception to the encryption safe harbor. Tennessee defines a breach as the acquisition of either unencrypted data or where encrypted data is acquired along with the encryption key.[58]

Outside of being a security best-practice and a possible mitigating factor in both legal responsibilities and risk, encryption safe harbors should give firms ample incentive to encrypt data both at rest and in transit. Whether or not a firm utilizes encryption depends on a host of factors including network architecture, firm structure, access to knowledgeable IT professionals, budgetary constraints, and sophistication of oversight within the firm. Regardless, encryption is an avenue best explored by firms of all sizes.

Partner Action Items:

- ☐ Understand if the applicable breach notification laws allow for encryption safe harbors;
- ☐ Communicate this data to relevant stakeholders including IT and staff;
- ☐ Consider implementing appropriate encryption for all computer assets, with a special emphasis on portable electronic devices;
- ☐ View Special Publication (NIST SP) 800-111, Guide to Storage Encryption Technologies for End User Devices for additional information on encryption;
- ☐ Update the firm's incident response plan as necessary.

Service Provider Requirements

Firms of all sizes now have some element of hosted data, colloquially known as "being in the cloud." Many small- and mid-sized firms may be entirely cloud-based. Large firms may still have servers in-house manned by full time IT staff, or a hybrid system which utilizes both a local server and a cloud provider. Regardless of size, nearly every business is at least utilizing cloud-based tax preparations software or transmits locally hosted data through their tax software provider.

Often, firms believe that because a service provider hosts the data, the hosting party will be responsible should a breach occur. However, this is not necessarily the case.

Michigan's breach notification law provides a common example of how limited the obligations of the service provider can be. A "person or agency that maintains a database that includes data that the person or agency does not own or license that discovers a breach of the security of the database shall provide a notice to the owner or licensor of the information of the security breach."[59]

Note that *nowhere* in the statute's wording does it mention that the provider is legally responsible for the data. Merely, it requires the provider to give notice to the firm. While such a revelation is not financially palatable to most firms, it does make sense from an insurance risk perspective. Should a breach occur at a major cloud provider, the cost of notification could be catastrophic and centralized to a relatively minor number of insurers. By minimizing the legal culpability of providers as it pertains to breaches, legislators have distributed the risk to exponentially more insurers and businesses.

Whether any one provider is contractually obligated to assist in notification or cover associated costs is beyond the scope of this book. However, it should be noted that having reviewed the contracts of over a dozen cloud providers, every contract contained a strict "hold harmless" clause for a breach in favor of the provider. While large firms may have the power to negotiate this limit of liability, small- to mid-sized firms will likely have to take such contracts as they are presented.

Partner Action Items:

- ☐ Understand how applicable breach notification laws generally view service provider requirements;
- ☐ Reference the firm's own contracts with service providers to view any indemnification clauses or "hold harmless" provisions. Consider having these contracts reviewed by a privacy attorney;
- ☐ Determine if/how your cyber policy will respond to a breach at a service provider;
- ☐ Reference the firm's cyber insurance application to determine if the insurer requested information on vendors indemnifying the firm for losses following a breach;
- ☐ Speak with your service providers to understand their view of liability;
- ☐ Communicate this data to relevant stakeholders including IT and staff;
- ☐ Update the firm's incident response plan as necessary.

Notice Requirements

Inevitably, all firms will face a breach at some point necessitating notices to clients. The content of these breach notice requirements is controlled by the states and vary greatly depending on the residency status of the client in question. There are, however, several shared elements that require understanding by you firm's leadership.

Credit Reporting Agency Notification

Many states have varying requirements to notify credit bureau agencies following a breach.

Certain states, such as Nebraska, have no apparent requirement to notify the credit reporting agencies of the breach of a consumer's personal data.[60] So, the onus would be on the consumer to notify the credit reporting agencies at their own discretion.

The states which do require notification of a breach to the credit reporting agency generally have a threshold on the number of consumers breached before reporting is required.

For example, Minnesota appears to have one of the lowest numbered thresholds at 500 consumers. Stating: "If a person discovers circumstances requiring notification under this section and section 13.055, subdivision 6, **of more than 500 persons at one time**, the person shall also notify, **within 48 hours**, **all consumer reporting agencies** that compile and maintain files on consumers on a nationwide basis, as defined by United States Code, title 15, section 1681a, of the timing, distribution, and content of the notices."[61]

Note that the 48-hour reporting time is particularly onerous and would likely require detailed levels of coordination at the breached firm. Most likely, this would be accomplished with a well-documented and thoroughly rehearsed incident response plan.

Other states, such as Texas, require higher levels of the number of customer's affected by a breach before notification is required and a much laxer requirement to timing. "If a person is required by this section to notify at one time **more than 10,000 persons** of a breach of system security, the person shall also **notify each consumer reporting agency**, as defined by 15 U.S.C. Section 1681a, that maintains files on consumers on a nationwide basis, of the timing, distribution, and content of the notices. The person shall provide the notice required by this subsection **without unreasonable delay**."[62]

Firms should note that the timing requirement can vary drastically by state. As a precautionary measure, firms should be ready to adhere to the strictest notification requirement found among all the various breach notification laws to which they must adhere. Having this information readily available in the firm's incident response plan can aid greatly in this endeavor and avoid additional regulatory inquiries.

Partner Action Items:

☐ Understand how applicable breach notification laws mandate threshold and timing requirements to credit reporting agencies;

☐ Communicate this data to relevant stakeholders including IT and staff;

☐ Update the firm's incident response plan as necessary;

☐ Review the firm's insurance policies, including cyber insurance policy, to determine if coverage is afforded for client notification following a breach.

Timing Requirements

The time that a firm is allowed to notify clients of a breach ranges from the ambiguous to the specific, and sometimes in between.

On the ambiguous side, most states contain a provision like that found in Georgia's breach notification law: "The notice shall be made

in the most expedient time possible and without unreasonable delay, consistent with the legitimate needs of law enforcement…"[63]

How, exactly, the state will effectively determine if a firm truly notified affected individuals expediently and without unreasonable delay is likely determined on a case by case basis. Regardless, no firm would want to test the limits of a state's patience in this area.

More definitively, 19 states declare specific notification time requirements for those persons affected.[64] On the higher end, Wisconsin mandates that notice must be given "within a reasonable time, **not to exceed 45 days** after the entity learns of the acquisition of personal information."[65]

Florida has a particularly illustrative example of notification timing requirements. They state that "Notice to individuals shall be made **as expeditiously as practicable and without unreasonable delay**, taking into account the time necessary to allow the covered entity to determine the scope of the breach of security, to identify individuals affected by the breach, and to restore the reasonable integrity of the data system that was breached, **but no later than 30 days after the determination of a breach** or reason to believe a breach occurred unless subject to an authorized delay for law enforcement purposes or an authorized waiver."[66]

One of the less-touted benefits of a cyber insurance policy is that most insurers have a pre-selected list of vendors to assist with breach response. This gives affected firms the ability to select vendors in each required area and to review contracts before a breach. In turn, this allows the firm to expeditiously respond to a breach considering various, state-imposed time requirements.

Partner Action Items:

☐ Understand how applicable breach notification laws mandate timing requirements to consumers;

- ☐ Communicate this data to relevant stakeholders including IT and staff;
- ☐ Consider reviewing the contracts of the firm's cyber insurance vendor list with legal counsel prior to a breach occurring;
- ☐ If possible, pre-select the appropriate vendors before a breach to ease time requirements;
- ☐ Update the firm's incident response plan as necessary.

How Notice Is Given Including Content Requirements

All states and territories require notification to individuals when their personal information has been breached. As is the trend, the method of notification, as well as the criteria for substitute methods of notification, vary by jurisdiction.

For primary methods of notification, most states generally allow for three types of notification:

1. A written notice;
2. A telephone notice;
3. An electronic notice that complies with the electronic records and signatures provisions of the Electronic Signatures in Global and National Commerce Act.[67]

This is seen directly in South Carolina's provision: "The notice required by this section may be provided by: **(1) written notice**; **(2) electronic notice**, if the person's primary method of communication with the individual is by electronic means or … **(3) telephonic notice**[.]"[68]

Conditionally, firms may elect to use substitute methods of notice. Certain states may require one to all of the following methods depending on their statute:

1. Email notification;
2. A conspicuous notice posted on the firm's website;
3. Notice given to major statewide media.[69]

However, such substitute notice methods are generally subject to several conditions as dictated by the states. These include, but are not limited to:

1. Exceeding a cost threshold for primary notices;
2. Exceeding a person threshold for primary notification;
3. Lack of contact notification to provide primary notification.[70]

For example, Rhode Island states that substitute methods of notification may be used if "the state agency or person demonstrates that **the cost of providing notice would exceed twenty-five thousand dollars ($25,000),** or that the affected class of subject **persons to be notified exceeds fifty thousand (50,000),** or the state agency or person **does not have sufficient contact information.**"[71]

In relation to how such a substitute notice is to be given, Rhode Island states "Substitute notice **shall consist of all of the following**: (A) **E-mail notice** when the state agency or person has an e-mail address for the subject persons; (B) Conspicuous posting of the **notice on the state agency's or person's website page**, if the state agency or person maintains one; (C) Notification to **major statewide media.**"[72]

For practical purposes, most firms will, in conjunction with legal counsel, elect to use a written notice sent via registered mail. Other primary methods of notice are often difficult to track or evidence. Substitute notification methods are often situationally dependent and unpalatable for firm management who are attempting to control negative publicity.

Regardless of which law(s) firms must adhere to following a breach, they should plan to comply with the strictest requirements across all states. To adequately prepare for such an event, they should understand where clients claim residency and how those states mandate notification requirements. While the firm's breach attorney should have ready access to these requirements, adequate planning can assist greatly in avoiding otherwise costly delays.

Partner Action Items:

☐ Understand how applicable breach notification laws mandate notification content requirements to consumers;

- ☐ Consider maintaining a master list of each client's state of residency;
- ☐ Communicate this data to relevant stakeholders including IT and staff;
- ☐ Update the firm's incident response plan as necessary;
- ☐ Legal counsel may be able to provide stock letters tailored to the relevant states before the breach occurs. Firms should consider approving these stock letters before a breach to avoid potentially costly delays.

State-level Enforcement Actions and Penalties

Notwithstanding federal-level actions brought by organizations such as the FTC and HHS OCR, many states have an enforcement action if a firm is not reasonably attempting to prevent a breach, or otherwise fails to adhere to the state's breach notification law. Often this power is held within the state attorney general's office.

First, firms should be aware that many breach notification laws require notification to state agencies following a breach. Thus, most firms may be legally obligated to notify the state of every breach of meaningful size. This can trigger an agency to begin its investigation or provide oversight to client notification.

As is now expected, each state has varying requirements. Those states that do require agency notification tend to include the following general information:

- The state agency that requires notification;
- The timing and method to the agency following discovery of a breach;
- A threshold of affected individuals that requires notification;
- Specific requirements on the information included with the notification to the agency, if any.

In Hawaii, for example, notification must be given to the Office of Consumer Protection without unreasonable delay if 1,000 or more residents are affected. Included in the letter will be the timing, distribution, and content of the notice to individuals.[73]

By comparison, Florida is much more exacting in their requirements. Notice must be given to the Department of Legal Affairs of the Office of the Attorney General no less than 30 days after a breach is believed to have occurred, and if it will affect 500 or more residents. Information included in the notice must include:

- Description of the breach events known at the time;
- Number of state residents actually or potentially affected;
- Any services being offered to residents without charge and directions on use;
- Contact information for the person overseeing the breach response;
- An explanation of any other actions taken in conjunction with providing notification.[74]

Due to the varied nature of notification requirements, it is imperative that firms work closely with legal counsel to ensure that they meet required notification standards in the time allotted to them. Failure to do so could result in stiff penalties as many states have a provision inside of their breach notification laws which allow the state to investigate and fine businesses for compliance failures.

Washington State's breach law allows for an innocuous sounding state enforcement. "The attorney general may bring an action in the name of [Washington], or as *parens patriae* on behalf of persons residing in [Washington], to enforce this section."[75]

In a recent case of *State of Washington v. Uber Technologies, Inc.*, firms were put on notice as to the serious nature of state-level enforcement actions.

Uber had known about their breach as early as November of 2016 when they were notified by a hacker who claimed to have access to Uber user information. Following an internal investigation, Uber confirmed that the hacker had indeed accessed the names and driver's license numbers of approximately 10,888 residents of Washington State.[76]

Rather than notify the appropriate law enforcement agency and affected consumers, Uber paid the intruder's demands and expected that the offender would delete the data and remain quiet. Not until more than a year after the discovery of the breach did Uber notify the state and consumers.[77]

Washington State specifically noted the following actions by Uber which were in violation of the state's laws:

- Uber was aware of the breach and had internally confirmed its existence;
- Uber understood that Washington State residents were affected by the breach;
- Uber failed to provide notification to affected residents in the maximum allotted time of 45 calendars days in accordance with Washington State breach notification law;
- Uber failed to provide notification to the appropriate Washington State Attorney General in the maximum allotted time of 45 calendar days;
- The failure to notify Washington State residents was a deceptive and unfair trade practice and is in violation of the state Consumer Protection Act.[78]

Uber's failure to adhere strictly with the law resulted in a $2.2 million dollar fine and untold bad publicity. This case should serve as a warning to all firms that they must strictly follow state notification requirements. Moreover, firms should also be prepared to do so before a breach occurs due to the stringent timelines in various state's notification laws which can incidentally change without warning.[79] Working closely with legal counsel before a breach can greatly assist in this endeavor.

Partner Action Items:

- ☐ Understand how applicable breach notification laws penalize firms for late notification to appropriate government agencies;

- ☐ Work with legal counsel to understand which government agencies require notification and the timing requirements thereof;

- ☐ Communicate this data to relevant stakeholders including IT and staff;

- ☐ Update the firm's incident response plan as necessary;

- ☐ Review the firm's insurance policies, including cyber insurance policy, to determine if coverage may be afforded for claims arising from late or inadequate state-level notification.

Client Claims Following a Breach

A minority of states contain provisions for a private right of action by consumers to bring a suit against a firm following a breach. Though these private rights of action may appear daunting, they are rarely pursued and even more rarely successful. Foremost, most states which do allow private right of action limit those actions to an error in the execution of the breach notice, and not necessarily to the loss of data.[80]

The preponderance of states does not explicitly allow a private right of action by consumers. They are either silent on the issue, limit action only to government agencies, or outright forbid the practice.[81]

Depending on the state, plaintiffs may use some or all of the following claims when litigating a data-breach-related claim.[82] For firms that have defended against a professional liability claim, such action may appear familiar:

- Negligence;
- Negligent Misrepresentation;
- Breach of contract;
- Breach of implied warranty;
- Invasion of Privacy/Publication of Private Facts;
- Unjust Enrichment;
- State Consumer Protection Laws.[83]

A separate avenue for plaintiffs to bring rise to a claim could come from an attempt to extend federal laws to local data breaches. Most often they will use the following federal laws to plead recovery: HIPAA/HITECH, the Stored Communications Act (SCA), The Fair Credit Reporting Act (FCRA), and of particular note to accounting firms, The Gramm-Leach-Bliley Act (GLBA). However, courts have been hesitant to apply these laws as requested by the plaintiffs. Most often actions brought under these statutes fail to proceed beyond the motion to dismiss as courts find they are ill-suited for consumer data-breach litigation, or the statues themselves lack private right of action.[84]

A more in-depth discussion on this topic is found on page 313.

Partner Action Items:

- ☐ Understand which clients, if any, reside in states which allow for a private right of action following a breach;
- ☐ Continuously monitor applicable breach notification laws for any changes;
- ☐ Communicate this data to relevant stakeholders including IT and staff;
- ☐ Update the firm's incident response plan and other internal documents as necessary;
- ☐ Determine if the firm's cyber insurance policy would cover a private right of action following a data breach.

Section 3: Notable State-Specific Privacy Laws

Though every state privacy law is worth reading and reflecting upon, certain state privacy laws are so specific and potentially burdensome in their requirements that they are worth their own notable mention. Failure to understand and abide by these laws, if applicable, can lead to increased risks for firms as well as potential coverage declinations.

California Consumer Privacy Act (CCPA)

Soon, there is a possibility that firms with California residents could see private actions increase dramatically with the upcoming implementation of the California Consumer Privacy Act (CCPA). However, there are various stipulations that will give the majority of firms solace.

Generally, the CCPA applies to companies which meet one or more of the following threshold requirements:

- Annual gross revenue exceeds $25,000,000;
- Buys, sells, shares, or receives the personal information of 50,000 or more consumers, devices, or households;
- 50% or more of the annual revenue of the business is derived from selling the personal information of a consumer.[85]

In practice, these thresholds mean that many small- to mid-sized accounting firms will likely not be subject to the law. However, there could be small firms that are participating in various practice areas, such as payroll processing or ERISA audits, that could potentially subject them to this law.

Under the CCPA, consumers would have the right to bring a private right of action if their information was accessed or stolen by unauthorized parties. Private actions can also be brought if their personal information was disclosed in a nonencrypted or nonredacted format due to the firm failing to properly implement reasonable cybersecurity measures.[86]

If an action is brought by a consumer, the CCPA provides for the following potential damages:

- Awards ranging from $100 to $750 per consumer, per incident, or actual damages if those are greater;
- Declaratory or injunctive relief;

- Any additional relief deemed proper by the court. [87]

While the CPPA will not become effective until January 1st, 2020, this should give firms pause for further consideration. Foremost, there will be a clear path for consumers to bring data-breach-related claims against the firm following a breach. Additionally, there will now be a defined avenue for consumers to bring claims after a breach if the firm failed to implement "reasonable" cybersecurity measures.[88]

Firms should note that the California Department of Justice will attempt to make this a self-sustaining program. To do so, they will need to raise more than $57.5 million in civil penalties related to the rule in order to cover the cost of enforcement. To achieve this outcome, businesses can be assessed up to $2,500 for each violation, or up to $7,500 for intentionally violating the CCPA.[89]

How firms that demonstrate "reasonable" cybersecurity measures will not likely be the subject of litigation. However, a good starting point would be the adoption, implementation, and continuous review of an appropriate cybersecurity framework such as the NIST CSF described in this book. Security consults and legal counsel can also assist in this endeavor. Whether other states will adopt similar legislation is, at this point, up for speculation.

If a firm were to face claims from clients following a breach, they are most likely to face a class-action claim. However, such a claim would likely be limited to large firms which held large quantities of personal client information. The rationale for this statement can be found on page 313.

As of publication, the CCPA is being amended with various laws put forward in the California Assembly. While the current proposals do not appear to materially change the substance of the law, this is not to say that a future amendment will not.[90] Therefore, it is imperative that any firm which believes it may be subject to the CCPA continues to stay abreast of any changes in the law.

Partner Action Items:

- ☐ Determine if your firm will be subject to CCPA;
- ☐ Work with legal counsel to review firm policies, procedures, and engagement letters for any additional liability in light of CCPA;
- ☐ Communicate this data to relevant stakeholders, including IT and staff;
- ☐ Update the firm's incident response plan and other internal documents as necessary;
- ☐ Review the firm's insurance policies, including cyber insurance policy, to determine if coverage may be afforded for CCPA related claims.

Massachusetts' 201 CMR 17

Massachusetts General Law Chapter 93H, containing regulation 201 CMR 17, warrants particular scrutiny here as it describes in detail various protocols that must be followed by firms. Known as the Standards for The Protection of Personal Information of Residents of the Commonwealth, 201 CMR 17 applies to, "all persons that own or license personal information about a resident of the Commonwealth."[91] Therefore, if a firm handles even one return for a Massachusetts' resident, they likely have responsibilities unseen and unprecedented in most other states.

None of the definitions in the law are particularly worrisome. Indeed, the first half of the law contains language and definitions common to many other state breach notification laws.[92]

Unique to this law is the requirement for a firm to create and utilize a <u>written</u> information security plan. This plan must include "administrative, technical, and physical safeguards" that are appropriate to the size of the firm and the amount of personal information stored.

Regardless, every firm is required to enact at the least the following measures in their information security program per section 17.03:

- Designated employee(s) to maintain the program;
- Identifying and evaluating external and internal risks;
- Implementation of training for permanent, temporary, and contract employees;
- A method to detect and prevent failures of the security system.
- Creation of security policies for employees who transport covered records off-site;

- Enact disciplinary actions against employees who violate the firm's information security program;
- Preventing terminated employees from accessing covered data;
- Reasonably limiting the firm's third-party service providers to those providers who maintain data security standards at least as strict as 201 CMR 17.00, as well as other applicable federal level regulations, and requiring them by contract to do so;
- Enact reasonable restrictions on the physical access of covered data;
- Consistent monitoring of the program and updating of safeguards as necessary;
- Mandatory minimum of an annual review of the program, or as business practices change;
- Documentation of actions taken in relation to breach of the firm's security, and well as a mandatory post-occurrence review to makes changes in business practices.[93]

In addition, firms will be required to include and maintain the following computer security requirements not seen in other states, as mandated in section 17.04:

- Protected user authentication protocols such as restricting and blocking access and control of password location/format;
- Restricting access, including segmented user permissions and assignment of unique user IDs;
- Encryption of all information transmitted either across public networks or wirelessly;
- System monitoring for unauthorized access or use of covered data;

- Encryption for all portable devices which contain covered data;
- Mandatory employee training on computer and personal security;
- Ensuring system security with updated firewall protection, security patches, virus definitions, and supported software.[94]

As shown in the ongoing case of *Commonwealth of Massachusetts v. Equifax, Inc.,* the Massachusetts Attorney General asserts that enforcement of the law does not require a breach or demonstrated harm done to consumers.[95]

In late 2017, the Massachusetts attorney general brought action against Equifax following their highly publicized breach of allegedly 143 million consumers. Within the attorney general's claim, she lists several violations of Massachusetts General Law, but specific to this discussion, multiple violations of the 201 CMR 17. Equifax allegedly violated:

- The responsibility to develop, maintain, and implement a written security plan suitable for the information being protected to meet the basic requirements expected of a business their size;
- The requirement to maintain security updates of their computer systems;
- The requirement to monitor systems for unauthorized access or use as required.[96]

Additionally, the attorney general is alleging that, by virtue of violating 201 CMR 17, Equifax also committed various unfair or deceptive trade practices in violation of Massachusetts G.L. c. 93A , § 2, committed deceptive acts or practices in violation of Massachusetts G.L. c. 93A , § 2, committed unfair acts or practices in violation of Massachusetts G.L. c. 93A , § 2, failed to safeguard personal information in violation of Massachusetts G.L. c. 93H , § 2, and failed to notify the appropriate parties as required by law following the breach in violation of Massachusetts G.L. c. 93H , § 3(b). [97]

As of publication, the two parties are currently in court. Regardless, no firm would want to test the limits of a state's attorney general in court for similar accusations.

Partner Action Items:

- ☐ Determine if 201 CMR 17 applies to your firm;
- ☐ Work with legal counsel or other compliance experts to review firm policies and procedures to ensure compliance if applicable;
- ☐ Communicate this data to relevant stakeholders, including IT and staff;
- ☐ Update the firm's incident response plan, business practices, and other internal documents as necessary;
- ☐ Determine whether the firm's cyber policy would cover 201 CMR 17 related claims and expenses.

23 NYCRR 500

23 NYCRR 500 was unveiled in March of 2017 by the New York Department of Financial Services (DFS). This law places specific requirements on companies to safeguard their consumers' data privacy. The impetus for this new law arose from the concerns of DFS that the financial services industry could face significant disruptions by cybercriminals.[98]

It is not immediately clear which entities must comply with this law as there is no definitive list provided by DFS within 23 NYCRR 500. The law only defines a "Covered Entity" as "any Person operating under or required to operate under a license, registration, charter, certificate, permit, accreditation or similar authorization under the Banking Law, the Insurance Law or the Financial Services Law."[99]

DFS has attempted to alleviate some of the confusion regarding who must comply. Notably, they clarified in a recent FAQ that non-profit mortgage brokers, health maintenance organizations (HMOs), and continuing care retirement communities (CCRCs) must also comply with the law.[100] While it is unlikely that CPA firms proper must comply with the law, certain subsidiary entities owned by the firm may require compliance. Firms may also provide technology-related services to clients that would fall under the purview of this statute, so at least a passing understanding of the law is advised. Currently, there exists a large amount of ambiguity regarding who must comply, so it is advised that firms consult legal counsel to determine applicability.

Covered entities must also be aware that the information to be protected may be far broader than that detailed by other state and territory breach notification laws. "Nonpublic Information" means any electronic information that is not publicly available. More specifically, it is defined as:

"(1) Business-related information of a Covered Entity the tampering with which, or unauthorized disclosure, access or use of which, would cause a materially adverse impact to the business, operations or security of the Covered Entity;

(2) Any information concerning an individual which because of name, number, personal mark, or other identifier can be used to identify such individual, in combination with any one or more of the following data elements:

(i) social security number;

(ii) drivers' license number or non-driver identification card number;

(iii) account number, credit or debit card number;

(iv) any security code, access code or password that would permit access to an individual's financial account or;

(v) biometric records.

(3) Any information or data, except age or gender, in any form or medium created by or derived from a health care provider or an individual and that relates to:

(i) the past, present or future physical, mental or behavioral health or condition of any individual or a member of the individual's family;

(ii) the provision of health care to any individual or;

(iii) payment for the provision of health care to any individual."[101]

Broadly speaking, 23 NYCRR 500 requires entities regulated by DFS to assess their cybersecurity to create a risk profile. These activities are quite analogous to those found in other cybersecurity frameworks, such as NIST CSF.

Once a risk profile is completed, the entity must implement a comprehensive data security plan to mitigate the risks that the entity has identified to any nonpublic information in its possession. While apparently simple, there are various mandatory requirements that firms must follow unless specifically exempted. Covered entities may be exempt from portions of the law, but no covered entity is entirely exempt from all portions of the law.

500.2: This section describes the cybersecurity program that covered entities shall maintain. Within the cybersecurity program, the entity must meet six core functions. These include identifying and assessing risks to nonpublic information; the use of policies, procedures, and controls to protect the entity's IT system and stored nonpublic information; detection of cybersecurity events; responding to events to mitigate harm; recovering from events to resume normal operations; and reporting of the events in conjunction with the law.[102]

The following are notable sections of the law with brief descriptions:

500.3: This section concerns the entity's mandatory written cybersecurity policy. Of note, the cybersecurity program must be approved by the governing body of the entity and based upon the previously completed risk assessment. The policy mandates fourteen specific areas to be addressed by the entity, if applicable. Notable amongst these areas are business continuity, disaster recovery, physical security, vendor management, and incident response. In particular, such areas are often not mandated by other laws, so special effort may be required to fully comply.[103]

500.4: Firms must, in accordance with this section, designate a qualified chief information security officer (CISO) to oversee and implement its cybersecurity program. What qualifies a person to be considered a, "qualified" CISO is not specified. To alleviate personnel shortages, firms may elect to use a third-party service provider to act as a CISO. Regardless of origin, the CISO must report on the cybersecurity program and risk at least annually to the governing body of the organization.[104]

500.5: This section mandates that covered entities must undergo continuous monitoring, or periodic vulnerability assessment and penetration testing.[105]

500.6: The "Audit Trail" section mandates that covered entities must meet two criteria. First, they shall maintain a system that can reconstruct material financial transactions to allow for normal operations for no less than five years. Second, they shall maintain a system that includes audit trails for no less than three years. This audit trail must be able to detect and respond to any cyber-event that could harm to the normal operations of the entity.[106]

500.7: Each covered entity must limit the access privileges of users to systems that contain nonpublic information. The access privileges to such systems must be reviewed periodically.[107]

500.8: Covered entities must assess the security of their applications. This shall include guidelines, standards, and written procedures to any organically developed applications. Further, entities must create similar protocols for externally developed applications. These actions must be periodically reviewed and updated by the CISO.[108]

500.9: This section mandates that covered entities shall conduct periodic and documented risk assessments and that those assessments must be updated as necessary to respond to emerging risks and changes to the entity. In particular, this section requires the risk assessment to contain policies and procedures that include: "(1) criteria for the evaluation and categorization of identified cybersecurity risks or threats facing the Covered Entity; (2) criteria for the assessment of the confidentiality, integrity, security and availability of the Covered Entity's Information Systems and

Nonpublic Information, including the adequacy of existing controls in the context of identified risks, and; (3) requirements describing how identified risks will be mitigated or accepted based on the Risk Assessment and how the cybersecurity program will address the risks."[109]

500.10: Particularly noteworthy is the requirement for a covered entity to maintain qualified cybersecurity personnel. Such personnel must be provided with updates and training necessary to combat current cybersecurity risks. In addition, the entity must verify that these personnel maintain and update their knowledge base.[110]

500.11: This section requires covered entities implement written policies and procedures to maintain the security of their IT system and nonpublic information held by any third-party service provider. In addition, the document must also include the due diligence performed by the entity as well as contractual protections as they relate to the third-party providers.[111]

500.12: Each covered entity is required to use effective controls to prevent unauthorized access to nonpublic information. This may include Multi-Factor Authentication (MFA) or other forms of Risk-Based Authentication (RBA). For any individual accessing the entity's internal network from an extern network, MFA should be used unless the CISO has authorized an equivalent or superior control in writing.[112]

500.13: This section concerns limitations on the retention of nonpublic information data. Exemptions are granted where law or regulations, such as those required by the state board of accountancy, require information to be held for longer. If no such exemption exists and nonpublic information is no longer required for legitimate business purposes, that information should periodically be disposed of in a secure fashion.[113]

500.14: A covered entity must monitor the activities of authorized users as well as detect any anomalous access of non-necessary information by authorized users. In addition, all personnel must provide periodic cybersecurity-awareness training that is updated to reflect current risks identified by the entity's risk assessment.[114]

500.15: The entity shall implement controls to include encryption for all nonpublic information. Nonpublic information sent over external networks shall be encrypted unless a necessary alternative is approved by the CISO. Nonpublic information at rest shall be encrypted unless a necessary alternative is approved by the CISO.[115]

500.16: This section covers the creation of the entity's written incident response plan. Included will be seven key areas, including subjects ranging from pre-breach planning to response and revision of the response plan.[116]

500.17: When a cybersecurity event has occurred, the entity is required to notify the DFS superintendent within 72 hours. This will occur whenever notice must also be given to another regulatory agency or government body, as well an event that could materially harm the entity's normal operations.[117] The quick notification mandate, in conjunction with the somewhat vague triggering actions, means that entities will likely need to have had dry runs through various notification scenarios to maximize the odds of compliance.

500.18: Generally speaking, information provided by the entity in accordance with 23 NYCRR 500 is still subject to the exemptions and limitations found in other state and federal laws.[118] Therefore, firms must also understand if other laws require stricter controls than those found in this law.

500.19: This section of the law deals with the exemptions that entities may qualify for. Recall that a covered entity may qualify for some exemptions but will not be exempt from all portions of the law.

Due to the ambiguity of the law, as well as the ambiguity of who must adhere to the law, firms are advised to seek legal counsel to assist in determining if they qualify for exemptions.[119]

500.20: As detailed in this section, 23 NYCRR 500 will be enforced by the superintendent of the DFS.[120] As of publication, the authors were unable to find any business that has been subject to fines and penalties under this law. It has been opined that enforcement actions will be brought by the DFS under the New York Banking Law. This would authorize penalties of up to $2,500 per day during the violation, $15,000 per day due to reckless conduct, or $75,000 due to willful violations.[121]

Firms should understand that adherence to 23 NYCRR 500 is not a "one and done" compliance issue. Adherence is a continual process that demands resources and personnel overseen by the highest authorities within the firm. In turn, those authorities will need to attest to various security practices and procedures to the DFS, often on an annual basis.

Partner Action Items:

☐ Determine if 23 NYCRR 500 applies to your firm;

☐ Work with legal counsel to review firm policies and procedures to ensure compliance, if applicable;

☐ Communicate this data to relevant stakeholders, including IT and staff;

☐ Update the firm's incident response plan and other internal documents as necessary;

☐ 23 NYCRR 500 can be found at: https://www.dfs.ny.gov/docs/legal/regulations/adoptions/dfsr f500txt.pdf;

☐ 23 NYCRR 500 FAQs page containing additional guidance can be found at: https://www.dfs.ny.gov/industry_guidance/cyber_faqs;

☐ Determine whether the firm's cyber policy would cover 23 NYCRR 500 related claims and expenses.

Section 4: Federal Cybersecurity Requirements for Firms

Firms are often surprised that they may be subject to various federal level cybersecurity/privacy laws. Certain statutes may be overarching, while others are specific to the practice area of the firm. Regardless, firms should be well familiar with their obligations. Failure to do so can lead to otherwise unnecessary breaches, potential declinations of coverage, and unwanted actions from regulators.

Origins of FTC Cybersecurity Oversight

It may seem odd to most firms that the Federal Trade Commission would have the ability to bring cases against companies following cybersecurity breaches. After all, Congress has never passed a law explicitly allowing the FTC to bring such cases. Rather, the FTC has used the interpretation of controlling statutes passed by Congress to become the de facto, cyber-breach regulatory body.

The FTC points to Section 5 of the Federal Commission Act, a law enacted over 100 years ago to claim authority in data-breach cases. Section 5 states that "unfair or deceptive acts or practices in or affecting commerce, are hereby declared unlawful."122

In 1980, the FTC attempted to assist businesses with understanding their interpretation of "unfair." The FTC had noted that "the concept of consumer unfairness is one whose precise meaning is not immediately obvious, and also recognize that this uncertainty has been honestly troublesome for some businesses and some members of the legal profession."[123]

Generally, the FTC would be looking for cases of substantial and unjustified consumer injury which "involves monetary harm, as when sellers coerce consumers into purchasing unwanted goods or services[13] or when consumers buy defective goods or services on credit but are unable to assert against the creditor claims or defenses arising from the transaction."[124]

Going further, the FTC noted, "the injury must not be outweighed by any offsetting consumer or competitive benefits that the sales practice also produces." And finally, "the injury must be one which consumers could not reasonably have avoided."[125]

In 1983, the FTC released a policy statement on deception to aid the public. In short, they noted that "the Commission will find deception if there is a representation, omission or practice that is likely to mislead the consumer acting reasonably in the circumstances, to the consumer's detriment."[126]

How precisely companies were and are supposed to structure their cybersecurity to avoid the FTC from bringing a claim based on, "unfair and deceptive trade practices" has never been detailed. Historically, when the FTC brought action against companies under its presumed cybersecurity enforcement authority, those companies rarely if ever challenged such action. Generally, companies who are threatened with a lawsuit accepted their maximum, 20-year consent orders to avoid public scrutiny.[127] As noted by the GAO, of the over 100 instances of privacy enforcement actions filed by the FTC in the last ten years, virtually all companies have acquiesced to changes in their business and security practices by agreeing to consent orders.[128]

Perhaps the first company to question whether the FTC had the authority to regulate and enforce cybersecurity was Wyndham Worldwide Corporation, a hotel chain, in the case of *F.T.C. v. Wyndham Worldwide Corp.*

In 2008 and 2009, Wyndham had been the victim of at least three breaches where hackers were able to access Wyndham's computer network. Through this access, the hackers were able to view customer's personal information including payment card numbers, expiration dates, and security access codes. As a result, more than 619,000 consumers were affected and suffered more than $10.6 million in fraud losses.[129]

In 2014, the FTC alleged that following the discovery of the first two breaches, Wyndham was negligent in their handling to prevent additional compromises in their network through "reasonable and appropriate security measures." The numerous failures of Wyndham, per the FTC included:

- Clear text storage of consumer's payment card data;
- Failure to employ firewalls;

- Lack of oversight in implementing security procedures and policies as necessary before hotels could connect their computers to the host network;
- Servers utilized operating systems that were no longer supported and thus could not receive updates or patches necessary to avoid publicly known security vulnerabilities;
- Servers could be accessed using default passwords and user IDs;
- Lack of management for devices which could access the network;
- No apparent monitoring of networks for malware which had previously been used to infiltrate the company network;
- Failing to limit access by third parties as necessary;
- Lack of stringent requirements for usernames and passwords.[130]

Rather than agree to a consent order by the FTC, Wyndham responded to the FTC by filing a lawsuit in federal court where they could fight the case.

Wyndham attempted to have the lawsuit dismissed on multiple grounds. Specific to this discussion, Wyndham asserted that the FTC's authority did not extend to data security. Congress had passed statutes to deal with cybersecurity in specific industries, but no such statue had granted the FTC authority to create data and cybersecurity standards. Further, they asserted that "it defies common sense to think that Congress would have delegated [this] responsibility to the FTC[.]"[131]

In response, the FTC asserted that it was acting with due authority under Section 5 of the FTC Act of 1914, and the district court disagreed with the assertions of Wyndham.[132] In particular, the court noted that "the FTC's unfairness authority over data security can coexist with the existing data-security regulatory scheme." [133]

Ultimately, the case was brought before the Third Circuit Court of Appeals. Here too, Wyndham was unsuccessful. The Court of Appeals affirmed FTC's ability to bring actions against companies alleged to have engaged in unreasonable computer and data security practices. [134]

Gramm Leach Bliley Act and the Safeguards Rule

Although accounting firms must adhere to applicable state and territory breach notification laws, there are additional requirements placed upon them at the federal level for being considered a financial institution. Most notable is the Gamm-Leach-Bliley Act (GLBA), also known as the "Financial Modernization Act of 1999." Under the GLBA, the FTC would be the most likely body to bring an action against an accounting firm.[135] Indeed, a recent report by the GAO noted that most interviewed stakeholders favored the FTC's continued enforcement practices and that their power to do so should be expanded.[136]

Whereas the states generally referred to Personally Identifiable Information as needing protection under their relevant breach laws, GLBA uses the term "nonpublic personal information." The GLBA describes 'nonpublic personal information' as the following:

"(A) The term "nonpublic personal information" means personally identifiable financial information:

(i) provided by a consumer to a financial institution;

(ii) resulting from any transaction with the consumer or any service performed for the consumer, or;

(iii) otherwise obtained by the financial institution."[137]

For purposes of firms researching their cybersecurity requirements under GLBA, the Safeguards Rule is the most immediately relevant.

Safeguards Rule

The GLBA required each designated agency or authority to establish standards and physical safeguards:

1) to ensure the security and confidentiality of customer records and information;

2) to protect against any anticipated threats or hazards to the
   security or integrity of such records, and;

3) to protect against unauthorized access to or use of such
   records or information which could result in substantial harm
   or inconvenience to any customer. [138]

The FTC, being granted authority to do so, has published
guidance on how they want the Safeguard Rule implemented within
firms. Specifically, the FTC notes that firms will be required to,
"develop a written [emphasis added] information security plan that
describes their program to protect customer information."[139]

The specifics of the plan are "allowed" to be flexible dependent
on firm size, services offered, and type of client information stored.

Regardless, the FTC requires every firm to:

- designate one or more employees to coordinate its
  information security program;

- identify and assess the risks to customer information in each
  relevant area of the company's operation and evaluate the
  effectiveness of the current safeguards for controlling these
  risks;

- design and implement a safeguards program and regularly
  monitor and test it;

- select service providers that can maintain appropriate
  safeguards, make sure your contract requires them to
  maintain safeguards, and oversee their handling of customer
  information, and;

- evaluate and adjust the program considering relevant
  circumstances, including changes in the firm's business or
  operations or the results of security testing and monitoring.

Regarding the above requirements, the FTC has placed particular importance on three areas: "Employee Management and Training; Information Systems; and Detecting and Managing System Failures." FTC guidance on this area is too lengthy to list, so every firm should consider visiting the following FTC website to glean further information:

> https://www.ftc.gov/tips-advice/business-center/guidance/financial-institutions-customer-information-complying

Recently, the FTC brought enforcement action against a nationwide tax preparer for, among other provisions, violating the Safeguards Rule.

In the Matter of TaxSlayer, LLC, the FTC brought action against TaxSlayer for allegedly allowing nearly 8,882 TaxSlayer accounts to be accessed by hackers from October 10th, 2015 until December 21st, 2015. The FTC charged TaxSlayer with violating the GLBA's Safeguards Rule.[140]

The FTC noted the following select violations of the Safeguards Rule, alleging TaxSlayer failed to:

- have a written information security plan until November 2015;
- failed to conduct a risk assessment;
- implement appropriate password requirements;
- implement risk-based authentication, such as two-factor authentication;
- failed to notify users when there was a material change made to their account. [141]

In their settlement with the FTC, TaxSlayer is "prohibited from violating the… Safeguards Rule of the Gramm-Leach-Bliley Act for 20 years." Further, TaxSlayer was required to obtain third-party compliance verification of these rules. biennially, for the following ten years.[142]

Such a case should serve as a stark warning to accounting firms of all sizes. Understanding the significance of the fact that only 8,882 people were affected but the FTC moved forward with an action is an indication that even smaller firms could be subject to other FTC actions. Failure to adopt security standards as deemed appropriate by the FTC's interpretation of the Safeguards Rule could result in legal action and significant trailing costs for years to come.

Regardless, compliance with GLBA is mandatory. Violation can result in up to five years in prison as well as potential fines. Firms can be fined $100,000 per violation. Officers and directors can face a $10,000 fine per violation.[143]

Firms should also note that the FTC periodically proposes amendments to its Safeguard and Privacy Rule under the GLBA. It is speculated that future proposals will more closely align FTC rules with notable cybersecurity standards such as the NY Department of Financial Services recent cybersecurity regulation, 23 NYCRR 500, and the NIST Cybersecurity Framework.[144] This should spur continued research by firms into understanding these regulations and how a similar adoption could impact their business.

Partner Action Items:

☐ Work with legal counsel to review firm policies and procedures to ensure compliance with FTC Guidelines;

☐ Review the FTC's cybersecurity guide at: **https://www.ftc.gov/system/files/documents/plain-language/pdf0205-startwithsecurity.pdf** ;

☐ Communicate this data to relevant stakeholders including IT and staff;

☐ Update the firm's incident response plan and other internal documents as necessary;

☐ Determine if your policy would respond to allegations of FTC Safeguards Rule violations. Most often this will be found as "Regulatory Investigation" coverage.

Securities and Exchange Commission (SEC) Regulation S-P

Regulation S-P sets the GLBA Safeguard Rule requirements for investment advisers, investment companies, brokers, and dealers.[145] For firms that own a broker/dealer or are RIA licensed with the SEC, they should be aware of how the SEC interprets and enforces Regulation S-P. Not only does this have insurance implications, but it can have a direct impact on business practices.

Broadly speaking, Regulation S-P advises firms on how they should maintain written information policies and procedures that address administrative, technical, and physical safeguards to protect client records and information. These policies and procedures must follow the same general goals of the GLBA; namely:

1) to ensure the security and confidentiality of customer records and information;
2) to protect against any anticipated threats or hazards to the security or integrity of such records, and;
3) to protect against unauthorized access to or use of such records or information which could result in substantial harm or inconvenience to any customer.[146]

Additionally, the SEC provides guidance under Regulation S-P as to how firms should dispose of consumer report information. Though sparse on specifics, "Disposal" means:

(A) The discarding or abandonment of consumer report information, or;
(B) The sale, donation, or transfer of any medium, including computer equipment [emphasis added], on which consumer report information is stored.[147]

In a recent Risk Alert, the SEC related the most common Regulation S-P compliance issues experienced by RIAs and broker-dealers.[148] For purposes of brevity, these entities will collectively be referenced to as, "firms" hereafter.

Privacy and Opt-Out Notices

Inspectors noted that firms failed in providing initial, annual, and opt-out notices to the customers. When these notices were provided, they often failed to accurately portray the firm's true policies and procedures. In addition, the privacy notices did not give adequate notice to the clients that they could opt-out of having their personal information shared with "unaffiliated third parties." [149]

Lack of policies and procedures

Inspectors found that firms did not have the required written policies and procedures as required by Regulation S-P. Firms did possess documents that restated the regulation but did not include the policies and procedures necessary for administrative, technical, and physical safeguards. The inspectors also found firms where policies had adequately addressed the Privacy Notice but did not contain written policies and procedures required by the regulation. [150]

Policies did not reasonably safeguard client information or were not implemented

Here, the inspectors found numerous errors in how firms with written policies did not implement those policies or the policies were inadequate to safeguard client information. This included lack of reasonable security on personal devices storing client information, lack of safeguard to prevent sending PII via unencrypted email, unsecured networks, unsecured physical locations, inadequate incident response plans, former employees who retained access, and lack of inventory for systems that maintained PII. [151]

Naturally, the SEC takes these violations seriously and has a website page dedicated exclusively to cyber-enforcement actions.[152] As an example of a Regulation S-P enforcement action, consider the cases involving Morgan Stanley Smith Barney.

In this case, trouble initially began for Morgan Stanley when the FTC began an investigation on allegations of unfair or deceptive trade practices. From 2011 until 2014, an employee had unduly gained access to and transferred the data of 730,000 customers to his personal server. In turn, this server was hacked by third parties, and the client information appeared on numerous websites. Ultimately, the FTC decided to close the case because they believed that Morgan Stanley had taken the necessary steps to protect against insider theft.[153]

In turn, the SEC conducted their own investigation *In the Matter of Morgan Stanley Smith Barney*. The SEC released a finding that Morgan Stanley had "failed to adopt written policies and procedures reasonably designed to protect customer data." As stated by the Director of the SEC Enforcement Division, "Given the dangers and impact of cyber breaches, data security is a critically important aspect of investor protection. We expect SEC registrants of all sizes to have policies and procedures that are reasonably designed to protect customer information[.]"[154]

Though the SEC's press release is worthy of a read in its own right, the basis of their enforcement action was that Morgan Stanley had violated Rule 30(a) of Regulation S-P, known as the "Safeguards Rule." Morgan Stanley did not admit or deny the SEC's findings but agreed to a $1,000,000 penalty. The employee was ultimately sentenced to 36 months of probation and agreed to a $600,000 restitution order.[155]

Greater guidance on how rules are applied should be investigated by firms who may fall under SEC Regulation S-P. Firms should seek guidance from their Compliance Officer and competent legal counsel.

Partner Action Items:

- ☐ Determine if your firm is subject to SEC Regulation S-P;
- ☐ Regulation S-P can be found at: https://www.sec.gov/rules/final/34-42974.htm#P80_19305;
- ☐ Work with legal counsel to review firm policies and procedures to ensure compliance with SEC Guidelines;
- ☐ Determine if your policy would respond to allegations of SEC Regulation S-P violations. Most often this will be found as "Regulatory Investigation" coverage;
- ☐ Communicate this data to relevant stakeholders including IT and staff;
- ☐ Update the firm's incident response plan and other internal documents as necessary.

SEC Custody Rule

The SEC Custody Rule, Rule 206(4)-2 under Section 206(4) of the Investment Advisers Act of 1940, is not a "cybersecurity" rule, *per se,* but can have internal cybersecurity controls and business practice implications.

In December of 2009, the SEC adopted amendments to the custody rule for investment advisors as it applies to the client's funds or securities. Notably, these amendments were created to provide an additional level of client safeguards when advisor had custody of client assets. Amongst provisions in the rule are requirements to maintain client assets with a qualified custodian, or to engage an independent CPA to conduct a surprise examination.[156]

Trouble began in June of 2012 for GW & Wade when a client's email account had been compromised, and a hacker posed as the client. The hacker then requested GW & Wade to wire a total of $290,000 via three separate wires to a foreign bank. Ultimately, the fraud was discovered, and the client was reimbursed the lost sum.[157]

In late 2013, the SEC issued an order instituting administrative proceedings *In the Matter of GW & Wade, LLC.* The SEC asserted that the firm was subject to the custody rule due to having pre-signed letters of authorization. This enabled GW & Wade to transfer client funds without obtaining a client's contemporaneous signature. Further, the SEC alleged that GW & Wade had "not adopted or implemented policies and procedures reasonably designed to prevent violations of the securities laws and rules governing custody of client assets or kept required books and records for certain custodied accounts" and had erred in its mandatory Form ADV disclosures.[158]

The SEC also noted that there were other practices within the firm that could have caused issues. This includes GW & Wades' being granted third-party delegation on clients' check-writing accounts, as well as login and password information for those accounts.[159]

GW & Wade ultimately consented to a censure and cease-and-desist order. They paid a $250,000 penalty.[160]

Partner Action Items:

- ☐ Determine if your firm is subject to SEC Custody Rule; he SEC Custody Rule can be found at: https://www.sec.gov/rules/final/2009/ia-2968.pdf;
- ☐ SEC Staff response to questions about the Custody Rule can be found at: https://www.sec.gov/divisions/investment/custody_faq_0305 10.htm;
- ☐ Work with legal counsel to review firm policies and procedures to ensure compliance with SEC Custody Rule Guidelines;
- ☐ Determine which policies may respond to allegations of SEC Custody Rule violations. This may be a professional liability policy, or a cyber policy dependent up the allegations;
- ☐ Communicate this data to relevant stakeholders, including IT and staff;
- ☐ Update the firm's incident response plan and other internal documents as necessary.

Red Flag Rule(s) – SEC & FTC

In 2012, the Dodd-Frank Wall Street and Consumer Protection Act amended the Fair Credit Reporting Act. Effectively, this transferred the rulemaking and enforcement authority for identity theft Red Flag Rules to the various agencies.

You have to mark one in the win column for the AICPA lobbying efforts which undoubtedly was part of the reason the FTC's authority to make accounting firms adhere to the Red Flag Rule ended with the Red Flag Program Clarification Act of 2010.[161] However, for firms with a broker-dealer or investment adviser registered with the state regulators may still have that portion of their firm needing to adhere to the FTC Red Flag Rule. The FTC has their own Red Flag Rules which roughly mirror those propagated by the SEC. Per the statute, a red flag means "a pattern, practice, or specific activity that indicates the possible existence of identity theft."[162]

Known as Regulation S-ID: Identity Theft Red Flags, but generally referred to as the "Red Flags Rule," the SEC requires financial institutions and creditors that offer any number of covered accounts to develop a written identity theft program.

The written plan concerning Red Flag Rules is used to help the firm meet the four following goals:

1) **Identification of relevant Red Flags:** Factors that should be considered include the type of covered accounts, the method it provides to open and access such accounts, as well as any previous incidents of identity theft. The sources of Red Flags should also be considered to include prior incidents of identity theft and any methods of identity theft that have been identified that would change the risk of identity theft. Categories of Red Flags should also be addressed, such as

reports from service providers, suspicious documents, and any other doubtful activity.

2) **Detecting Red Flags:** Firms should obtain and verify proper ID of anyone opening a covered account. They should also monitor all transactions and verify the validity of a covered account requesting a change of address.

3) **Preventing and mitigating identity theft:** When Red Flags are detected, the firm must respond appropriately. This could include customer contact, notifying law enforcement, changing methods of access, or even no response if that is warranted.

Updating the Program

The firm's written plan should be a living document that requires periodic updates. Such updates should reflect the evolving risk to customers based on factors such as changing methods of identity theft, experience by the firm, and changes in available methods to detect, mitigate, or prevent such theft.

In the Matter of Voya Financial Advisors, Inc., was the third known action brought against a firm for violating Regulation S-P (the Safeguards Rule), and the first action brought against a firm for violating the Identity Theft Red Flags Rule.[163]

Per the SEC, at least one person impersonating Voya's contractor representative interacted over the phone with Voya's tech-support line to reset three representative's web portal passwords. These web portals allowed access to customer information. [164]

On two occasions, the impersonator used phone numbers that the firm had previously flagged as being associated with fraudulent activity. Regardless, Voya's support staff reset the three passwords and provided temporary passwords via phone. In two of those instances, Voya staff had also provided the username of the representative to the impersonator. [165]

The first indication that foul play had occurred happened three hours following the first impersonator request when a representative whose account had been affected called Voya's support staff. He notified the staff that he had received an email confirming the password on his account had been changed, but he had never requested such action be initiated. [166]

Voya responded to the intrusion but failed to prevent the intrusion of two other representative accounts using the same attack vector. Ultimately, the impersonators were able to use the obtained usernames and passwords to gain access to at least 5,600 customer's personally identifiable information. There were no known fraudulent transfers of money or securities from the affected customer's accounts. [167]

Though Voya had policies and procedures to protect their customer's information as well as to prevent and respond to cybersecurity incidents, SEC alleged that they were not "reasonably designed to meet these objectives." More specifically, Voya policies were not designed properly for their representatives, and they did not identify those representatives and customers which were higher risk and thus required additional security measures. As such, SEC alleged that Voya violated Regulation S-P (Safeguards Rule). [168]

Finally, Voya had written and adopted a Theft Prevention Program. However, their program was deemed to have been an additional violation of the Red Flag Rule. The SEC alleged that it was not reviewed and updated as necessary to include changes to customer risks seen at the time. The SEC also alleged that Voya did not provide adequate training to their employees to properly identify and respond to identity theft red flags. [169]

Though Voya did not admit or deny the allegations of the SEC, they agreed to be censured in addition to paying a $1 million penalty.[170]

Partner Action Items:

☐ Determine if your firm is subject to the SEC or FTC Red Flag Rules;

☐ Work with legal counsel to review firm policies and procedures to ensure compliance with applicable SEC and FTC Guidelines;

☐ Determine which policies may respond to allegations of SEC or FTC Red Flag Rule violations. This may be a professional liability policy, or a cyber policy; dependent up the allegations;

☐ Communicate this data to relevant stakeholders, including IT and staff;

☐ Update the firm's incident response plan and other internal documents as necessary.

Section 5: Other Cybersecurity and Privacy Regulations

Beyond the various state and federal laws, firms may also be subject to a litany of other cybersecurity regulations. Whether any one firm is subject to these laws will depend upon the business practices and services being rendered. Once again, failure to understand and adhere to applicable laws can lead to unwanted regulatory inquiries and potential declinations of coverage.

GDPR – EU General Data Protection Regulation

The European Union's General Data Protection Regulation became effective in mid-2018. This regulation is notable in that it greatly expanded the definition of personal data to be protected, the jurisdiction to apply and enforce GDPR was increased, the consent requirements became more stringent and gave greater rights to the individual to control their data – including the right to erase that data, and includes very hard penalties among other requirements.[171]

To fully explain the intricacies of GDPR in such a limited space would be impossible. However, there are a few key points, starting with definitions, that firms should understand. Generally speaking, GDPR is structured to protect the processing of personal data of EU citizens.[172]

Processing means "'[A]ny operation or set of operations which is performed on personal data or on sets of personal data, whether or not by automated means, such as collection, recording, organization, structuring, storage, adaptation or alteration, retrieval, consultation, use, disclosure by transmission, dissemination or otherwise making available, alignment or combination, restriction, erasure or destruction."[173]

Personal Data means "any information relating to an identified or identifiable natural person ('data subject'); an identifiable natural person is one who can be identified, directly or indirectly, in particular by reference to an identifier such as a name, an identification number, location data, an online identifier or to one or more factors specific to the physical, physiological, genetic, mental, economic, cultural or social identity of that natural person." [174]

As shown from the definitions, if a firm is performing nearly any service that involves the personal data of an EU individual, or the firm maintains any data on an EU individual, the firm may be subject to

GDPR. This could reasonably include sign-up forms for newsletters on websites, the tracking of IP addresses for marketing purposes, or even an EU individual finding the firm's ad via an Internet search.

Additionally, GDPR contains a provision that allows EU member states to adapt the rules contained in portions of GDPR by determining more specific requirements.[175] Conceivably, this could result in a situation where a firm subject to GDPR must also be required to stay compliant with the various stipulations of each EU member state. Such an endeavor is certain to be expensive and time-consuming.

Penalties

Article 58 of the GDPR lists over 20 investigative, advisory, and corrective powers.[176] Notably, Article 58(2)(i) allows for administrative fines in conjunction with, or instead of, all the other powers listed in the article. Including other actions listed in GDPR, this allows regulators to fine firms the greater of up to €10,000,000 or 2% of the firm's worldwide revenue from the previous year.[177] Article 58(2) also allows for a public reprimand which could damage brand value as well as demanding compliance within a specific time frame. The latter action could specifically lead to significant costs and turmoil in a company that must now work to meet an imposed timeframe that it may otherwise have rejected as being too disruptive to operations.[178]

Businesses with company locations inside the EU have been pursued for years by regulators. Whether fines will be levied against non-EU businesses without EU-territory representation remains speculative. Issuing fines against entities where the EU lacks jurisdiction could undermine the gravitas that the EU is hoping to wield with this law.

Regardless, wholly based U.S. companies may agree to submit to GDPR fines for practical business purposes. The business may comply to avoid appearing out of step with current data security standards which could impact future revenue.[179] They may also acquiesce if pressured by other businesses who are registered under the EU-US Privacy Shield agreement so that these other businesses are not found to be non-compliant with GDPR. [180]

For any US-based business which has voluntarily registered under the EU-US Privacy Shield agreement, they are likely bound to any enforcement actions, fines, or injunctions imposed under GDPR.[181]

Exemptions

Given the confusing definitions, potentially excessive cost of compliance, and the high cost for non-compliance, many firms are naturally interested in any part of the regulation that would definitely exempt them from participating in GDPR. Unfortunately, most, if not all, of the possible exemptions are currently speculative in nature.

There does not appear to be any blanket exemption for small businesses. GDPR makes no compliance exemption for the amount or frequency of data collected. Article 2 does contain limited exemptions, but these do not appear relevant to businesses as they would mainly apply to personal or household activities and the action of member states.[182] The UK's Information Commissioner's Office (ICO), an independent regulatory body responsible for enforcing GDPR in the UK, has specifically stated, "You'll have to comply with the GDPR regardless of your size if you process personal data."[183] There may be, although, some exemptions for parts of the regulation that are determined on an individual basis.

Given the complexity and ambiguity of the regulation, the determination of specific clauses will likely remain the subject of litigation for years to come. Firms are advised to immediately seek competent legal counsel familiar with GDPR to determine their own compliance exemptions or requirements. Most firms will not have the resources, or will, to fight prolonged legal battles in this arena.

Partner Action Items:

☐ Seek legal counsel to give a qualified opinion on whether your firm is subject to GDPR;

☐ Determine if your firm's cyber policy would cover GDPR related actions;

☐ Communicate this data to relevant stakeholders, including IT and staff;

☐ Update the firm's incident response plan and other internal documents as necessary.

APEC - Asia-Pacific Economic Cooperation

The Asia-Pacific Economic Cooperation (APEC), is a group of 21 Pacific Rim member economies that was created to encourage free and open trade.[184] Notably, the United States is also a member country.[185] While still relatively unknown, APEC comprises 55% of the world's real GDP and 44% of world trade.[186] Thus, there is the possibility of significant growth in relevance in the coming years.

APEC is a large organization with varied goals. For the purposes of cybersecurity and cyber insurance, the voluntary APEC Privacy Framework is the most important for this discussion. The framework consists of the following nine principles:

- Preventing Harm
- Notice
- Collection Limitations.
- Uses of Personal Information
- Choice
- Integrity of Personal Information
- Security Safeguards
- Access and Correction
- Accountability

While the framework is voluntary, certification must come from a certified CBPR Accountability Agent. Currently, there are three accountability agents worldwide, with two in the United States.[187] Only a firm certified by an APEC Accountability Agent can claim to be a participant of the APEC CBPR system. The APEC CBPR system can be thought of as somewhat analogous to EU-US Privacy Shield discussed later.[188]

Within the United States, the Federal Trade Commission (FTC) is the primary enforcement agency regarding violations of the CBPR system. In July of 2016, the FTC began enforcement when it sent a letter to 28 companies that falsely claimed APEC CBPR system participation. This came on the heels of the FTC's first-ever settlement with a company that had allegedly misrepresented participation.

In the Matter of Very Incognito Technologies, Inc., a corporation d/b/a Vipvape, the FTC gave notice to companies nationwide that it will take CBPR enforcement seriously.

In its complaint, the FTC alleged that Vipvape had made statements on its website that related to their participation in the APEC CBPR system. However, Vipvape was never certified to participate by any Accountability Agent. The FTC discovered this alleged oversight by quickly referencing a website that lists all certified companies, www.cbprs.org.[189]

The FTC, therefore, asserted that VipVape had violated Section 5(a) of the Federal Trade Commissions Act, and their actions constituted, "deceptive acts or practices."[190]

In the settlement agreement, VipVape neither admitted nor denied the allegations made by the FTC. The FTC ordered numerous actions to be taken by VipVape, including the following:

- Acknowledgment of the receipt of the order;
- For 20 years, the business must deliver the order to all relevant and necessary principals, officers, directors, managers, members, employees, agents, and representatives;
- VipVape must obtain a signed and dated acknowledgment of the order within 30 days of delivery;
- Within 60 days, VipVape must submit a compliance report;
- VipVape will have 14 days to submit compliance notices regarding material changes to their business;

- For 20 years, they must maintain specific records as listed in the order and retain those records for a minimum of five years;
- Continued compliance monitoring as dictated by the FTC.[191]

Would a cyber policy cover an APEC related claim?

Unfortunately, there does not appear to be any definitive legal action that can be referenced. Likely it would depend on how the claim arose and what allegations were brought against the firm.

If the FTC were to investigate a firm following a breach for failure to adhere to the APEC Framework, this might be covered under a regulatory coverage. Firms will need to reference their own policy language to determine how their insurer defines regulatory actions and policy territory.

If a firm falsely or mistakenly claims APEC compliance on their website, coverage will likely depend on the opposing party's allegation, but nonetheless, are unlikely to be afforded coverage. While many cyber policies provide coverage for media liability claims, they also tend to include exclusions for false or misleading advertising.

Looking toward the future, APEC could gain ever greater relevance. In September of 2018, the final draft of the United States-Mexico-Canada Agreement (USMCA) was released. Within the final draft, it was noted that APEC CBPR is a valid method of facilitating cross-border information and data transfers.[192]

Partner Action Items:

- ☐ Understand if the firm is a certified member of APEC;
- ☐ Continuously monitor changes to APEC's framework to maintain compliance;

☐ Check that your firm is adequately protecting all covered data appropriately;

☐ Communicate this data to relevant stakeholders, including IT and staff;

☐ Update the firm's incident response plan and other internal documents as necessary;

☐ Determine if the firm's cyber insurance policy would cover an APEC related claim.

EU-US & Swiss-US Privacy Shield frameworks

The EU-US Privacy Shield replaced the International Safe Harbor Privacy Principles after the latter was deemed to be invalid.[193] Broadly speaking, Privacy Shield is a voluntary framework that regulates the transmission of personal data for commercial reasons that occur between the European Union and the United States.[194] The Swiss-US Privacy Shield is identical to the EU-US Privacy Shield.

The Department of Commerce maintains a list of companies that have voluntarily joined Privacy Shield. FTC acts as the enforcement body for the program within the United States. Failure to fully comply with the principles of the Privacy Shield Framework will be enforced under Section 5 of the FTC Act which prohibits unfair and deceptive acts.[195]

Naturally, the Privacy Shield is a complex undertaking with seven privacy principles:

- Notice
- Choice
- Accountability for Onward Transfer
- Security
- Data Integrity and Purpose Limitation
- Access
- Recourse, Enforcement and Liability[196]

In addition to the above privacy principles, Privacy Shield also contains 16 supplemental principles which either augment or explain the privacy principles. These include:

- Sensitive Data
- Journalistic Expectations
- Secondary Liability
- Performing Due Diligence

- The Role of the Data Protection Authorities
- Self-Certification
- Verification
- Access
- Human Resources Data
- Obligatory Contracts for Onward Transfers
- Dispute Resolution and Enforcement
- Choice - Timing of Opt Out
- Travel Information
- Pharmaceutical and Medical Products
- Public Record and Publicly Available Information
- Access Requests by Public Authorities[197]

To date, the FTC has but a handful of enforcement actions related to Privacy Shield. The actions have focused on a lack of proper registration or failures to maintain accurate privacy policies reflecting the status of their programs.[198] It has been reported that the FTC is looking to bring a greater number of actions against companies that show "substantial violations" of the Privacy Shield.[199]

Consider the allegations made by the FTC *In the Matter of SecurTest, Inc.*

SecurTest is a Florida-based company that provides employment background checks, drug testing, and other employment-related services.[200] The FTC alleged that SecurTest published statements related to its participation in the EU-US Privacy Shield framework on its website. One such alleged statement was the following:[201]

SecurTest, Inc. complies with the EU-US Privacy Shield Framework and the Swiss-US Privacy Shield Framework as set forth by the US Department of Commerce regarding the collection, use, and retention of personal information transferred from European Union and Switzerland to the United States, respectively. SecurTest, Inc. has certified to the Department of Commerce that it adheres to the Privacy Shield Principles. If there is any conflict between the terms in this privacy policy and the Privacy Shield Principles, the Privacy Shield Principles shall govern. To learn more about the Privacy Shield program, and to view our certification page, please visit https://www.privacyshield.gov/The [sic] terms of this policy apply to SecurTest's Web site and Background Screening Solutions, except where noted.

In its complaint, the FTC alleged that SecurTest had begun its Privacy Shield application with the Department of Commerce in September of 2017. In October of 2017, SecurTest had added a note on the bottom of its webpage noting that their application was pending. Although they allegedly failed to meet the certification timelines as established by the Department of Commerce, SecurTest continued to display the EU-US Privacy Shield paragraph shown previously, on its website. [202]

FTC subsequently contacted SecurTest regarding the matter. SecurTest subsequently completed the necessary steps to participate in the Privacy Shield framework and received certification on August 31, 2018. [203]

The FTC alleged SecurTest to have violated Section 5 of the FTC Act. [204]

In its decision and order, the FTC mandated SecurTest to engage in the following:

- Acknowledge the order;

- Deliver a copy of the order to all relevant parties within the business and have them acknowledge the order in writing within 30 days;
- Submit a compliance report to the FTC within 60 days;
- Submit a compliance notice to the FTC within 14 days of any material changes to the business;
- Create records for 10 years, and keep for 5 years, as they pertain to the order;
- Adhere to compliance orders as deemed necessary by the FTC;
- The order will be effective for 20 years.[205]

For firms who are currently, or are contemplating, adherence to the Privacy Shield Frameworks, there are various insurance implications to consider.

Most importantly, firms will need to be careful regarding how they complete any section on their cyber insurance application regarding federal or international security and privacy laws affecting their business. Privacy Shield requires an annual re-certification as well as year-round compliance. Failure to adhere to these mandates could be deemed a material misrepresentation by an insurer leading to a potential coverage declination.

In addition, firms will need to reference the relevant language in their cyber insurance policy. At a minimum, they will need to determine if a regulatory proceeding brought by the FTC in regard to the Privacy Shield frameworks would be considered a covered claim. It is unlikely that any follow-on compliance costs will be covered, though firms should also consider them when looking for coverage.

Partner Action Items:

- ☐ Requirements to participate in the EU-US Privacy Shield can be found at: https://www.privacyshield.gov/article?id=Requirements-of-Participation;
- ☐ Determine if your firm is currently a participant in the EU-US or Swiss-US Privacy Shield frameworks;
- ☐ Reference your cyber policy to determine if "regulatory proceedings" are considered a covered claim;
- ☐ Work with relevant stakeholders, including IT and Legal, to ensure year-round compliance within the framework;
- ☐ Update the firm's incident response plan as necessary.

Payment Card Industry Data Security Standards (PCI DSS)

Payment Card Industry Data Security Standards (PCI DSS) compliance is not legally mandated, but rather is founded and governed by the major credit card companies such as Visa, Mastercard, Discover, and American Express.

On their website, PCI DSS lists the following six goals. Numerous requirements exist within each goal:

- **"Build and Maintain a Secure Network":** Includes the use of a firewall and checking that default system passwords are changed;

- **"Protect Cardholder Data":** Includes protecting cardholder data that is stored, along with the encryption of cardholder data when it is sent across public networks;

- **"Maintain A Vulnerability Management Program":** Includes the use of anti-virus software and maintaining secure applications and systems;

- **"Implement Strong Access Control Measures":** Includes physical safeguards to cardholder data and the implementation of unique IDs to everyone with computer access;

- **"Regularly Monitor and Test Networks":** Includes the regular testing of computer security systems and well as the monitoring of access to the computer network;

- **"Maintain an Information Security Policy":** Includes the maintenance of a policy that addresses security for both contractor and employees.[206]

Many firms mistakenly believe that if they are using a third-party payment processor, PCI DSS does not apply to them, and thus coverage for PCI DSS is unnecessary in their cyber policy. Of note, the PCI DSS website states, "If you accept or process payment cards, the PCI Data Security Standards apply to you." Firms should also refer to their Merchant Service Agreement to assess any further liability.

When a firm decides to utilize a third-party payment processor, they will often be asked to complete one of the PCI DSS Self-Assessment Questionnaire and Attestation of Compliance forms. The depth of these forms will depend upon the circumstances of the firm, as there are nine different types of questionnaires available.[207]

For a firm where the payment card is not present and all payment processing functions are fully outsourced, they would likely be required to complete "Self-Assessment Questionnaire A and Attestation of Compliance." Firms should understand that they are attesting to various security controls that must be adhered to.

Assuming a firm uses a webpage for billing purposes which is hosted by a payment processor, how could a firm reasonably be subject to PCI DSS fines, penalties, or assessments?

Outside of a sophisticated attack, it could be as simple as an email breach where clients had sent the firm their credit card information via email despite the firm warning otherwise. Another common example could be physical copies of billing information data being stolen from the firm.

Regardless of the myriad scenarios that could lead to a breach, it is worth noting that credit card companies and banks do not take lightly to payment card breaches which result from non-compliance with PCI DSS. While the total fines are generally not made public, it has been estimated that fines for non-compliance can range from $5,000 to $500,000, with large businesses facing fines in the millions.[208] Such fines do not include assessments for additional Operational Reimbursement and Fraud Recovery Costs as detailed in the latter mentioned case of *P.F. Chang's China Bistro, Inc. v.*

Federal Insurance Co.[209] Further, the ability to utilize the payment card system could be revoked entirely leading to potentially severe income issues.[210]

Indeed, even if firms were to purport that they had adhered to PCI DSS standards, such representations may not persuade the FTC that a firm has enacted reasonable security standards. Such was the case of *FTC. v. LifeLock, Inc.*

In 2010, the FTC brought a complaint against LifeLock, a popular identity theft protection company. In their complaint, the FTC alleged that LifeLock advertisements regarding the protection of their customers were misleading as there was no definitive way to guarantee against identity theft. Furthermore, LifeLock was not adhering to advertised controls such as encryption and "need to know" access rights.[211]

FTC Chairman Jon Leibowitz noted, "While LifeLock promised consumers complete protection against all types of identity theft, in truth, the protection it actually provided left enough holes that you could drive a truck through it."[212]

As an additional word of warning concerning a previous explanation of state-level actions, the following attorneys general participated in the LifeLock settlement: Alaska, Arizona, California, Delaware, Florida, Hawaii, Idaho, Illinois, Indiana, Iowa, Kentucky, Maine, Maryland, Massachusetts, Michigan, Missouri, Mississippi, Montana, Nebraska, Nevada, New Mexico, New York, North Carolina, North Dakota, Ohio, Oregon, Pennsylvania, South Carolina, South Dakota, Tennessee, Texas, Vermont, Virginia, Washington, and West Virginia.[213]

Ultimately, LifeLock agreed to a $12 million settlement. Additionally, they agreed to a biennial third-party assessment of a broad data and cybersecurity program.[214]

Trouble returned for LifeLock approximately five years later when the FTC filed a contempt proceeding. Following an investigation, the FTC alleged the numerous deficiencies in LifeLock's 2010 order. In particular, they failed to, "maintain reasonable security measures to protect its users' sensitive personal data, including credit card...and bank account numbers [underline added]..." This, despite LifeLock asserting that they had complied with PCI DSS and that there was no evidence of a breach having affected their customers.[215]

Notably, the FTC commission issued a stark warning on their view of the difference between certification and compliance. "Certifications alone will not suffice to meet those obligations if we find evidence of security failures that put consumer information at risk...PCI DSS certification is insufficient in and of itself to establish the existence of reasonable security protections [underline added]... [T]he existence of a PCI DSS certification is an important consideration in, but by no means the end of, our analysis of reasonable security."[216]

The FTC noted that a previous case had called for "additional significant protections, including the implementation of risk assessments, certification of untrusted networks, and certification of the assessor's independence and freedom from conflicts of interest."[217]

Under the terms of the settlement, LifeLock was required to deposit $100 million into the U.S. District Court for the District of Arizona's registry. Of that, $68 million would be used to refund fees paid by class-action consumers who alleged injuries noted by the FTC. Any money not specified for use in consumer actions would be "provided to the FTC for use in further consumer redress."[218]

Regardless of whether firms consider the FTC's arguments to be pedantic, they should consider how the PCI Security Standards

Council described their data security standards before the U.S. House Financial Services Committee. "PCI Standards, <u>along with many other tools</u> [underline added], will provide a strong baseline for card data protection programs."[219]

Meeting baseline standards of PCI DSS compliance and evidencing appropriate and reasonable security measures before the FTC are two very different undertakings. Firms must take additional cybersecurity measures suitable to their firm's exposure to maximize their chances of avoiding FTC actions.

Partner Action Items:

- ☐ Determine if your firm is subject to PCI DSS. You will likely need to reference your Merchant Services Agreement (MSA);
- ☐ Continuously monitor compliance with PCI DSS requirements to assure compliance at all times. Failure to do so could result in a declination of coverage;
- ☐ Check that the firm is adequately protecting all covered payment card data appropriately;
- ☐ Communicate this data to relevant stakeholders, including IT and staff;
- ☐ Update the firm's incident response plan and other internal documents as necessary;
- ☐ Determine if the firm has coverage for any PCI DSS-related claims and associated expenses.

AICPA/IRS Requirements

The AICPA seemingly has nothing to say regarding the enforcement of cybersecurity within firms. It appears that they wholly defer to the FTC and IRS when dealing with cybersecurity.

In Publication 1345, *Handbook for Authorized IRS e-file Providers of Individual Income Tax Returns,* the IRS noted, "Failing to take necessary steps to implement or correct your security program may result in sanctions from the FTC. Failures that lead to an unauthorized disclosure may subject you to penalties under sections 7216 and/or 6713 of the Internal Revenue Code (I.R.C.)."[220]

I.R.C. 7216 notes in part, "Any person who is engaged in the business of preparing, or providing services in connection with the preparation of, returns of the tax imposed by Chapter 1, or any person who for compensation prepares any such return for any other person, and who knowingly or recklessly…discloses any information furnished to him for, or in connection with, the preparation of any such return…shall be fined not more than $1,000, or imprisoned not more than 1 year, or both, together with the costs of prosecution [underline added]."[221]

I.R.C. 6713 notes in part, "Imposition of penalty: If any person who is engaged in the business of preparing, or providing services in connection with the preparation of, returns of tax imposed by chapter 1, or any person who for compensation prepares any such return for any other person, and who…discloses any information furnished to him for, or in connection with, the preparation of any such return…shall pay a penalty of $250 for each such disclosure or use, but the total amount imposed under this subsection on such a person for any calendar year shall not exceed $10,000 [underline added]… Exceptions: The rules of section 7216(b) shall apply for purposes of this section."[222]

Outside of immediate monetary penalties assessed by the IRS, firms registered as Electronic Return Originators (EROs), or Transmitters, may have additional concerns. As stated in IRS Publication 1345, "Providers with problems involving fraud and abuse may be suspended or expelled from participation in IRS e-file, be assessed civil and preparer penalties or be subject to legal action."[223] Regarding e-file, the IRS noted in a late 2018 Tax Tip that they "may treat a violation of the FTC Safeguards Rule as a violation of IRS Revenue Procedure 2007-40."[224]

As a brief synopsis of Revenue Procedure 2007-40, the IRS stated, "This procedure specifies the requirements for participating as an Authorized IRS e-file Provider and is the official set of rules that govern participation in IRS e-file. The procedure revises [previous Revenue Procedures] by providing for denial of application or revocation of an Authorized IRS e-file Provider's participation in IRS e-file if it has been enjoined from filing returns by a federal or state court injunction or other legal action that would prevent its participation in the program."[225]

More succinctly, if a firm fails to properly secure client data, they could:

- have their e-file access revoked or suspended;
- be subject to action by the FTC;
- face penalties and possible prison sentences by the IRS.

As firms are investigating their adherence to the FTC Safeguards Rule, they should reference IRS Publication 4557, *Safeguarding Taxpayer Data: A Guide for Your Business*. This is a short guide with convenient checklists to assist firms in understanding their compliance requirements. The publication appears to provide non-mandatory guidance on security best-practices but is based upon The FTC Safeguards Rule.

Publication 4557 is unique in that it attempts to assist accounting firms with directly safeguarding taxpayer data. Keep in mind that the included "Safeguards Rule Checklist" does not guarantee full compliance with the FTC's interpretation of the Safeguard Rule. However, it is a good starting point for most firms looking to increase their cybersecurity posture and awareness.

It is unknown at the time of publication whether the IRS has investigated and fined a firm for violations of IRC 7216 or IRC 6713 following a breach of confidential client information. Further, it is unknown if the IRS has sanctioned an e-file Provider for a breach of their computer system. However, if tax fraud continues to plague the IRS and large dollar losses accumulate, it is conceivable that action will eventually be taken.

Were such fines, penalties, and actions to befall a firm, there are two primary policies that may respond: professional liability and cyber insurance policies.

Foremost, many firms would look to their professional liability policy. While most professional liability policies do include a sublimit for regulatory proceedings and disciplinary actions, they generally cover between $5,000 and $50,000 for defense costs but do not typically cover monetary fines, assessments, or penalties. Whether the policy would respond to an IRS proceeding or hearing is likely speculative as the defense is limited to actions brought by entities regulating the practice of accountancy.[226]

Finally, firms may also look toward their cyber insurance policy for coverage. The inclusion and applicability of coverage and defense for regulatory claims varies by insurer and policy. Thus, firms should investigate the coverage features, and definitions therein, with scrutiny.

Partner Action Items:

- ☐ IRS Publication 1345: Handbook for Authorized IRS e-file Providers of Individual Income Tax Returns can be found for free at: https://www.irs.gov/pub/irs-pdf/p1345.pdf;

- ☐ IRS Publication 4557 can be found for free at: https://www.irs.gov/pub/irs-pdf/p4557.pdf;

- ☐ Continuously monitor IRS publications for any changes in the law;

- ☐ Check that the firm is adequately protecting all covered data appropriately;

- ☐ Communicate this data to relevant stakeholders, including IT and staff;

- ☐ Update the firm's incident response plan and other internal documents as necessary.

American Bar Association Requirements

For CPAs also licensed as attorneys or those firms who specialize in work performed by CPA/JDs, the American Bar Association has additional guidance concerning data security. While it may seem strange that hackers would attempt to specifically infiltrate an attorney's computer, the information stored on those computers could be worth big money.

In one notorious example, hackers gained access to some of the country's largest law firms to access confidential client information. Their ultimate goal was to utilize that information with insider trader schemes.[227]

While large firms are obvious targets, smaller firms may inadvertently fall in the crosshairs of ideologically driven hackers. In 2012, the law firm of Puckett & Faraj was targeted by the hacktivist group "Anonymous." The firm was known for defending U.S. military service members accused of war crimes. The following is a series of emails allegedly from the firm of Puckett & Faraj, released by Anonymous after the breach:[228]

One of the firm leaders apparently first learned of the breach via the news.

From: "███████████" <███@puckettfaraj.com>
Date: Fri, 3 Feb 2012 13:54:57 -0500
Subject: Damage assessment
Cc: ███████   <███████@puckettfaraj.com>,
            ███<███████@puckettfaraj.com>
To: ███████████ <████████████████████>

████,

News agencies are reporting that our website was hacked and that the
hackers claim our emails and sensitive personal information was taken.
Is that possible?

Neal
████████████

Puckett & Faraj, PLLC
1800 Diagonal Rd, Suite 210
Alexandria, VA 22314
703.706.9566
www.puckettfaraj.com

Here, a firm member who was cc'd on the previous email vents his frustration concerning their cloud service provider:

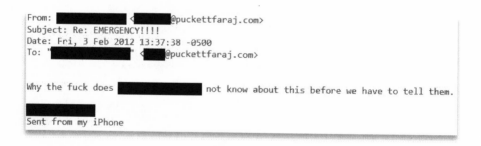

From: ████████████ <██████@puckettfaraj.com>
Subject: Re: EMERGENCY!!!!
Date: Fri, 3 Feb 2012 13:37:38 -0500
To: "████████████████" <██████@puckettfaraj.com>

Why the fuck does ████████████████ not know about this before we have to tell them.

████████████
Sent from my iPhone

Here is a portion of the email sent from the cloud service provider to the firm:

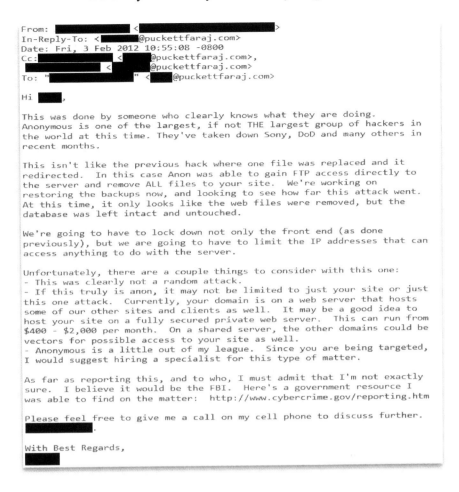

```
From:          ████████ < ███████████████ >
In-Reply-To: < ████ @puckettfaraj.com>
Date: Fri, 3 Feb 2012 10:55:08 -0800
Cc: ████████ < ████ @puckettfaraj.com>,
   ████████ < ████ @puckettfaraj.com>
To: " ████████ " < ████ @puckettfaraj.com>

Hi ████ ,

This was done by someone who clearly knows what they are doing.
Anonymous is one of the largest, if not THE largest group of hackers in
the world at this time. They've taken down Sony, DoD and many others in
recent months.

This isn't like the previous hack where one file was replaced and it
redirected.  In this case Anon was able to gain FTP access directly to
the server and remove ALL files to your site. We're working on
restoring the backups now, and looking to see how far this attack went.
At this time, it only looks like the web files were removed, but the
database was left intact and untouched.

We're going to have to lock down not only the front end (as done
previously), but we are going to have to limit the IP addresses that can
access anything to do with the server.

Unfortunately, there are a couple things to consider with this one:
- This was clearly not a random attack.
- If this truly is anon, it may not be limited to just your site or just
this one attack.  Currently, your domain is on a web server that hosts
some of our other sites and clients as well.  It may be a good idea to
host your site on a fully secured private web server.  This can run from
$400 - $2,000 per month.  On a shared server, the other domains could be
vectors for possible access to your site as well.
- Anonymous is a little out of my league.  Since you are being targeted,
I would suggest hiring a specialist for this type of matter.

As far as reporting this, and to who, I must admit that I'm not exactly
sure.  I believe it would be the FBI.  Here's a government resource I
was able to find on the matter:  http://www.cybercrime.gov/reporting.htm

Please feel free to give me a call on my cell phone to discuss further.
████████ .

With Best Regards,
████████
```

An email sent by a hacker to a member of the firm confirmed the breach:

```
From: ████ @gmail.com
Subject: HAHAHAHA
Date: February 3, 2012 12:53:24 PM EST
To: ████ @puckettfaraj.com

YOU GOT OWNED, YOU SICK, TWISTED RUBBISH
```

Here, a member of the firm acknowledges to their mother that they are in serious trouble:

```
On Fri, Feb 3, 2012 at 2:35 PM, ████████████████
<████████@comcast.net> wrote:

Mom, this group who hacked the law firm has stolen
all our Emails and client information.  They may
have the ability to send you Emails by |
impersonating me. Please don't answer any emails
from ████@puckettfaraj.com.  We are on hold with
Google trying to get the Emails completely shut
down.

This may completely destroy the Law Firm.

████████
```

Assuredly, high-profile episodes such as the one above spurred the American Bar Association (ABA) into action. In mid-2017, ABA released an update to the arguably antiquated Formal Opinion 99-413, via Formal Opinion 477R, *Securing Communication of Protected Client Information*. This opinion, while lengthy, fundamentally detailed "a lawyer's ethical responsibility to use reasonable efforts when communicating client confidential information using the Internet."[229]

This opinion included a brief description of the Duty of Competence, the Duty of Confidentiality, and the Duty to Communicate as they relate to cybersecurity. While it did not specify what "reasonable steps" a lawyer should take, it did offer the following considerations that should be understood:

- The nature of threats;
- Where client information is stored and how it is transmitted;

- The use of cybersecurity tools to prevent disclosure of confidential client information;
- How a client's electronic communications should be protected;
- Labeling of confidential client information;
- The training of attorneys and staff members on information security;
- Providing due diligence on technology vendors.[230]

Picking up where Formal Opinion 477R ended, the ABA more recently issued Formal Opinion 483, *Lawyers' Obligations After an Electronic Data Breach or Cyberattack.* With this new guidance, the Standing Committee on Ethics and Professional Responsibility has provided detailed guidance on an attorney's obligations to both former and current clients when either the client or the firm has become the victim of a data breach.

While Formal Opinion 483 is exhaustive and should be read by anyone who believes they may be required to follow its mandates, there are a few key points worthy of further consideration.

Per the ABA, a "data breach" is defined as "a data event where material client confidential information is misappropriated, destroyed, or otherwise compromised, or where a lawyer's ability to perform the legal services for which the lawyer is hired is significantly impaired by the episode."[231] This greatly expands an attorney's obligations beyond information specifically mentioned in other statutory regimes noted in this book.

To comply with this provision, firms should understand whether their cyber policy allows for voluntary notifications. Whether any one cyber insurer will agree to adhere to the obligations seen in this opinion is unknown and should be investigated by the firm prior to the purchase of a cyber insurance policy.

When a data breach is detected or suspected, a lawyer has the duty to act "reasonably and promptly" to both mitigate damage and stop the breach.[232] Performing these actions faithfully will require foresight by the firm and likely require an incident response plan.

According to the opinion, the Model Rules do not impose different standards on a physical breach or an electronic breach. [233] This should give firms pause to assess both the physical and digital security of their clients' confidential information.

Following the detection of a breach, a lawyer should conduct a post-breach investigation to verify that the intrusion has been halted. Following the stoppage, a lawyer should assess what data was lost or accessed.[234] Most commonly, this could be accomplished with a computer forensic expert.

When a lawyer knows or should have known that a data breach occurred, they must provide a notice to their current client(s) "to permit the client to make informed decisions regarding the representation." [235]

Interestingly, Opinion 483 does not explicitly require lawyers to notify formal clients of a data breach. However, the ABA does mention that attorneys should reference any contractual obligations they may have, as well as any other regulatory or statutory requirements to which they must adhere. [236]

The ABA also makes reference to a firm's document retention schedule/policy. This is meant to limit the amount of information that would fall into the hands of unauthorized parties and ultimately require notification by the lawyer.[237]

Formal Opinion 483 then circles back to the previously mentioned Formal Opinion 477R to discuss how the ABA views, "reasonable" security. A firm is not required to be "invulnerable or impenetrable," but they are obliged to make a reasonable effort. What, "reasonable" means is ultimately a term that will be defined depending on the firm. As referenced in the ABA Cybersecurity Handbook:

"Although security is relative, a legal standard for "reasonable" security is emerging. That standard rejects requirements for specific security measures (such as firewalls, passwords, or the like) and instead adopts a fact-specific approach to business security obligations that requires a "process" to assess risks, identify and implement appropriate security measures responsive to those risks, verify that the measures are effectively implemented, and ensure that they are continually updated in response to new developments."[238]

While this may not be particularly enlightening, firms may find greater guidance in cybersecurity, such as NIST CSF, to evidence a "reasonable" cybersecurity posture. NIST CSF is covered later in this book, though there are numerous other frameworks or formalized approaches that may fulfill this obligation.

In total, both Formal Opinions contain a litany of references to various Model Rules that have implications on cybersecurity and thus require constant vigilance. In addition, each state's Bar Association may have additional requirements that warrant further study. As stated by the ABA, violations of the Model Rules can lead to significant sanctions; to include:

- Disbarment;
- Suspension;
- Probation;
- Reprimand;
- Admonition by disciplinary counsel;
- Reimbursement for fees associated with the disciplinary action;
- Limitation by the court on a respondent's future practice.[239]

From all this, firms should understand that by employing JDs within their practice, they may be subjecting themselves to greater cybersecurity requirements. These additional requirements will need to be understood and dealt with before a firm can confidently complete a cyber insurance application without risking a declination in coverage for material misrepresentations.

Partner Action Items:

- ☐ Formal Opinion 483; Lawyers' Obligations After an Electronic Data Breach or Cyberattack can be found for free at: https://www.americanbar.org/content/dam/aba/images/news/formal_op_483.pdf;
- ☐ Understand if your firm is subject to any ABA cybersecurity rules;
- ☐ Continuously monitor those rules for any changes;
- ☐ Check that your firm is adequately protecting all covered data appropriately;
- ☐ Communicate this data to relevant stakeholders including IT and staff;
- ☐ Update the firm's incident response plan and other internal documents as necessary;
- ☐ Determine if the firm's cyber insurance or professional liability policy would cover actions brought by the ABA – or equivalent state-level bodies – for breach related claims.

Financial Industry Regulatory Authority (FINRA)

FINRA, the Financial Industry Regulatory Authority, is a self-regulatory organization that oversees several areas, including broker-dealers. For firms that operate a broker-dealer, they should understand and continuously assess FINRA's view of cybersecurity.

It does not appear that FINRA has any specific cybersecurity mandates that broker-dealers must follow, though FINRA rule 4370 does require a business continuity plan that may require disclosures on data backup and recovery methods and procedures.[240]

To date, the only discovered FINRA disciplinary action mentioning cybersecurity revolved around the format of electronic record retention.

In 2017, FINRA imposed fines on 12 firms alleging significant deficiencies in preserving customer records in a non-alterable format. Per the report, both federal securities laws and FINRA rules mandate that business-related records in electronic format are to be kept in a, "write once, read many" (WORM) format. This data format is deemed crucial by the SEC for "monitoring compliance with applicable securities laws, including antifraud provisions and financial responsibility standards."[241]

FINRA also found that three of the 12 firms also failed in their retention requirements under certain record retention rules.

Recently, FINRA issued recommendation and best practices to address the most common cybersecurity risks for broker-dealer firms, the *Report on Selected Cybersecurity Practices – 2018*. They acknowledge that the report does not create a legal opposition nor does it create a new legal requirement for broker-dealers to follow. Topics include:

- Branch controls such as written security plans (WSPs), asset inventories, technical controls, and a branch review program;

- Useful tips on countering common social engineering ploys such as "phishing;"
- A discussion on insider threats with useful countermeasures;
- Penetration testing;
- Mobile device security.

More immediately useful for most firms would be FINRA's *Small Firm Cybersecurity Checklist*. This checklist is derived from the NIST Cybersecurity Framework and FINRA's 2015 Report on Cybersecurity Practices. However, the website mentions that the checklist does not create a safe harbor for any law, so firms will still need to perform their own due diligence.

Finally, FINRA has issued at least one investor alert urging consumers to question their brokerage firms about the topic of cybersecurity. Questions included the naming of safeguards, reimbursement of assets following a breach, and whether the brokerage monitors the customer's assets to ascertain whether their information has been unduly used or stolen.[242] Firms should be ready to answer these questions without hesitation as consumers become savvier of cybersecurity in their lives.

Partner Action Items:

- ☐ FINRA's *Small Firm Cybersecurity Checklist* can be found at: http://www.finra.org/industry/small-firm-cybersecurity-checklist;
- ☐ FINRA's *Report on Selected Cybersecurity Practices – 2018* can be found at: https://www.finra.org/sites/default/files/Cybersecurity_Report_2018.pdf;

- ☐ FINRA's *Small Firm Business Continuity Plan Template* can be found at: http://www.finra.org/industry/small-firm-business-continuity-plan-template;
- ☐ If your firm falls under the oversight of FINRA, make sure that you are following are required security practices;
- ☐ Continuously monitor for any changes made by FINRA regarding cybersecurity;
- ☐ Communicate this data to relevant stakeholders, including IT and staff;
- ☐ Update the firm's incident response plan and other internal documents as necessary;
- ☐ Determine if the firm's cyber insurance policy covers a claim brought by FINRA following a data breach.

FARS/DFARS: For Government Contracts

Within the Code of Federal Regulations, Title 48 is commonly referred to as the "Federal Acquisition Regulation" (FAR). This regulation governs the formation and administration of contracts with the federal government. Within FAR, there are more than 20 supplements, but the cybersecurity requirements within the Department of Defense FAR Supplement (DFARS) are the most important for firms with Department of Defense (DoD) contracts. Broadly speaking, DFARS governs the majority of procurements made by DoD, NASA, General Services Administration (GSA), and all branches of the armed forces.

DFARS contains a relatively new provision known as Safeguarding Covered Defense Information and Cyber Incident Reporting (DFARS 252.204-7012).[243] If a firm stores, processes, or transmits covered defense information, they are likely subject to the 7012 regulation. Per the DoD, covered defense information is defined as "unclassified controlled technical information (CTI) or other information as described in the CUI Registry...that requires safeguarding/dissemination controls AND IS EITHER marked or otherwise identified in the contract and provided to the contractor by DoD in support of performance of the contract; OR collected/developed/received/transmitted/used/stored by the contractor in performance of contract."[244]

The CUI Registry is quite extensive and contains numerous categories and subcategories. Depending on the engagement and specialty of the firm, they could be handling information from any number of CUI categories.

To remain compliant with DFARS 252.204-7012, firms and their legal counsel should be aware that the regulation contains two main provisions.

The first deals with protecting the covered defense information via NIST Special Publication 800-171 Protecting Controlled Unclassified Information in Nonfederal Systems and Organizations. Proper compliance with this framework can require significant time and resources as it covers policies, process, secure IT configurations, and possibly additional hardware and security-related software.[245]

NIST SP 800-171 contains the following fourteen specific requirements:

- **Access Control** – Who can view this data?
- **Awareness and Training** – Are those who can view the data trained properly?
- **Audit and Accountability** – Can the firm identify and track who accesses the system?
- **Configuration Management** – Can the firm establish, maintain, and enforce secure configuration requirements?
- **Identification and Authentication** – Does the firm possess the ability to verify the identity of users, devices, or process prior to viewing the information?
- **Incident Response** – Does the firm have a system for testing and handling incidents?
- **Maintenance** – How will routine maintenance be handled and who is responsible?
- **Media Protection** – How does the firm handle hard copy and electronic records, including backup storage?
- **Personnel Security** – Are those allowed access to information appropriately screen before access and is there access revoked upon termination?
- **Physical Protection** – Does the firm limit the physical access to systems and is access recorded?

- **Risk Assessment** – Are there routine vulnerability scanning and risk assessments of the organization and its systems?
- **Security Assessment** – How will the firm continuously assess and improve their security controls?
- **System and Communications Protection** – Are communications monitored, controlled, and protected at crucial internal and external system boundaries?
- **System and Information Integrity** – How is the system integrity maintained and monitored for intrusions?[246]

While that may seem relatively straightforward, firms should understand that within the fourteen requirements, there are an additional 118 basic and derived security requirements.[247] If the firm wants to vary from the standards present in NIST SP 800-171, they will need to submit a request in writing to the Contracting Officer, who will forward it for consideration to the DoD CIO.[248] In certain circumstances, subcontractors must also adhere to DFARS 252.204-7012.

If the firm wants to use an external cloud provider to store, process, or transmit covered information, the firm must contractually require and ensure that the cloud provider meets the security requirements listed in the Federal Risk and Authorization Management Program (FedRAMP).[249] The cloud provider must still meet the requirements of DFARS 252.204-7012 pertaining to "cyber incident reporting, malicious software, media preservation and protection, access to additional information and equipment necessary for forensic analysis, and cyber incident damage assessment."[250] Any IT system or service other than the cloud provider requirements are still subject to the security restrictions found in DFARS 252.204-7012.[251]

The second main provision deals with the rapid reporting of cyber incidents and cooperation with the DoD.

Per the regulation, cyber incidents are "actions taken through the use of computer networks that result in a compromise or an actual or potentially adverse effect on an information system and/or the information residing therein." When a cyber incident is discovered, the firm will review the incident in accordance with the regulatory requirements and report the incident within 72 hours.[252]

If it is determined that malicious software was on the computer system that contributed to the incident, the firm must submit the offending code to the DoD's Cyber Crime Center. From there, the DoD can decide to formally assess the damage caused by the incident. During this assessment, the firm may be required to submit the media to the DoD and further aid in their evaluation.[253]

Interestingly, there is no requirement within the statue for the government to verify that firms are adhering to this regulation. Nor is there any specific type of certification that firms must obtain to demonstrate compliance. Furthermore, the DoD has stated that it will not accept or recognize any assessments or certifications by third parties. However, by signing the contract, the firm is agreeing to adhere to the terms of the contract, which likely include security requirements as stated in DFARS 252.204-7012.[254]

Failure to follow the safeguarding requirements of DFARS 252.204-7012 could result in detrimental actions against the contractor per DFARS 252.204-7009, Limitations on the Use or Disclosure of Third-Party Contractor Reported Cyber Incident Information:

"A breach of these obligations or restrictions may subject the Contractor to –

(i) Criminal, civil, administrative, and contractual actions in law and equity for penalties, damages, and other appropriate remedies by the United States, and;

(ii) Civil actions for damages and other appropriate remedies by the third party that reported the cyber incident, as a third-party beneficiary of this clause."[255]

Firms should be aware that the government is increasingly taking cybersecurity more seriously than before and may investigate, with the intent to prosecute, contractors who fail to adhere to their requirements. As an example, in December of 2017, the DOJ's National Security Division, and the U.S. Attorney's Office for the Eastern District of Virginia investigated Netcracker Technology Corporation (NTC).[256]

NTC is a software engineering firm that specializes in network solutions for large corporations. Like many large software companies, NTC used both American and foreign staff to develop software.[257]

Through a series of contracts, NTC provided services to the DoD's Defense Information System Network (DISN). This network operates the services for the governments classified and unclassified networks. Due to a series of misunderstandings regarding contract language and requirements, it was ultimately discovered that foreign nationals without the required security clearances were performing work on the contract. Further, the NTC server was stored in Moscow where the Russian Intelligence Services could legally monitor all network traffic, compromising the project. The contract with NTC was immediately canceled, and their work product was removed from DISN.[258]

NTC was subsequently investigated by the DOJ's National Security Division and the U.S. Attorney's Office for the Eastern District of Virginia. NTC denied that it had engaged in any wrongdoing but agreed to comply with an Enhanced Security Plan

(ESP), likely to avoid criminal prosecution.[259] The agreement includes both three-year and seven-year provisions.[260]

Within the three-year provision, NTC must seek the "non-objection" of the investigation government bodies before bidding on any new local, state, or federal contracts as the prime contractor, or as a sub-contractor. The seven-year provision includes retaining a third-party auditor to asses NTC's adherence with the ESP, and annual reports on NTC's adherence with the ESP. Among numerous other provisions, the agreement includes a $35 million fine to be paid to the United States Treasury if it is determined that NTC has failed in their responsibilities to uphold their promises as set forth in the plan.[261]

Partner Action Items:

☐ Determine if your firm must comply with DFARS 252.204-7012 Safeguarding Covered Defense Information and Cyber Incident Reporting;

☐ Consider seeking legal counsel to assist with compliance;

☐ Visit the CUI categories: https://www.archives.gov/cui/registry/category-list;

☐ NIST SP 800-171 (Rev. 1) Protecting Controlled Unclassified Information in Nonfederal Systems and Organizations can be found at: https://csrc.nist.gov/publications/detail/sp/800-171/rev-1/final;

☐ NIST SP 800-53, *Security and Privacy Controls for Federal Information Systems and Organizations* will provide more detail on the controls mentioned in NIST SP 800-71 (Rev. 1), and can be found at: https://csrc.nist.gov/publications/detail/sp/800-53/rev-4/final;

☐ FedRAMP can be found at: https://www.fedramp.gov/resources/documents/.

HIPAA/HITECH

The Health Insurance Portability and Accountability Act (HIPAA) and its partial update via the Health Information Technology for Economic and Clinical Health Act (HITECH Act), are quite expansive. Indeed, these laws alone could, and do, comprise entire books dedicated to their nuances. For the purposes of cybersecurity law and its implications on cyber insurance, two specific provisions will be addressed here: the Privacy Rule, and the Security Rule.

Generally speaking, HIPAA applies to "Covered Entities." As defined by HHS, the following are considered covered entities:

- Health care providers which includes providers like doctors, clinics, psychologists, dentists, chiropractors, nursing homes, and pharmacies if they are transmitting PHI in an electronic form;
- Health plans, including health insurance companies, HMOs, company health plans, and various government health programs such as Medicare or Medicaid;
- Health care clearinghouses which process nonstandard health information they have received from a different entity.[262]

The addition of HITECH greatly expanded the reach of HIPAA by adding a new class of entity referred to as a "Business Associate" (BA). Generally speaking, a business associate is a person or organization that performs services which require the covered entity to disclose PHI to that organization. This could include claims processing, billing, legal, or accounting services among others. The HIPAA Administrative Simplification Regulation Text defines a business associate as the following:

(i) A Health Information Organization, E-prescribing Gateway, or other person that provides data transmission services with

137

respect to protected health information to a covered entity and that requires access on a routine basis to such protected health information;

(ii) A person that offers a personal health record to one or more individuals on behalf of a covered entity;

(iii) A subcontractor that creates, receives, maintains, or transmits protected health information on behalf of the business associate.[263]

Any subcontractor, or subcontractor of a subcontractor and so on…, that creates, receives, transmits, or maintains PHI on behalf of a BA, is automatically considered a BA in their own right.[264] Ergo, if an accounting firm is acting as a subcontractor to a BA, even without a formal BA agreement (BAA), they will automatically be deemed a BA under HIPAA and must adhere to all applicable laws and safeguards.

Specifically excluded are the following:

(i) A health care provider, with respect to disclosures by a covered entity to the health care provider concerning the treatment of the individual;

(ii) A plan sponsor, with respect to disclosures by a group health plan (or by a health insurance issuer or HMO with respect to a group health plan) to the plan sponsor, to the extent that the requirements of § 164.504(f) of this subchapter apply and are met;

(iii) A government agency, with respect to determining eligibility for, or enrollment in, a government health plan that provides public benefits and is administered by another government agency, or collecting protected health information for such purposes, to the extent such activities are authorized by law;

(iv) A covered entity participating in an organized health care arrangement that performs a function or activity as described by paragraph (1)(i) of this definition for or on behalf of such organized health care arrangement, or that provides a service as described in paragraph (1)(ii) of this definition to or for such organized health care arrangement by virtue of such activities or services.[265]

Data to be protected under HIPAA/HITECH includes information quite similar to information considered PII in the various state and territory breach notification law. Generally, such information is referred to as Protected Health Information (PHI).

As stated in the regulation, PHI means:

[I]ndividually identifiable health information:

    (i) Transmitted by electronic media;

    (ii) Maintained in electronic media, or;

    (iii) Transmitted or maintained in any other form or
        medium.[266]

This is a very broad definition, and could include, but is not limited to: fingerprints, voiceprints, photographs, X-rays, Social Security number, name, address, employer's name, medical record number, account number, health plan number, and more.[267]

Information excluded from being considered PHI is stated as follows in the regulation:

[I]ndividually identifiable health information:

    (i) In education records covered by the Family Educational
        Rights and Privacy Act, as amended, 20 U.S.C. 1232g;

    (ii) In records described at 20 U.S.C. 1232g(a)(4)(B)(iv);

    (iii) In employment records held by a covered entity in its
        role as employer, and;

    (iv) Regarding a person who has been deceased for more than
        50 years.[268]

Antipodal to PHI is the term "De-identified Health Information." This is an altered type of information that does not allow for identification of the person. There are very specific elements required to de-identified information under the privacy rule, but they can be summarized by two primary methods. [269] Either a qualified statistician can make a formal determination, or specific identifiers can be removed.[270]

Unbeknownst to many accounting firms, they may be considered a business associate handling PHI. Referencing the above, firms can be business associates by definition, not necessarily solely through a contract, though a contract may be necessary. Services, where a firm may fall under these rules, could include providing an audit of internal controls, basic bookkeeping and accounting services, consulting services, and litigation support.[271] Indeed, the HHS lists "CPA Firms" as an example of a business associate on their website.[272]

Privacy Rule:

The Privacy Rule is the portion of HIPPA which, unsurprisingly, deals with privacy and confidentiality of PHI – also known as "individually identifiable health information" (IIHI). The rule provides federal-level protections but does not supersede any other federal, state, or local law which would require greater protections on PHI. Covered Entities (CEs) must comply fully with the Privacy Rule. Business Associates (BAs) must only comply with certain sections of the rule.

As a reminder, HIPAA defines CEs to include:

- Health plans;
- Health clearinghouses;
- Health care providers that transmit health information in electronic form for transactions.[273]

For Covered Entities (CEs), the Privacy Rule has the following four major components:

1. A CE must notify individuals of their privacy rights and how the individual's information can be used. Generally, this is accomplished with a notice of privacy practices (NPP). The NPP should detail how the CE will use and disclose PHI, the legal duties and privacy practices borne by the CE, and the individual's rights in regard to PHI – such as a restriction of disclosure in certain circumstances.[274]

2. Each CE must adopt and implement certain privacy procedures. These privacy procedures should minimize the request, disclosure, and amount of PHI in use.[275]

3. The CE shall train their employees to understand mandatory privacy procedures.[276]

4. An individual at each CE shall be designated as being responsible for ensuring that privacy procedures are followed and implemented. These tasks will be accomplished with a Privacy and Security Officer.[277] In addition, the privacy officer must create policies and procedures for persons to submit complaints regarding the CE's HIPAA compliance with a specified person.[278]

The Privacy Rule states that Business Associates are directly and/or contractually liable for any use or disclosure of PHI that is not allowed under the Privacy Rule, or as further dictated by its Business Associate Agreement (BAA). BAs may also be liable for various other shortcomings such as a failure to limit the disclosure and use of PHI, or to fail in providing breach notifications to the CEs. Finally, violations of HIPAA will subject BAs to the same civil and criminal penalties as those experienced by CEs.[279]

The penalties for violating the Privacy Rule are significant. The penalty amounts can range from $100 to $50,000 or more per violation. The calendar year cap for violations is $1,500,000.[280] As such, firms should be well acquainted with any and all obligations they may have in regard to the Privacy Rule.

Security Rule:

The security rule is perhaps the most important HIPAA rule in regard to cybersecurity as its goal is to protect the confidentiality of PHI in electronic form (ePHI). The Security Rule applies to ePHI while it is being transmitted, stored, or maintained. The provisions of this rule are generally mandatory to both CEs and BAs unless otherwise specified.

Broadly speaking, the Security Rule mandates a number of essential functions; such as:

- Keeping ePHI secure at all times;
- Ensuring that their workforce is complying with the rule;
- Protecting against unauthorized disclosures of ePHI from reasonably anticipated threats or errors.[281]

To accomplish these goals, the Security Rule has three organizational levels of safeguards. The three organizational levels of safeguards are Administrative safeguards, Physical safeguards, and Technical safeguards. Each safeguard is comprised of "standards." In turn, some of those standards may be broken into further, "implementation specifications" to provide a more detailed explanation of implementing a standard.

Administrative Safeguards

Administrative safeguards comprise the majority of safeguards that must be implemented. The administrative safeguards include:

- A security management process which implements policies and procedures which will "prevent, detect, contain, and correct security violations." This will include specific implementation of risk analysis, risk management, sanction policy, and information system activity review;
- An assigned security official who is responsible for the requirements of the administrative safeguards;
- Policies and procedures regarding the access of ePHI by appropriate staff members, as well as the denial of access for those staff not cleared to view ePHI. Specific implementations include authorization and supervision, clearance procedures, and termination procedures;
- The implementation of policies and procedures regarding the access of ePHI including the isolation of health care clearinghouse functions, access authorization, and initiation and modification of access;
- Mandatory security awareness training to include security reminders, protection for malware, log-in monitoring, and password management;
- Security incident procedures to deal with various types of incidents;

- Contingency plans for dealing with emergencies such as system failures or natural disasters. This would specifically include data backup plans, disaster recovery plans, as well as the testing and updating the plan;
- A periodic evaluation – both technical and non-technical – to test the entity's compliance with the various administrative safeguards;
- Business associate contracts and other arrangements to ensure that BAs safeguard ePHI appropriately.[282]

To evidence that entities are adhering to the administrative safeguards appropriately, each entity must adhere to certain documentation requirements. This includes a six-year document retention policy, a review of those documents to ensure confidentiality, and updates to those documents as threats evolve or arise.[283]

Physical Safeguards

Physical safeguards are designed to protect a firm's computer system and ePHI from unauthorized physical access. Within the physical safeguards rule, there are three primary standards:

- Facility access controls which limit the physical access of information systems to only those people which are authorized access. This includes contingency operations, facility security plan, access control and validation procedures, and maintenance records;[284]

- Workstation use and security, including the appropriate functions to be performed at those workstations, how those functions will be performed, and the physical environment of those workstations that have access to ePHI.[285] Per a recent HHS sub-regulatory guidance, this also includes portable electronic devices such as laptops, tablets, and smartphones;[286]

- Device and media controls which concern the accountability, receipt, storage, back-up, and disposal of hardware and electronic media in and out of the facility;[287] In recent newsletter guidance from the HHS, they identified numerous questions that entities should consider when developing device and media controls. These questions include whether the entity has a record that tracks the media and devices through their entire lifecycle and whether workplace members, including management, are appropriately trained on the safeguarding of ePHI.[288]

Technical Safeguards

Any information system that contains ePHI requires entities to develop and implement technical policies and procedures to safeguard that data. While the regulations are technology- and vendor-neutral, they require entities to implement those safeguards which are reasonable and appropriate for their organization. More specifically, technical safeguards include the following five standards:

- Entities must develop and implement access controls for any information system that contains ePHI. This will include unique user identification and emergency access procedures for obtaining ePHI during an emergency. In addition, this may include automatic logoffs and encryption/decryption of ePHI.[289]

- At their discretion, and consistent with internal risk analyses, entities may implement hardware, software, and procedural mechanisms to examine and record the activity on their systems that contain ePHI.[290]

- Entities must develop and implement policies and procedures to protect the integrity of ePHI from any improper destruction or alteration.[291] This may be accomplished by electronic means.[292]

- Entities must implement policies and procedures to verify that anyone seeking access to ePHI is authentic and authorized to do so.[293]

- When ePHI is being transmitted over an electronic network, entities will ensure that the information is guarded from unauthorized access.[294] This may be accomplished with integrity controls or encryption.[295]

Policies, Procedures, and Documentation Requirements

In addition to complying with the Security Rule, entities must also comply with various document retention policies and procedures. Entities shall:

- Retain documents required by this rule for six years from their creation, or the date of when they were last in effect, whichever is longer;

- Make those documents available to any individual who is responsible for implementing the required procedures;

- Maintain a record of actions, activities, or assessments that are required to be documented by the rule;

- Periodically review and update the documents as operational or environmental factors change the security of ePHI to ensure their confidentiality and security.[296]

Breach Notification Rules

Per HIPAA, a Breach means "the acquisition, access, use, or disclosure of protected health information in a manner not permitted...which compromises the security or privacy of the protected health information."[297]

Any PHI that is accessed, used, or disclosed is presumed to be a breach. This is unless the CE or BA can successfully demonstrate via risk assessment that there is a low probability of misuse based upon at least the following four factors:

- The nature and extent of the PHI involved and the likelihood of re-identification;
- The unauthorized person to whom the disclosure was made, or who used the PHI;
- Whether PHI was actually viewed or acquired;
- The extent to which any risks to the PHI have been mitigated.

As a warning, many breach notifications by a CE will result in an enforcement investigation. These investigations often result in a CE or BA making large payments to the government as well as acquiescing to a corrective action plan (CAP).[298] These plans can be lengthy and burdensome, so all efforts should be made by CEs and BAs to ensure strict compliance with the law.

Furthermore, breach notifications involving PHI are consistently the most expensive on a per-record basis.[299] While CEs are required to provide notice to affected individuals, those responsibilities may delegate that responsibility to a BA.[300] For any firm serving as a BA, such notices could prove financially burdensome and will have serious implications on prudent limits available under their cyber insurance policy. Firms should seek legal counsel to assist in reviewing their BAA to determine if they are liable for breach notifications to individuals, or liable to reimburse the CE for breach notification costs.

Business Associate Agreements and Cloud Computing

HIPAA requires that CEs obtain contractual assurances from BAs that they will adhere to all applicable security issues. Broadly speaking, the statute requires the following two implementation specifications:

- BA contracts must provide that the BA will comply with applicable HIPAA security standards for protecting ePHI. Any subcontractors that create, receive, maintain, or transmit ePHI on behalf of the BA must agree to comply with the HIPAA security standards via their own contract. BAs must report any security incident to the CE immediately.

- BA contracts with their own subcontractors will apply the same standards as stated between CEs and BAs.[301]

As cloud computing becomes more prevalent, these implementation specifications could pose additional risks to CEs and firms acting as BAs. Recently, HHS released guidance on complying with HIPAA when entities utilize cloud service providers (CSPs). Most notably, HHS stated, "[w]hen a covered entity engages the services of a CSP to create, receive, maintain, or transmit ePHI (such as to process and/or store ePHI), on its behalf, the CSP is a business associate [underline added] under HIPAA. Furthermore, when a business associate subcontracts with a CSP to create, receive, maintain, or transmit ePHI on its behalf, the *CSP* subcontractor itself is a business associate [underline added]. This is true even if the CSP processes or stores only encrypted ePHI and lacks an encryption key for the data. Lacking an encryption key does not [underline added] exempt a CSP from business associate status and obligations under the HIPAA Rules. As a result, the covered entity (or business associate) and the CSP must enter into a HIPAA-compliant business associate agreement (BAA), and the CSP is both contractually liable for meeting the terms of the BAA and directly liable for compliance with the applicable requirements of the HIPAA Rules."[302]

As such, CSPs that are business associates are still responsible for implementing appropriate controls under the Security Rule. HHS states that the CSP and their customer – in this case, a BA or CE – should confirm how each party will address their Security Rule requirements. For firms that have control over which security features are present at the CSP, HHS warns that OCR will consider any shortcomings in these choices in their investigation of the CSP and/or the firm. In addition, the BA and CSP must ensure that both parties are still staying compliant with the Privacy Rule.[303]

Therefore, if a firm is currently, or could be considered a BA under HIPAA, they should consider whether their CSP is HIPAA compliant. This would likely avoid many of the potential pitfalls inherent with such a complex set of rules and regulations. OCR, as a matter of policy, does not endorse, recommend, or certify any CSPs. [304] Firms should engage legal counsel when selecting and reviewing contract language of CPs.

Partner Action Items:

- ☐ Determine if your firm is, or could reasonably be construed as, a CE or BA under HIPAA/HITECH;
- ☐ Determine if the firm has entered into any BA agreements;
- ☐ Determine if the firm's CSP is compliant, as applicable;
- ☐ Continuously monitor applicable breach notification laws for any changes;
- ☐ Check that your firm is adequately protecting all covered data appropriately;
- ☐ Communicate this data to relevant stakeholders, including IT and staff;

☐ Determine which, if any, of the firm's insurance policies would cover a claim regarding failures of the Privacy or Security Rules.

Notable OCR Enforcement Action Examples

Business Associate Agreement Case

In April of 2017, the U.S. Department of Health and Human Services (HHS) took a public position with CEs on how seriously it takes Business Associate Agreements (BAAs).

Earlier in 2015, the HHS Office of Civil Rights (OCR) had begun a compliance review of the CE, The Center for Children's Digestive Health. This came after OCR had initiated an investigation of a BA which was storing inactive medical records for the center. Of concern to OCR was that the CE began providing PHI to BA in 2003, but neither party had been able to produce a signed BAA.[305]

Through its investigation, OCR determined various deficiencies. Foremost, the CE failed to obtain necessary assurances from the BA, via the written agreement, that the BA would safeguard the PHI as required by law. As such, the CE unlawfully disclosed the PHI of thousands of individuals to the BA, potentially violating the Privacy Rule.[306]

In addition to a $31,000 payment, the CE was required to carry out an extensive corrective action plan (CAP) that focused on numerous compliance requirements. These requirements included sending all policies and procedures to HHS for review and approval, collecting signed compliance certifications from all its staff, maintaining BAA documentation for six years after contract termination, and disclosing various BAA information to HHS.[307]

Enforcement Actions Against Business Associates

In what was the first enforcement action by HIPAA regulators against a BA, federal regulators have put all business associates on notice.

In February of 2014, six nursing homes separately sent notifications to the HHS OCR regarding a breach of unsecured ePHI.

Two months later, OCR notified the Catholic Health Care Services of the Archdiocese of Philadelphia (CHCS) of an investigation regarding its compliance with HIPAA rules. CHCS was a nonprofit that provided management and information technology services and was the sole corporate parent, of the six nursing homes. [308]

In its findings, the OCR alleged that the CHCS failed to adhere to the HIPAA Security Rule with the following actions:

- CHCS failed to conduct an assessment of potential risks and vulnerabilities to ePHI.
- CHCS failed to implement security measures necessary to reduce risks and vulnerabilities as required. [309]

In addition to a $650,000 Resolution Amount, CHCS agreed to an extensive CAP.[310]

Cloud Providers as HIPAA Business Associates

In 2016, HHS surprised many when it argued that at least some cloud providers could be considered business associates. Previous to this ruling, cloud providers had successfully argued that they fell within the "conduit exception" of HIPAA's business associate status. Later that year, HHS clarified its position on CSPs as BAs with an FAQ guidance.[311]

Problems began in 2013 when HHS received a breach notification from Oregon Health & Science University (OHSU), deemed to be a covered entity under HIPAA. That breach centered around a stolen laptop containing unsecured ePHI. Later that year, OHSU notified HHS of another breach involving unauthorized access of ePHI at a CSP without a required business associate agreement.[312]

Subsequently HHS's OCR investigated the matters and acknowledged that OHSU had implemented policies and procedures compliant with most HIPAA rules. However, it had erred in disclosing ePHI to the CSP without BAA resulting in a breach of over 3,000 individuals. In addition, OHSU violated HIPAA by not obtaining a BAA with the CSP, and among other violations, failed to implement the necessary policies and procedures to address security violations and incidents.[313]

Per the HHS Resolution Agreement, OHSU agreed to pay a $2,700,000 resolution amount (fine) and comply with a corrective action plan (CAP).[314]

HIPAA will enforce actions against defunct companies.

HHS has signaled that even out-of-business associates will be liable for improper retention and disposal of PHI in accordance with the Privacy Rule.

In 2015 HHS's OCR fielded an anonymous complaint that a "dumpster diver" had attempted to exchange medical records for cash at a shredding and recycling facility. Following an investigation, OCR determined that FileFax, an out-of-business BA, had either left PHI in an unlocked truck in their parking lot or allowed an individual to remove the PHI from the FileFax facility who disposed of it in an unsecured location.[315]

Regardless of the cause, the court-appointed receiver for FileFax agreed to a $100,000 resolution amount. The receiver also agreed to a CAP, which among numerous other provisions, mandated appropriate disposal of the remaining records containing PHI in accordance with HIPAA standards.[316]

In light of this resolution agreement, it is clear that HHS is taking document security seriously. Any firm with access to medical records should ensure that they are maintained, secured, and destroyed properly. If OCR is willing to pursue action against a bankrupt company for a relatively small infraction, they will certainly pursue an operating firm.

Cyber-Attacks Can Result in Significant Settlements

Potentially unavoidable cyber-attacks will not deter HHS from investigations and penalties.

In 2015, Anthem, an American health insurance company, filed a breach report with HHS after discovering that unauthorized individuals had gained access to their IT systems. This was accomplished via an undetected and continuous cyber-attack. Anthem later discovered that the attackers had infiltrated their computer system through a spear-phishing email after at least one employee had responded to the email. A subsequent OCR investigation revealed that the attackers had stolen the ePHI of nearly 79 million people, including names, social security numbers, medical identification numbers, and dates of birth.

Numerous potential violations of the Privacy Rule and Security Rule were noted, including Anthem's failure to:

- Conduct an accurate and thorough risk analysis of risks to ePHI;
- Implement procedures to regularly review IT system activity records;
- Identify and address detections of the incident which lead to the breach;
- Implement adequate technical policies and procedures to ensure that only authorized persons had access to ePHI.[317]

As a result, Anthem agreed to a record-setting $16 million settlement with HHS, including a comprehensive corrective action plan (CAP). [318]

The OCR Director noted, "The largest health data breach in U.S. history fully merits the largest HIPAA settlement in history[.] Unfortunately, Anthem failed to implement appropriate measures for detecting hackers who had gained access to their system to harvest passwords and steal people's private information. We know that large health care entities are attractive targets for hackers, which is why they are expected to have strong password policies and to monitor and respond to security incidents in a timely fashion or risk enforcement by OCR."[319]

State Attorneys General May Enforce HIPAA Violations

In 2015, the Indiana attorney general reminded entities who must remain compliant with HIPAA that the states may sometimes action.

In 2013, then dentist Joseph Beck had hired a data company to securely destroy paper records of his former patients. In an investigation by a local news station, it was alleged that 63 boxes, comprising over 7,000 files, of former patients were discovered in a dumpster. The new station alleged that it discovered names, addresses, social security numbers, credit cards numbers, and other health information in the files.

Beck subsequently entered into a consent order with the Indiana attorney general. As part of order, Beck was fined $12,000 and agreed to a CAP.[320] Indiana joins the ranks of numerous other states which have recently enforced actions against those they believe have violated HIPAA.[321]

For this, firms should take away two main points. First, small entities are not immune to HIPAA-related enforcement actions. Second, electronic disclosures may gain nationwide attention, but physical documents still require care in accordance with HIPAA mandates.

Private Rights of Action

While several patients have filed private lawsuits involving HIPAA violations, none so far appear to be successful. Also, HIPAA contains no explicit private right of action. As a federal law, HIPAA both explicitly and implicitly preempts state laws that are contrary to HIPAA – except in a case where a state's law is more rigorous than HIPAA in regard to privacy protection.

An illustrative case of courts generally refusing to extend a private right of action can be found in the case of *Hope Lee-Thomas v. Labcorp.*

Lee-Thomas was a hospital patient who was instructed to submit her medical information on a computer in close proximity to a separate intake station. She asserted that her health information was visible to another patient who was using the separate intake station. Upon discovery of this alleged violation, she informed the lab technician and took a photograph of the two stations.[322]

Early the following month, Lee-Thomas sent a letter to the hospital informing them of a possible HIPAA privacy violation. She then registered a complaint with the Department of Health and Human Services Office of Civil Rights (OCR). [323] While both complaints were denied by their respective oversight agencies, the District of Columbia informed Lee-Thomas of her right to bring a private action before the D.C. Superior Court.[324]

When bringing her action in front of the D.C. Superior Court, Lee-Thomas's sole complaint rested with her assertion that the computer station violated HIPAA's privacy protections. Though she filed her lawsuit *pro se* (on her own behalf and without formal legal representation), and thus was subject to a "less stringent standard than formal pleadings," she was unsuccessful.[325]

The court dismissed her claim because HIPAA provides no private cause of action. Subsequent to this definitive statement, the court wrote in length, referencing numerous cases which have reaches the same conclusion.[326]

While HIPAA does provide civil and criminal penalties for improperly disclosed or handled information, the statute specifically entrusts those actions with HHS and each state's attorney general.[327] Firms can rest a little easier knowing that individual plaintiffs will likely be unsuccessful with individual actions.

HIPAA Audit Program

Firms acting as BAs may be curious as to how they could be subject to an investigation by HHS's OCR.

The most direct method would be a party notifying HHS of a complaint involving HIPAA. Under HIPAA, HHS has the authority to conduct compliance reviews and engage in investigations where there has been an alleged violation of any rules therein. Namely, this would include alleged violation of the Privacy, Security, and Breach Notification Rules.

However, there is a separate program whereby OCR will investigate compliance and implementation of HIPAA standards without an alleged violation.

In 2016, OCT implemented its Phase 2 HIPAA Audit Program. This program is designed to "review the policies and procedures adopted and employed by covered entities and their business associates to meet selected standards and implementation specifications of the Privacy, Security, and Breach Notification Rules."[328]

The audit program is focused on evaluating the compliance of randomly selected businesses who are not currently facing an open investigation or undergoing a compliance review. OCR has indicated that they will be instructing CEs to list and identify their BAs with included contact information. They will use both desk and on-site audits.[329]

HHS has indicated that these audits are intended primarily as a "compliance improvement activity." However, if the audit report prepared by OCR brings to light a serious compliance issue, they may begin a compliance review.[330]

TCPA – Telephone Consumer Protection Act

The Telephone Consumer Protection Act (TCPA) was enacted in the early 1990s to govern telecommunications commerce. In short, it attempts to regulate the tools that a telemarketer would use, such as automatic telephone dialing systems and voice recordings, as well as the type of telephone line that is contacted. All three types of lines are covered, including wireless phones, landlines, and fax lines.[331] The TCPA does not govern the transmission of emails.[332]

Cyber insurance policies may offer coverage for media liability claims. However, claims relating to TCPA are often explicitly excluded from coverage.

For example, one prominent cyber insurer specifically notes the following "Spam" exclusion:

"...based upon or arising out of any actual or alleged violation of any federal, state, local, or foreign statutes, ordinances, regulations, or other laws regarding or relating to unsolicited telemarketing, solicitations, emails, faxes, text messages, mobile video messages, or any other communications of any type or nature, including but not limited to the Telephone Consumer Protection Act, CAN-SPAM Act, or any anti-spam or do-not-call statutes, ordinances, or regulations."[333]

To elucidate this point, consider the case of *Flores v. ACE American Insurance Company.*

The insured in the underlying case, GrubHub, Inc., was a food-ordering company that faced a class-action claim for allegedly violating the TCPA. The plaintiffs alleged that the violation came as a result of sending text messages to customers without their consent. Ultimately, GrubHub settled with the plaintiffs, agreed to a consent judgment, and assigned their rights against their insurer, ACE

American. Notably, ACE American had denied coverage to GrubHub, so with this assignment, the class plaintiffs proceeded to attempt collection from the insurer.[334]

When the insurer filed a motion to dismiss, the court held that there were two primary exclusions which prevented coverage.

GrubHub's cyber policy contained an exclusion for any claim, "alleging, based upon, arising out of or attributable to any unsolicited dissemination of faxes, emails or other communications by or on behalf of the Insured to multiple actual or prospective customers of the Insured or any other third party, including but not limited to actions brought under the Telephone Consumer Protection Act.."[335]

A further exclusion stated that there was no coverage for any claim, "alleging, based upon, arising out of or attributable to false, deceptive or unfair business practices or any violation of consumer protection laws."[336] Here, the court specifically noted that the TCPA is considered a "consumer protection" law, thus no coverage would be afforded. [337]

If a cyber policy explicitly excludes coverage, firms may look toward their general insurance policies for advertising injury or property damage provisions. Whether courts will require general insurance policies to defend insureds for claims alleging a violation of the TCPA is a complex legal area unto itself. Broadly speaking, it depends upon the policy, the state where the case is being decided, and type of medium used to transmit the data.[338] This area of the law is often exceedingly complex and seemingly contradictory.[339] Therefore, firms should seek competent legal counsel to address their compliance and insurance concerns.

Partner Action Items:

- ☐ The FTC's Complying with the Telemarketing Sales Rule can be found for free at: https://www.ftc.gov/tips-advice/business-center/guidance/complying-telemarketing-sales-rule;
- ☐ Understand if your firm is subject to TCPA;
- ☐ Continuously monitor the TCPA for any changes to the law or its interpretations;
- ☐ Communicate this data to relevant stakeholders, including IT and staff;
- ☐ Determine if any of the firm's insurance policies would cover a TCPA related claim.

CAN-SPAM – Controlling the Assault of Non-Solicited Pornography and Marketing Act

Digital marketing is a necessity for the modern firm. However, there are limitations a firm can go to market their services. Firms should consider the Controlling the Assault of Non-Solicited Pornography and Marketing Act (CAN-SPAM) enacted in 2003. Though somewhat of a misnomer, the act is broadly designed to protect consumers from unsolicited, bulk, commercial email (UCE) sent by online marketers. UCE can generally be classified as bulk emails for the advertising of goods or services that were not sent to the recipient with their approval and where no previous business relationship could be implied.[340]

Unlike many other laws, the CAN-SPAM Act preempts all other state laws in the area of UCE. However, it does preserve states' common law rules and statutory provisions to the extent they would prohibit email that is false or deceptive.[341]

Email messages sent from commercial entities must generally adhere to the following requirements:

- Email header information cannot be false or misleading;
- There should be no deceptive subject lines;
- An opt-out mechanism should be included;
- The sender's physical address should be included;
- The message should be identified as an advertisement or solicitation.[342]

The FTC is the primary enforcer of alleged CAN-SPAM violations, though other federal agencies such as the SEC and FCC may also have enforcement authority. State attorneys general and other state agencies may also bring an action where state residents were affected.343 Interestingly, Internet service providers (ISPs) can also bring claims for certain CAN-SPAM violations.[344]

The cost of non-compliance to firms can be crippling. The FTC alone notes, "Each separate email in violation of the CAN-SPAM Act is subject to penalties of up to $42,530, so non-compliance can be costly."[345] At the state level, statutory damages are limited to $2,000,000 with a $6,000,000 cap for willful, knowing, or aggravated violations.[346]

With such sizeable penalties on the line for firms, they will certainly be looking towards their insurance policies to provide a financial backstop should they run afoul of CAN-SPAM. Unfortunately, standard general liability policies often exclude coverage for these types of claims.[347]

Furthermore, many cyber insurance policies generally exclude coverage for any CAN-SPAM, or similar type, claims. As shown previously, one prominent cyber insurer specifically notes the following "Spam" exclusion:

"...based upon or arising out of any actual or alleged violation of any federal, state, local, or foreign statutes, ordinances, regulations, or other laws regarding or relating to unsolicited telemarketing, solicitations, emails, faxes, text messages, mobile video messages, or any other communications of any type or nature, including but not limited to the Telephone Consumer Protection Act, CAN-SPAM Act, or any anti-spam or do-not-call statutes, ordinances, or regulations."[348]

Another prominent cyber insurer did not explicitly name the CAN-SPAM act as being excluded from coverage. However, it did note a broad exclusion for "a Claim brought by or on behalf of any state, federal, local or foreign governmental entity, in such entity's regulatory or official capacity; but this exclusion will not apply to the Regulatory Defense & Penalties insuring agreement[.]" The Regulatory Defense & Penalties agreement within the policy only provides coverage for penalties and claims expenses arising from data breaches or security events.[349]

Thus, it is reasonable to assume that no cyber insurance coverage would be afforded from at least these prominent cyber insurers for CAN-SPAM related claims.

Given these considerations, firms should, at a minimum, seek input from legal counsel and compliance experts regarding their marketing practices to determine if they reasonably conform to CAN-SPAM.

Partner Action Items:

☐ The FTC's CAN-SPAM Act: A Compliance Guide for Business can be found at: https://www.ftc.gov/tips-advice/business-center/guidance/can-spam-act-compliance-guide-business;

☐ Understand if your firm is subject to TCPA;

☐ Continuously monitor the TCPA for any changes to the law or its interpretations;

☐ Communicate this data to relevant stakeholders, including IT and staff;

☐ Determine if any of the firm's insurance policies would cover a TCPA related claim.

Americans with Disabilities Act (ADA)

A growing concern for firms in the modern age is the conflicting rulings seen at various circuit courts of appeal on whether their website needs to be ADA-compliant. At the heart of the matter is whether ADA Title III's definition of "public accommodations" extends to the Internet, and thus a firm's website. Generally, ADA applies to any firm with 15 or more employees.[350]

Currently, the First, Second, and Seventh Circuit Courts of Appeals have held that a website can be considered a place of public accommodation without a direct connection to any physical place. However, the Third, Sixth, Ninth, and Eleventh Circuit Courts of Appeals have found that a public accommodation must be a physical place. However, they also noted that a good or service which is provided by a public accommodation – such as through a website – might fall under the purview of the ADA if there is a sufficient nexus to a business's physical location.[351]

Complicating matters, Stephen E. Boyd, Assistant Attorney General for the Department of Justice, recently responded to a letter sent by a group of U.S. House Representatives regarding ADA-compliant websites. In his September 2018 response letter, Boyd noted:

"[T]he Department has consistently taken the position that the absence of a specific regulation does not serve as a basis for noncompliance with a statute's requirements. Absent the adoption of specific technical requirements for websites through rulemaking, public accommodations have flexibility in how to comply with the ADA's general requirements of nondiscrimination and effective communication. Accordingly, noncompliance with a voluntary technical standard for website accessibility does not necessarily indicate noncompliance with the ADA."[352]

How firms should interpret this "guidance" from the DOJ is ultimately dependent on a conversation between them and their attorney. Though in the broadest sense, it is generally advisable to voluntarily comply rather than be forced through legal action.

More definitely, the U.S. Architectural and Transportation Barriers Compliance Board, also known as the United States Access Board, has a more definitive say. By way of background, the Access Board is an independent federal agency that coordinates amongst the other federal agencies to enforce accessibility standards.

Within their 2017 publication, the Information and Communication Technology (ICT) Standards and Guidelines, the Access Board noted that federal contractors, agencies, and vendors are subject to Section 508 of the Rehabilitation Act of 1973. Thus, federal contractors, agencies, and vendors must have their websites and other electronic material accessible to disabled individuals. To accomplish this, they stipulated that covered entities should adhere to Web Content Accessibility Guidelines 2.0 Levels A and AA (WCAG 2.0 AA) by January 18, 2018.[353]

For clarification, WCAG 2.0 contains four main principles for accessible website designs. They should be perceivable, operable, understandable, and robust. The four levels of conformance with WCAG 2.0 include Level A, Level AA, and Level AAA.[354] Level A is the minimum level of conformance, and Level AA is the conformance generally cited by the DOJ and various courts.[355] Level AAA may be impossible to meet for certain types of content, so it is not recommend by the originating authors for entire sites.[356]

Given the unique nature of ADA related website claims, it is difficult to determine how any insurance policies would respond to such actions. Broadly speaking, cyber insurance policies will respond to regulatory proceedings, but only when initiated by a data breach or security breach.

More applicable may be a firm's Employment Practices Liability Insurance (EPLI) policy if it offers coverage for third-party claims. However, this is far from assured, and firms should consult their own policies for clarification. Even if a policy were to respond to the claim, they may still lack coverage for any costs necessary to bring their website into compliance, as well as for any relief awarded by the court.

Partner Action Items:

☐ Work with legal and compliance experts to determine if your website should be ADA-compliant. If so, consider if your firm will make the website WCAG AA Level AA compliant;

☐ Continuously monitor ADA accessibility laws and applicable cases for any changes;

☐ Communicate this data to relevant stakeholders, including IT and staff;

☐ Determine if any of the firm's insurance policies would cover an ADA related claim.

A Note on Other Foreign "Cyber" Laws

Firms should be aware that many foreign nations have their own statutes which may require additional research if residents of those countries are engaged in business with the firm, or if the firm has offices in those countries. Due to the number of foreign laws, in conjunction with the unknown nature of their legal systems by these authors, they will not be covered in this book.

While the laws naturally vary between nations, firms should begin their search by looking for consumer protection, cybercrime, data protection and privacy, and electronic transaction laws. It is *highly* advised that firms engage legal counsel familiar with foreign laws in this area as applicability and enforcement may vary greatly.

Partner Action Items:

☐ Consult the United Nations Conference on Trade and Development:
https://unctad.org/en/Pages/DTL/STI_and_ICTs/ICT4D-Legislation/eCom-Cybercrime-Laws.aspx;

☐ If you believe that you may be subject to foreign statute, it is recommended that you seek assistance from legal counsel immediately;

☐ Determine if your policy's coverage territory would respond to cyber-related claims in foreign countries;

☐ Determine if your policy would respond to a cyber-related regulatory claim brought by a foreign power.

Section 6: Potential Coverage in Non-Cyber Insurance Policies

Coverage for "cyber"-related losses is not necessarily to be found exclusively in dedicated cyber policies. Dependent on the type of loss and the policies carried by the firm, coverage may be found elsewhere. It is advisable that firms first start from a position of believing they have no insurance for these types of losses so they can thoroughly investigate how their different policies may respond to the various loss scenarios. Commonly carried policies that may include coverage for specific losses include commercial, crime, and professional liability, employment practices, D&O, and tech E&O type policies.

Commercial Insurance Policies

While many firms may believe that insurance coverage for data breaches – hereafter referred to as "cyber insurance" – is only found in dedicated policies, that is not necessarily the case. When firms assess their cyber insurance needs, there are various policies that may contain coverage elements which may, or may not, respond based upon the scenario. Failure to properly assess the coverage of the firm may lead to losses that would otherwise have been covered.

Before cyber insurance became well-known, businesses would often look toward their commercial insurance policy for coverage if a cyber policy was not available for coverage. Within a firm's commercial insurance policy, they will likely see three primary types of coverage:

Coverage A – covering property damage and bodily injury;

Coverage B – covering personal and advertising injury;

Coverage C – covering medical payments associated with bodily injury.[357]

Coverage B is the most likely to be investigated for possible coverage following a breach.

Of note in commercial insurance, these policies are generally designed cover property damage as a covered loss. Most policies of this type specifically exclude damage to the insured's owned property. Rather, coverage is afforded if they damage another's property or person.

There have been a few cases were companies successfully argued that certain data breach associated losses should be covered under their commercial insurance policies Coverage A provisions.[358] However, most courts have acquiesced to hold that the loss of data is not considered tangible property and thus cannot be covered under a commercial insurance policy.[359] In a case as recent as 2014, the court further limited recovery under a Coverage A dispute as hard drives contain "abstract and intangible" data, and thus a firm could not argue coverage for damage to "tangible property."[360]

Should a firm seek to find data-breach coverage under a commercial insurance policy, they may consider Coverage B provisions. Coverage B generally indemnifies a firm for personal or advertising injury. Personal injury would refer to three general categories:

"(1) false arrest, malicious prosecution, or willful detention;

(2) libel slander, or defamation of character, and;

(3) invasion of privacy, wrongful eviction, or wrongful entry."[361]

Advertising injury is generally understood to cover "publication offenses, misappropriation of ideas, and infringement of copyright or trademark offenses."[362]

Should a firm attempt data-breach coverage under Coverage B, they can expect insurers to sternly challenge such a claim. Courts have thus far been conflicting in their reasoning to uphold or dismiss such cases.

In the case of *Travelers Indemnity Co. of America v. Portal Healthcare Solutions, LLC*, Portal, a healthcare company, faced a class-action claim from customers following a data breach which allegedly exposed their healthcare records. In turn, Portal sought coverage for the claim under their commercial general liability policy with Travelers Indemnity Company. Portal's policy contained coverage for "electronic publication of material that...gives unreasonable publicity to a person's private life[.]"[363]

Travelers proceeded to bring a claim against Portal, alleging that the exposure of material did not equate to the publication of material, so no coverage should be afforded. They argued, in part, that no publication could have occurred because the insured had no intention to publish the healthcare records and there was no indication that anyone had viewed the material. Ultimately, the district court, as well as the Fourth Circuit court, sided with Portal. Their reasoning was that the distinction held between "advertent" and "inadvertent" publication was irrelevant. Regardless of the intent, the exposure of the customer's medical records was a publication that otherwise resulted in unreasonable publicity to their private lives.[364]

In stark contrast to the previous case was *Zurich American Insurance Co. v. Sony Corp.* Sony sought to recover under its commercial general liability policy following a breach of its Play Station Network which allegedly exposed the names, addresses and credit card data of roughly 77 million users. Within Sony's policy was a provision that covered for the "[o]ral or written publication, in any manner, of material that violates a person's privacy."[365]

While at face value, this provision would appear to afford coverage, ultimately, the judge found in favor of Zurich. His rationale was that a publication would only occur if Sony were the ones to have published the data in question. The information had been obtained by a third-party hacker and without the permission of Sony. Thus, coverage, in this case, was denied.[366]

Perhaps the Sony case would lead firms to believe that if they mistakenly, but otherwise purposefully, exposed data, this would lead to a covered loss. A common example would be placing multiple clients' files into a client-accessible folder meant for one person. Unfortunately, coverage may still be denied.

In the case of *Creative Hospitality Ventures, Inc. v. United States Liability Company*, Creative faced a lawsuit for violating the Fair and Accurate Credit Card Transaction Act due to printing greater than the last five numbers of the consumer's credit card number on receipts. Upon facing the lawsuit, Creative Hospitality Ventures sought coverage under Coverage B of their commercial insurance policy.[367]

At face value, this would appear to be a covered loss as Creative Hospitality Ventures published the consumer data. However, the court did not agree. In its holding, the U.S. Court of Appeals for the Eleventh Circuit argued that coverage was denied because it did not consider receipts to fit the policy definition of "publication." Under the court's reasoning, a publication meant the "act or process of issuing copies...for general distribution to the public." Though the business printed the receipts, they were not meant for "general distribution to the public" and thus would not be considered publications. Hence, coverage was denied.[368]

Even if insurance companies are successful in their bid to deny coverage for data-breach-related claims brought under commercial liability policies, they would generally prefer to avoid the negative publicity and associated court costs. Thus, insurers are continually opting to refine their policy language with specific exclusions. Often, the source of these exclusions comes from the Insurance Services Office (ISO), a body which provides standardized policy language that can be altered by insurers for their own purposes.

In response to these manners of claims, ISO has offered the following specific endorsements which may already be found in a firm's commercial insurance policy, though this is not a definitive list:

- CG 21 08 05 14 (Exclusion: Access Or Disclosure Of Confidential Or Personal Information (Coverage B Only)). Precludes coverage under Coverage B for disclosure or access to personal or confidential information. Specifically, this excludes coverage for notification costs, credit monitoring expenses, forensic examination and investigation expenses, expenses for public relations to handle the event, and any other related cost, loss or expense.

- CG 21 07 05 14 (Exclusion: Access Or Disclosure Of Confidential Or Personal Information And Data-Related

Liability: Limited Bodily Injury Exception Not Included). This endorsement further excludes coverage for property damage or bodily injury that results from the disclosure or access of computer data or the loss or damage of computer data.

☐ CG 21 06 05 14 (Exclusion: Access Or Disclosure Of Confidential Or Personal Information And Data-Related Liability: With Bodily Injury Exception). Similar to the previously listed endorsement, this clarifies that bodily injury that results from the damage or loss of computer data is not to be excluded.369

Recently, certain insurers offering commercial general liability policies have been offering small endorsements to their base policies. Generally, coverage has been capped at $10,000 of coverage which is drastically insufficient for most firms. Additionally, the coverage elements offered lag behind those offered in dedicated cyber policies, so most firms have elected to eschew such minimalist coverage.

While limited coverage may be afforded under a commercial insurance policy, definitive coverage may be unknown until the case is decided. More extensive coverage features than those found in a commercial insurance policy may be found in a dedicated cyber policy.

For most firms, the cost to litigate nuanced insurance policy language will likely be far greater than the purchase of a dedicated cyber insurance policy. As more commercial liability insurance policies are litigated, insurance companies will continue to refine coverage elements and exclusions to specifically avoid coverage for data-breach-related claims. Thus, coverage for future claims brought in this sphere will likely be even more difficult.

Partner Action Items:

☐ Determine what "cyber"-related claims may be covered under your firm's commercial insurance policy. This will likely require the assistance of a competent legal broker and/or legal counsel;

☐ Continuously monitor the coverage afforded under your firm's commercial insurance policy for any changes;

☐ Communicate this data to relevant stakeholders including IT and staff;

☐ Update the firm's incident response plan and other internal documents as necessary.

Commercial Crime Policies

Firms often purchase a crime policy if they are handling large sums of money and are concerned about an internal misappropriation by staff. Firms may also purchase, or attempt to rely on, a crime policy for specific data-breach-related funds which are often the loss of funds via fraudulent wiring instructions. Of interest to this discussion, crime policies often offer coverage for computer crime and funds transfer fraud. These will be discussed in turn.

Computer Crime

Take, for example, a common policy provision found within a popular provider of crime policies for computer crime.

Computer Crime coverage:

"1. Computer Fraud: The Company will pay the Insured for the Insured's **direct loss of, or direct loss from** damage to, Money, Securities and Other Property directly **caused by Computer Fraud**."[370]

Computer Fraud is later defined in the policy as:

"The use of any computer to fraudulently cause a transfer of Money, Securities or Other Property from inside the Premises or Financial Institution Premises:

1. to a person (other than a Messenger) outside the Premises or Financial Institution Premises, or;

2. to a place outside the Premises or Financial Institution Premises." 371

From the above, it can be extrapolated that coverage under a crime policy often requires the wrongful act to directly cause the damages being sought by the insured. In the context of computer-related fraud, this could mean that the losses incurred by the fraud must relate to negative acts committed on the insured's computer.

However, insurers will often question coverage for certain computer-fraud losses with arguments of causation.

To illustrate this point, consider the case of *Apache Corp. v. Great American Insurance Co.*, a case hinging on social engineering.

By way of background, the fraud began when one of Apache's staff members received a phone call from a person purporting to be from a known and legitimate vendor of Apache. The caller requested that Apache change the bank account number of the vendor. In response, Apache notified the caller that they would need to submit such a request on the vendor's letterhead. In response, Apache received a duplicitous email containing a counterfeit letter on the vendor's letterhead to confirm the change in banking information. To the credit of the Apache employee, they called the phone number listed on the fake letterhead to authenticate the banking details. Once confirmed, Apache wired roughly $7 million via their computer inputs to a fraudulent account.[372]

Thankfully, Apache was able to recoup some of the money lost, which was likely due to an internal controls error at the bank.[373] However, not all was recoverable, and in response, Apache filed a claim with their crime policy insurer, Great American Insurance Company. In response, Great American Insurance Company sought to deny coverage.[374]

Relevant to this claim was the policy language being relied upon by both parties similar to policy listed above. Specifically, the policy covered computer fraud damages for the "loss resulting directly from the use of any computer to fraudulently cause a transfer of that property" to a third party. Great American argued that the loss was not due directly to computer usage.[375]

The Fifth Circuit Court subsequently agreed with Great American. The court held that the loss did not arise directly from the use of a computer. The email was incidental to the Apache employee authorizing the transfer of funds. In a clear warning to all firms holding a crime policy, the court cited a previous, similar ruling by holding that "'[C]omputers are used in almost every business transaction, reading this provision to cover all transfers that involve both a computer and fraud at some point in the transaction would convert this Crime Policy into a 'General Fraud' Policy', essentially covering losses from all forms of fraud rather than a specified risk category."[376]

Such rationale by the courts has been upheld in numerous other cases of similar construction.[377] Thus, it is important for every firm to carefully read their own policy language with competent legal counsel to clarify their own coverage. Otherwise, a firm could discover that their policy does not cover what is conceived of by a plain language policy assessment.

Funds Transfer Fraud

Many crime policies purchased by firms also offer coverage for funds-transfer fraud. As social engineering-fraud schemes become more painful and prevalent for firms, this is a policy provision worthy serious consideration. However, firms should not blindly believe any funds-transfer loss can be covered by this policy provision.

Take, for example, a common policy provision found within a popular provider of crime policies for funds-transfer fraud:

Funds transfer fraud coverage:

"Funds Transfer Fraud means:

1. an electronic, telegraphic, cable, teletype or telephone instruction **fraudulently transmitted** to a Financial Institution directing such institution to debit a Transfer Account and to transfer, pay or deliver Money or Securities from the Transfer Account which instruction **purports to have been transmitted by the Insured**, but was in fact

fraudulently transmitted **by someone other than the Insured without the Insured's knowledge or consent**, or;

2. **a fraudulent written instruction**, other than one covered under [a different insuring agreement] issued to a Financial Institution directing such Financial Institution to debit a Transfer Account and to transfer, pay or deliver Money or Securities from such Transfer Account by use of an electronic funds transfer system at specified intervals or under specified conditions, which written instruction **purports to have been issued by the Insured** but was in fact fraudulently issued, Forged or altered **by someone other than the Insured without the Insured's knowledge or consent**."[378]

This definition further states, "Funds Transfer Fraud does not include Social Engineering Fraud or Computer Fraud."[379]

Thus, coverage does not necessarily apply if an employee is duped by a hacker into transferring firm or client funds. To sophisticated purchasers of insurance, such exclusions did not sit well in the age of social engineering. For this reason, crime-policy insurers began offering coverage for social engineering. This too will undoubtedly come with its own unique coverage restrictions that should be investigated by the firm.

Social Engineering Fraud Coverage

Within the social engineering fraud coverage endorsement, some insurers will name a specific exclusion if the money transfer was initiated by an authorized person.

For example, take the case of *Aqua Star (USA) Corp. v. Travelers Casualty & Surety Co.* Aqua Star's troubles began when a hacker sent a fake email to their treasury manager requesting that they change the bank account number of a known vendor. The employee then changed the account number in their internal spreadsheet used to track bank account numbers for vendors. Aqua Star was ultimately defrauded of over $700,000 when funds were sent to the wrong address. In response, they filed a claim with their crime insurance policy provider.[380]

Travelers attempted to deny coverage due to the following exclusion for any "loss resulting directly or indirectly from the input of Electronic Data by a natural person having the authority to enter the Insured Computer System."[381]

The court agreed with Travelers. Specifically, the court noted in their holding, "[A]n indirect cause of the loss was the entry of Electronic Data into Aqua Star's Computer System by someone with authority to enter the system, [the named exclusion] applies. None of Aqua Star's arguments to the contrary...justify another conclusion."[382]

As crime policies have evolved, some insurers have begun to eliminate the authorized person's exclusion in their social engineering fraud coverage. However, coverage sublimits in this area tend to be small – typically ranging from $100,000 to $250,000 – due to the unpredictability of large dollar losses.[383] Should firms elect to insure against social engineering fraud through a crime policy, they should take note of the coverage and exclusions listed in the policy with competent legal counsel.

Partner Action Items:

- ☐ Determine what "cyber"-related claims may be covered under your firm's crime policy. This will likely require the assistance of a competent legal broker and/or legal counsel;
- ☐ Continuously monitor the coverage afforded under your crime policy for any changes;
- ☐ Communicate this data to relevant stakeholders, including IT and staff;

☐ Update the firm's incident response plan and other internal documents as necessary.

Professional Liability Policies

In response to the onslaught of data-breach-related claims, professional liability carriers have sought to refine and limit their scope of liability. Most commonly this is done via an endorsement which first seeks to amend the definition of a data breach in relation to a professional liability claim. Specifically, this can be accomplished by defining privacy claims and client network damage claims. Effectively, this may result in an overlap of coverage between a firm's professional liability policy and third-party coverage features found in a dedicated, cyber-liability policy, though this is not necessarily detrimental.

Privacy Injuries

One nationwide, leading, professional liability insurer specializing in accounting firms defines a privacy injury as the following:

"*Privacy Injury* means:

    (1) any unauthorized disclosure of, inability to access, or inaccuracy with respect to, non-public personal information in violation of:

    (a) an *Insured's* privacy policy, or;

    (b) any federal, state, foreign or other law, statute or regulation governing the confidentiality, integrity or accessibility of non-public personal information, including but not limited to, the Health Insurance Portability and Accountability Act of 1996, Gramm-Leach-Bliley Act, Children's Online Privacy Protection Act, or the EU Data Protection Act.

    (2) an *Insured's* failure to prevent unauthorized access to confidential information provided to the *Insured* by another, or created by an *Insured* for another, where such information is subject to the terms of a confidentiality

agreement or equivalent obligating the *Insured* to protect such information on behalf of another."[384]

Put succinctly, a privacy claim would generally mean a claim alleging a privacy injury due to a firm rendering professional services. Most commonly, this element of coverage would generally provide for a firm facing a private right of action suit from a client following a breach. Private rights of action, as they relate to data-breach laws, were discussed earlier in this book. In a similar vein, this could also cover a claim due to breach of a contractually obligated confidentiality agreement.

Client Network Damage

As defined by one prominent insurer, "Client Network Damage Claim means a demand for money or services received by an Insured, including service of suit or institution of arbitration proceedings, alleging Network Damage to an Insured's client's computer network in the rendering of an Insured's rendering of Professional Services."

"Network Damage means:

(1) the unscheduled or unplanned inability of an authorized user to gain access to a network, or;

(2) the suspension or interruption of the operation of any network, or;

(3) the unauthorized access to, destruction of, addition to, deletion of, or alteration to information maintained on the network of an Insured's client."[385]

Client network damage would generally cover damage done to a client's network if the firm's computer system sent malicious code to a client. Another scenario could include damage to a client's network, such as downloading malware while a staff member was providing outsourced CFO or Client Accounting Services. Whether this would afford coverage to damages done to the clients of the firm's client is unknown and has yet to be tested.

Additional coverages found in such endorsements may include a small, sublimit of coverage for responding to regulatory proceedings brought by a jurisdiction for violating sections of a breach notification law. Of note, none of the endorsements assessed provided coverage for damages that could be awarded. These endorsements provide a small amount – typically around $12,500 – for expenses related to the defense of such regulatory claims.

Misappropriation of Client Funds

Found within most professional liability policies is a sublimit for insider theft. Specifically, this would cover the firm if a staff member were to misappropriate funds from a client. This would not cover the theft of the firm's funds by a staff member. Such coverage would likely need to be obtained from a crime policy's employee theft coverage provision.

When contemplating the threat of employee theft, it is crucial that the firm considers the sublimit. Many insurers offer a basic coverage of $100,000, often included in base policy language. At the firm's request, this can be increased, generally to no greater than $2 million.[386] If higher limits are needed, it may be necessary to consider a crime policy or fidelity bond.

Should a firm suffer a loss greater than their policy's stated misappropriations sublimit, it is unlikely that they will be able to recover full policy limits. Such a scenario was seen in the case of *CAMICO Mutual Insurance Company v. Heffler Radetich & Saitta, LLP.*

In this case, Heffler was appointed by the court to act as a claims administrator for a $490 million settlement. A senior accountant was assigned to assist in the administration of the settlement. Through a series of fraudulent acts, the accountant was able to work with co-conspirators to file over $5 million in fake claims. A class-action claim was brought against Heffler for damages due to the accountant's crimes.[387] In turn, Heffler submitted a claim to its professional liability carrier.

Due to the outsized nature of the claim in relation to the $100,000 sublimit carried by Heffler, CAMICO filed suit against Heffler seeking a declaratory judgment to affirm that no coverage beyond the sublimit was obligated. In response, Heffler filed counterclaims for:

"(1) declaratory judgment that CAMICO has a duty to defend and indemnify not limited by the $100,000 sublimit, and;

(2) bad faith."[388]

Ultimately, the court held wholly in favor of CAMICO. In its holding, the court stated that "[a]s Heffler notes, CAMICO's primary reason for denying coverage was the $100,000 sublimit for misappropriation, misuse, theft, or embezzlement. The Court has concluded that the denial of coverage on this ground was proper." [389] This decision was later affirmed on appeal by the United States Court of Appeals for the Third Circuit.[390]

While CAMICO was found to have acted good faith to the policy limits offered and accepted by the firm in question, another case displays how careful firms should be when seeking coverage for claims arising from a staff member's theft of client funds.

In the case of *Bryan Brothers, Inc. V. Continental Casualty Company*, the accounting firm had been a policyholder for multiple, continuous years. During these successive policy renewals, they employed an on-site, part-time, account clerk who was responsible for basic ledger and bookkeeping activities. Beginning in 2002, until discovery in 2009, the clerk began to misappropriate client funds from several of the firm's clients. This was done by withdrawing from the accounts of numerous clients. To cover her tracks, the clerk made "checks drawn on client accounts payable to herself and others" while manipulating internal documents. No other employees of the firm were aware of her activities.[391]

In 2009, the owners of the firm discovered her theft, and upon admission to the clients, subsequently faced multiple claims. In response, Byran Brothers submitted multiple claims to their professional liability insurance carrier, Continental Casualty Company.[392]

Continental Casualty subsequently denied coverage.[393]

Foremost, Continental Casualty argued that though the clerk has perpetrated fraud against multiple clients, the claims arising from multiple clients would fall under the definition of interrelated acts. Thus, sole acts committed by the clerk during the active policy period would likewise be grouped in with all acts committed prior to the policy renewal.[394]

If successful in arguing that all claims were interrelated, Continental Casualty was effectively limiting their own future, potential liability in regard to defending against multiple claims and protecting any damages awarded from the policy.

Of utmost importance, in this case, was the policy language being relied upon for Continental Casualty's denial of coverage for all claims, "In accordance with all the terms and conditions of this policy, we will pay on your behalf all sums in excess of the deductible, up to our limits of liability, that you become legally obligated to pay as damages and claim expenses because of a claim that is both made against you and reported in writing to us during the policy period by reason of an act or omission in the performance of professional services by you or by any person for whom you are legally liable **provided that**: [...] 2. **prior to the effective date of this Policy, none of you had a basis to believe that any such act or omission, or**

interrelated act or omission, might reasonably be expected to be the basis of a claim;..."[395]

Continental argued that the clerk's knowledge of her fraud prior to the effective date of the policy would preclude coverage. In short, the clerk fell under the definition of "you" as stated in the policy and thus should have reasonably believed that her actions could bring rise to a claim. Ergo, she should have reported herself as having committed ongoing fraud.[396]

Continental further denied coverage that would otherwise have been afforded under the innocent insured provision of Bryan Bryans Policy. The policy stated, "If coverage under this policy would be excluded as a result of any criminal, dishonest, illegal, fraudulent or malicious acts of any of you, we agree that the insurance coverage that would otherwise be afforded under this Policy will continue to apply to any of you who did not personally commit, have knowledge of, or participate in such criminal, dishonest, illegal, fraudulent or malicious acts or in the concealment thereof from us."[397]

Continental argued that the innocent insured provision would not apply because coverage was denied on the grounds of the clerk's knowledge of her ongoing fraud, not the fraud itself. While Bryan Brothers considered the provision ambiguous, the court was not persuaded.[398]

Ultimately, the court held in favor of Continental Casualty on all counts as it found the Bryan Brothers' arguments unpersuasive. The firm appealed the decision and lost again.[399] The total amount of funds that Bryan Brother lost due to bringing a claim against their insurer, as well as defending and settling the multiple claims brought by their own clients, is unknown.

Firms who could find themselves in circumstances where staff members could impose an internal threat to client funds should consider the following:

☐ Investigate any misappropriations sublimit inside the professional liability policy;

☐ Check that the sublimit, if available, would cover a catastrophic loss due to interrelated acts;

☐ Understand the prior knowledge provision and its relation to policy renewal.

Professional Liability Policy Cyber Endorsements

Firms should pay notice to the limits and sublimit within policy endorsements. Additionally, attention should be paid to the definitions of what is covered as their pertain to endorsement sublimits. These endorsements will look attractive as it appears to offer adequate limits at a reasonable price. "Buyer beware" as coverage elements vary greatly by insurer.

Third-party cyber endorsement limits are the least likely to be used by a firm following a breach.[400] As a reminder, third party claims are generally classified as private rights of action, class-action claims, and regulatory investigations. Not incidentally, those limits are often listed at the beginning of the cyber endorsement.

Take, for example, the following real-world endorsement found within a common accountant's professional liability policy:[401]

Claims for Network Damage/Extortion Demands	
Limit applicable to all claims for network damage in the aggregate	$500,000
Sublimit applicable to all extortion demands in the aggregate	$75,000
Deductible applicable to each claim for network damage	$5,000
Deductible applicable to each extortion demand	$5,000
Privacy Event Expenses	
Limit applicable to all privacy event expenses in the aggregate	$75,000
Deductible applicable to each privacy event	$0

To those not familiar with the intricacies of this line of insurance, the endorsement above appears to offer a half-million-dollar cyber policy for what amounted to roughly $560. However, it is necessary to carefully examine the definition of the bolded words to determine how this endorsement would respond to a real-life breach. Once again, the failure of the firm to provide due diligence on their own endorsements could lead to catastrophic losses or critical gaps in coverage.

As it turns out, the definition of the $500,000 sublimit of "Network Damage" generally limits coverage to claims brought by clients if they alleged that you infected their computer through the rendering of professional services.[402]

"Extortion Demands," sub-limited to $75,000 in coverage, can generally be understood to cover the extortion demands for a threatened or actual ransomware event.[403] Ransomware demands, minus a few noteworthy cases, rarely exceed $2,000[404]. Considering the listed deductible for an extortion demand is $5,000, it is difficult to see when most firms would consider this a useful policy feature.

Finally, featured is the generically named "Privacy Event Expenses" with a total $75,000 in coverage. When referencing the definitions section this endorsement, it covers the following:

- Notification costs to clients potentially affected by a breach;
- Costs associated with adhering to breach notification laws, including the notification of clients affected by the breach;
- Costs associated with computer forensics to determine the scope and nature of the breach;
- Attorney's fees to assist with regulators and for compliance with breach notification laws;
- Call center costs;
- Remediation of the deficiency that led to the breach.[405]

While a basic listing of features, it does not appear to cover the following widely available elements often found in dedicated cyber policies. For practical purposes, these terms will be further defined later in the book.

- Business interruption costs;
- Regulatory fines, awards, and penalties;
- Crisis management and public relations;
- Contingent business interruption;
- System failure business interruption;
- Cybercrime;
- Social engineering;
- Reputation risk.

In contrast to the above endorsement, a cyber endorsement was offered to the same firm, but with different coverages and for $480. This endorsement was a $100,000 per event with a unique aggregate schedule based upon the number of professionals at the firm.

Coverage elements included:

- **Privacy Breach Response Costs**: This includes $100,000 in coverage to respond to claims brought by clients following a breach alleging "breach of confidentiality, infringement, or violation of any right to privacy, including, but not limited to, a breach of your privacy policy or public disclosure of a person's private information" Coverage also generally covers claims arising out of state breach notifications and other associated federal statutes.
- **Notification Expenses**: Included is a $100,000 limit for attorney's fees, legal expenses, forensics, public relations, the cost to mail notifications, and any related advertising expenses.

- **Breach Support and Credit Monitoring Expenses**: This includes a $100,000 sublimit for providing credit monitoring and identity theft education services.
- **Network Asset Protection**: This $100,000 generally covers the loss of digital assets and/or defined special expenses. This would include the cost to return your system to the same state as before the event, as well as the costs incurred by the firm for staff to assist in returning the computer system to pre-event status. Special expenses could include the costs to mitigate further damage the firm's computer system, preservation of evidence, purchasing of licenses to restore functionality, and client notification to inform of the degradation, interruption or ceasing of the firm's system.
- **Cyber Extortion**: A $100,000 sublimit for the ransom paid by a firm to terminate the attack. This would loosely cover both threats to the firm's system as well as ransomware events.
- **Cyber Terrorism**: This provision offers a $100,000 sublimit in the event that a person or group breaches your system with the intent to cause destruction or to further a belief. This could include being caught in a large-scale, state-sponsored attack which results in damage to the firm's network.

Annual Aggregate Limits

Number of Professionals	Aggregate Limit
Up to 5	$100,000
6 to 10	$200,000
11 to 15	$300,000
16 to 20	$400,000
21 to 200	$500,000

When assessing the total limits available for breach-related claims available via endorsement to an accountant's professional liability policy, the market lacks coherency. Combined first- and third-party limits on these endorsements range from $50,000 to $500,000.[406] Whether one carrier's endorsement is superior to another's depends on the firm's needs and the sublimits offered per coverage feature.

Depending on the rating mechanism of the carrier, small- to large-sized firms will often be able to purchase a dedicated cyber policy with higher limits and more coverage features for less than a policy endorsement. Due to their structure and rating scheme, professional liability policy cyber endorsements are often designed for sole proprietors or very small firms with minimal staff and PII exposure.

Social Engineering and Funds Transfer Loss Coverage

Given a sizable social engineering or funds transfer loss of money owned by a client but controlled by the firm, coverage might be sought under a firm's professional liability policy. The rationale for this would be that the claim arose due to a claim brought by the client against the firm for professional services rendered.

Unless otherwise specifically excluded, an all-risk policy may require the insurer to respond to such a claim with defense expenses and potential damages awarded to the plaintiff. The ability for a named peril or ambiguously defined policy to respond to such an event is much more dubious. It could be subject to a court ruling whose merits are decided on a case-by-case basis.[407]

Regardless, firms should seek to clarify coverage with their professional liability insurer. Should the insurer not comment on the coverage specifics of their own policy, firms are advised to seek competent legal counsel for clarification. When in doubt, firms should seek appropriate coverage under a dedicated cyber policy or appropriate endorsement of a professional liability policy even if they believe that there may be duplication in coverage. Waiting until a loss occurs is no time to hurriedly search for potential coverage.

Partner Action Items:

☐ Determine what "cyber"-related claims may be covered under your firm's professional liability policy. This will likely require the assistance of a competent legal broker and/or legal counsel;

☐ Continuously monitor the coverage afforded under your professional liability policy for any changes;

☐ Communicate this data to relevant stakeholders, including IT and staff;

☐ Update the firm's incident response plan and other internal documents as necessary.

Employment Practices Liability Insurance Policies

Employment Practices Liability Insurance (EPLI) Policies generally cover wrongful employment act claims against the firm. Common claims where an EPLI policy would respond include allegations of discrimination, harassment, and wrongful termination from employees. Certain policies may also cover temporary or leased workers and claims from third parties bringing claims of sexual harassment or discrimination.[408]

While it is feasible that an employee could bring a claim following a data breach, it is unlikely that an EPLI policy would respond to such a claim. Many EPLI policies are constructed as "named peril" policies. This means that only those wrongful employment acts listed in the policy will be covered.

Assuredly, some enterprising plaintiff's attorney, or business without a proper cyber policy, may find a novel claim construction alleging coverage under an EPLI Policy. However, as of publication, the authors were unable to find the record of a single case where an EPLI policy has responded to a cyber claim. It is conceivable that an EPLI policy could respond to an Americans with Disability Act (ADA) claim related to a firm's website. However, this would be highly circumstantial and dependent upon the allegations made in the claim as well as unique wording of the policy.

Partner Action Items:

☐ Determine what, if any, "cyber"-related claims may be covered under your firm's EPLI policy. This will likely require the assistance of a competent legal broker and/or legal counsel;

☐ Continuously monitor the coverage afforded under your EPLI policy for any changes;

☐ Communicate this data to relevant stakeholders, including IT and staff;

☐ Update the firm's incident response plan and other internal documents as necessary.

Director and Officers Liability Insurance (D&O) Policies

Director and Officers Liability Insurance (D&O) policies generally cover claims against an officer or director for allegations of wrongful acts they committed while acting in their professional capacity. Companies often seek coverage under their D&O policy for claims involving a breach of fiduciary duty, theft of intellectual property, misrepresentations, or failure to adhere with workplace laws – often employment-related.

Thus, it would seem strange that companies would look toward their D&O policy to assist with at least partial insurance coverage following a data breach. Unlike most other lines of insurance, there does yet appear to be any widespread exclusions to coverage in D&O policies following a data breach. However, if D&O insurers begin finding themselves covering claims which they believe should have been covered under a cyber policy, firms may quickly find a new exclusion on their policies.[409]

The most prominent case of possible data-breach-related coverage found in a D&O policy was shown in *Spec's Family Partners, Ltd. v. Hanover Insurance Company.*

Prior to the case, Spec's had entered in a Merchant Agreement with First Data Merchant Services to process payment cards for transactions occurring at Spec's. Subsequently, it was found that Spec's credit card network had been hacked for roughly one and a half years.[410]

As a result of the breach, First Data asserted that there was, "conclusive evidence of a breach of the cardholder environment at Spec's." Further, Spec's was not in compliance with their PCI DSS requirements, and thus, First Data incurred costs related to the breach. First Data sent a demand letter to Spec's for the associated case management fee, reimbursement costs, and fines which totaled $7,624,846.21. They also demanded documentation that Spec's prove they were now PCI DSS compliant by an attestation of compliance by a third-party qualified security assessor. Early the following year, First Data notified Spec's that the costs of the breach would increase by another $1,978,019.49. These funds, to which Spec's believed they were entitled, were to be held in reserve accounts by First Data.[411]

In turn, Spec's provided both letters from First Data to its D&O insurer, Hanover Insurance Company, as a claim. Initially, Hanover denied coverage but later agreed to provide for defense, subject to a reservation of rights letter.[412] To recoup the reserve account funds, Spec's filed a suit against First Data.

Initially, Hanover complied with a defense funding agreement, but eventually they decided that litigation expenses were not "defense expenses."[413]

Previously, Spec's had purchased a Private Company Management Liability (D&O) policy from Hanover. The policy contained the following pertinent clauses:[414]

Corporate Entity Liability: We will pay "Loss" which the "Insured Entity" is legally obligated to pay because of "Claims" made against the "Insured Entity" during the "Policy Period" and reported to us during the "Policy Period" for any "Wrongful Act" to which this insurance applies."

"Claim" means:
1. Any written demand presented for monetary "Damages" or non-monetary relief for a "Wrongful Act," or;
2. Any complaint or similar pleading initiating a judicial, civil, administrative, regulatory, alternative dispute or arbitration proceeding, including any appeal result from it, to which an "Insured" is provided notice and which

subjects an "Insured" to a binding adjudication of liability for monetary or non-monetary relief for a "Wrongful Act."

"Loss" means the amount the "Insured" is legally obligated to pay for "Damages" and "Defense Expenses" for a covered "Claim" under this Coverage Part. "Loss" does not include:

1. Any amounts which an "Insured" is obligated to pay as a result of a "Claim" seeking relief or redress in any form other than monetary "Damages;"

The policy had included a number of exclusions. Central to Hanover's attempt to deny coverage was the following:

This insurance does not apply to:

"Loss" on account of any "Claim" made against any "Insured" directly or indirectly based upon, arising out of, or attributable to any actual or alleged liability under a written or oral contract or agreement. However, this exclusion does not apply to your liability that would have attached in the absence of such contract or agreement.[415]

Ultimately, Hanover was successful at the district court level in arguing that the policy excluded coverage for claims that had arisen as a result of the merchant services agreement between First Data and Spec's. Immediately following the decision, Spec's appealed.

In June of 2018, a three-judge panel of the Fifth Circuit reversed the ruling of the district court and remanded the case back to the district court for additional proceedings.[416]

The logic of the Fifth Circuit in remanding the case was somewhat puzzling. The court held that the policy exclusion stated previously did not necessarily apply. The demand letters by First Data referenced Spec's non-compliance with PCI DSS standards and monetary relief but was "wholly separate from the Merchant Agreement." The demands for security, as well as requests for prompt payment from First Data ", implicate theories of negligence and general contract law that imply Spec's liability for the assessments separate and apart from any obligations "based upon, arising out of, or attributable to any actual or alleged liability under" the Merchant Agreement."[417]

Ultimately, it should be noted that the circuit court was not explicitly finding the existence coverage existed for Spec's. Merely, they concluded that when assessing policy language in favor of Spec's, there is a possibility for some or all of the claim to be covered.[418] The case is currently ongoing and is assuredly being watched closely by D&O insurers.

Perhaps most puzzling is why Spec's was attempting to find coverage for a data breach and PCI DSS expenses under their D&O Policy. Cyber policies often have contractual liability exclusions, but most have an exception that provides for PCI DSS-related costs. Many come with this coverage as a standard option. Whether Spec's neglected to purchase a cyber policy, or their policy, for whatever reason, did not contain PCI DSS coverage, is speculative. Of further speculation is what other costs Spec's incurred as a result of the breach that was not involved in the above litigation and thus is wholly borne by Specs. Regardless, they could have saved the time, effort, and litigations costs seen in this case with a simple policy coverage assessment.

Partner Action Items:

☐ Determine what, if any, "cyber"-related claims may be covered under your firm's D&O policy. This will likely

require the assistance of a competent legal broker and/or
legal counsel;

☐ Continuously monitor the coverage afforded under your
D&O policy for any changes;

☐ Communicate this data to relevant stakeholders, including IT
and staff;

☐ Update the firm's incident response plan and other internal
documents as necessary.

Tech E&O Policies

As accounting firms continue to acquire or organically develop computer-related services, the probability that these services are covered by a separate insurance policy is increasing. Common offerings in this range can include software installation, client training, hardware sales, and various types of computer-related consulting services. As these practice areas fall outside the scope of traditional accounting-related services, firms will often need to seek coverage from a Technology Errors and Omissions Professional Liability (Tech E&O) policy.

At its most basic, Tech E&O policies are designed to cover firms from third-party claims. Often such claims would arise due to the failure of a product or an error or omission in the performance of the technology service offered. This could include programming errors, failure to discover a crucial flaw, and implementation problems. Common claim allegations could include failure in the consultation process, deficient services rendered under the contract, or lack of work completion.[419]

More immediately useful for firms facing a breach of PII would be any first-party coverage elements found in their Tech E&O policy. As stated elsewhere in this book, first-party costs are those costs to a firm following a covered event that they would otherwise be responsible for without a dedicated cyber insurance policy. Generally, these would be found under a "Privacy Notification Costs" policy provision, or some analogously named provision.

Common first-party coverage features in these policies can include forensic, legal, notification, credit monitoring, and call center costs. However, the limits or availability for these features vary by policy and could be subject to numerous sublimits that could result in unanticipated costs.

While Tech E&O policies continue to evolve in their coverage features, their first-party coverage elements and limits are generally more limited than those found in a dedicated cyber insurance policy. They may also lack necessary third-party features such as coverage for PCI DSS fines, penalties, and assessments.

Of particular note for any firm insured under a Tech E&O policy would be the source of the breach which might trigger coverage. Even if the accounting firm proper is named on the declarations page as a named insured, this does not necessarily mean that a breach of the accounting firm would be covered.

These types of policies have definitions for both "Professional Services," and "Technology Based Services" that vary by insurer.

The definition of "Professional Services" will often specifically exclude any activities offered by white-collar professionals such as accountants, architects, lawyers, and engineers.

"Technology Based Services" further limits coverage which would not include any services offered by an accounting firm.

Therefore, if the breach arose in the system of the technology provider and affected the clients of the technology provider, there would likely be first-party coverage. If the breach arose in the system of the technology provider and affected the clients of the provider *as well as* the clients of the accounting firm, any costs related to the accounting firm's clients may not be covered.

Therefore, it is prudent that any accounting firm carrying a Tech E&O policy understand what entities are covered under the policy, but also contemplate how various scenarios could potentially afford or deny coverage. In all likelihood, it would generally be simpler to have a dedicated cyber insurance policy cover both the firm and the technology provider under one policy to avoid ambiguities and potential pitfalls.

Technology Services Coverage in Miscellaneous E&O Policies

Certain firms may have technology services endorsed on a "Miscellaneous E&O" policy form. These style of Tech E&O policies vary widely in their coverages and endorsement language. They will often contain manuscript endorsements that are unique to the firm and its circumstances. As such, they are beyond the scope of this book. If a firm has technology services endorsed under a Miscellaneous E&O they are advised to seek competent legal counsel to ascertain coverage elements.

Partner Action Items:

☐ Determine what, if any, "cyber"-related claims may be covered under your firm's Tech E&O policy. This will likely require the assistance of a competent legal broker and/or legal counsel;

☐ Continuously monitor the coverage afforded under your Tech E&O policy for any changes;

☐ Communicate this data to relevant stakeholders, including IT and staff;

☐ Update the firm's incident response plan and other internal documents as necessary.

Section 7: Dedicated Cyber Insurance Policies

While coverage for various "cyber"-related incidents and claims may be found in more traditional policies, firms are generally better served by dedicated cyber insurance policies. However, these comparatively new types of insurance are far from standardized. Basic terms could provide radically different coverage elements depending on the insurer. Firms must become familiar with all aspects of a dedicated cyber policy to maximize their chances of being covered when an incident occurs.

Concerning Admitted vs. Non-Admitted Policies

Upon completion of an application, firms may be offered terms by multiple insurance companies. Often this can be done after completing only one application. Before a firm starts to consider coverage options, they need to understand the differences between policies being offered by admitted and non-admitted insurance companies. In a line of insurance where catastrophic, cyber-related losses such as those seen with "NotPetya" appear to actuarially undefinable and thus unforeseeable, no firm would want to file a claim to discover that no funds are available.

Admitted Carriers

For a carrier to qualify as being "admitted," they must file an application with the state's insurance commissioner for each state in which they want to do business in. In turn, the state's Insurance Commission will review the insurance company's application to ensure that they are adhering to that state's unique insurance requirements. This will include a strict review of the company's policy filing, forms, and rates.

Almost without exceptions, insurance companies have a greater depth of knowledge and expertise than could be expected of the average consumer. A primary benefit to consumers of purchasing an admitted policy is that the state's stricter oversight should protect them from predatory or abusive behaviors by the insurance company who may otherwise include tricky or deceptive policy language.

As admitted insurers sell policies, a portion of the premiums paid to them will be ceded to the state's guaranty fund. Should an admitted company become insolvent, the handling and payment of claims are taken over by the state's guaranty fund. In turn, the guaranty fund will specify a limit on the dollar amount allowed to be paid out for a claim, often based on policy limits carried by the firm.

Given the rapidly changing coverage options offered by cyber insurance carriers, it is often difficult for new or smaller insurance carriers to file admitted cyber insurance policies. Filing for an admitted policy is expensive and lengthy. Depending on the state, the process could take years to complete. Weathering this task takes significant expertise and capital. Once this is completed, the market may have shifted into offering new coverage features not available in an admitted cyber policy form.

Non-Admitted Carriers

Insurance companies who fall into this category at the primary insurance level are often referred to as "surplus lines" carriers or companies. Non-admitted carriers are generally subject to token oversight by the state's Surplus Lines Office. This oversight is generally limited to administrative measures such as collection of applicable surplus lines taxes attached to policies, but these likely do not include the myriad of consumer protection measures found during an admitted filing.

Generally, the majority of cyber insurance policies on the market are offered by non-admitted carriers, though the exact percentage remains unknown. This is done so that cyber insurance carriers can quickly modify rates and coverage features without undergoing the lengthy and expensive process necessary for admitted filing with state insurance commissioner for oversight. [420]

Should a non-admitted carrier become insolvent, a receiver will generally take control of the remaining assets. The receiver generally takes an accounting of all the liabilities and creditors of the company and submits a distribution plan for court approval. Within that plan would be the current claims submitted by the firm. In the interim, firms would need to fund and steer their own defenses and settlements while hoping that the estate may eventually reimburse some of those expenses.

A notable exception would be many non-admitted policies offered by various Lloyd's syndicates under different trade names who alleged that they write approximately one-third of the world's cyber insurance. In the early 20th century, Lloyd's created a "chain of security" comprised of three layers to pay claims should a member become insolvent. The first layer, noted as £51 billion in 2017, is a trust held by the specific Lloyd's syndicate. The second layer known as the "member's funds" was noted at £24 billion. The third layer, known as the Central Fund, was noted at roughly £3 billion.[421]

Whether a firm should choose an admitted carrier over a non-admitted carrier is circumstantial. Admitted carriers may provide more stability in the event of a catastrophic cyber loss affecting numerous business around the world. Further comfort may be found in the state guaranty fund. Non-admitted carriers may offer more policy features, but firms may not have the oversight provided by the state insurance commissioner to avoid potentially questionable practices. Nor would firms who hold a non-admitted cyber policy have the ability to access the state's guarantee fund should the carrier experience financial difficulties following a catastrophic loss.

Cyber Insurance Applications

Typically, a firm will need to complete a lengthy application for cyber insurance, though in special instances conditional applications and quotes may be available.[422] While traditional insurance applications often fall upon a specified partner within the firm to complete, placing this responsibility on one individual is inadvisable for cyber insurance.

The ability of an accounting firm partner to successfully complete a cyber application with no inputs from other parties in an acceptable fashion is rare. The questions often appear pedantic in their wording and would require inputs from additional stakeholders to avoid a potential declination. Other entities which should ideally be involved include IT, legal, compliance, and HR. Each stakeholder may have different takes on the questions posed, and flaws in business processes or security can be identified and remedied before the application is submitted.

Regarding the structure of the applications, they can be broadly categorized into the following four categories. Once again, this underscores the need for a firm to engage all relevant stakeholders to answer the questions as thoroughly as possible.

1. **Organizational:** This would include fundamental information about the firm. Questions could include industry type, employee count, disclosures of revenue, assets, and even audited financial statements.

    Included in this category would be questions concerning the type and amount of first-party and third-party sensitive information held or processed by the firm such as PHI or PII. Depending on the insurer, they may ask for exact record counts or will settle for a range count; i.e. 50,000 – 100,000 records.

The application will also ask how the firm manages its relationship and security with outsourced service providers. Questions may focus on whether the firm outsources its IT security functions to a third party or whether third parties have access to the firm's network. Be aware that certain insurers may request the breach history of these third parties as well as any contracts in force between the firm and these providers.[423]

Finally, insurers are obviously interested in the loss history of the applicant as it pertains to data breaches. Firms who have been breached in the past may need to fill out lengthy questionnaires to satisfy the interests of the underwriter.

2. **Technical:** This section is mainly on the technical controls implemented by the firm to address their cybersecurity as well as their network architecture. While the information collected is relatively basic, the idea is to help the underwriter determine a basic risk rating.

    Additionally, questions may delve deeper into the type of controls implemented by the firm – for example: "Does the firm operate an intrusion detection system?" or, "Does the firm utilize two-factor authentication for all applications storing sensitive information?".

    Other questions may focus on access to data, both physical and digital. Such questions could focus on physical access to the building and server room, or whether the firm has procedures to revoke access following employee termination.[424]

3. **Policies and Procedures:** This section generally deals with data and information management within the firm. Questions often focus on the information that the firm would process or sell to third parties. Other common questions would include the data retention and data destruction policy within the firm.

For an accounting firm with an updated data retention policy, this should be easily describable, but firms should check to see whether their internal policy is being strictly followed and whether their policy requires updating. [425]

Additionally, this section will inquire into the firm's network use and security policies. While insurers are unlikely to ask for a copy of such documents, it is still good practice to have these policies and procedures documented and updated regularly after being approved by the firm's leadership and assessed by legal counsel. Firms may also be further asked about penetration testing, vulnerability scanning, and incident response plans.[426]

4. **Legal and Compliance:** This section within the application will ask the firm about their adherence to various laws, regulations, and standards. This could include questions on PCI/DSS and GLBA compliance – hence, their inclusion in this book.[427]

When completing the application, firms should be aware that additional controls, such as encryption and penetration/vulnerability scanning, may lower the yearly premium paid. Also, some insurers will require certain controls be implemented and maintained as a prerequisite to coverage. However, the implementation of such controls may outweigh the reduced premium or be unnecessary depending on the firm structure.

As a practical matter, applications may only provide space for a yes or no answer, while others will ask for lengthy explanations. If the firm is ever in doubt as to the answer or there is not a definitive answer to the question posed, consider an addendum of explanation(s) provided to the underwriter. There is no need to be bashful and risk a potential denial of coverage.

Furthermore, firms should understand how different insurers define different terms on their application. For example, two different applications from different insurers may ask about "Cyber Crime." Understand that this term could have three different meanings. Cybercrime coverage may generally only cover the loss of client funds; or, it may only cover the loss of business funds; and thirdly, it could cover both. As such, firms should seek clarification of any terms they deem ambiguous so they can properly fill out their application and minimize uninsured exposures or material misrepresentations.

Each question posed by an insurer deserves to be heavily scrutinized and investigated. Cyber applications are not like a professional liability application that can be readily completed by a single partner the day before renewal. To complete the application with the lowest possibility of a material oversight, all stakeholders should be involved, including IT, HR, legal, fellow partners, and anyone else who may provide greater insight. As will be discussed in a later chapter, misrepresentations will be the future Holy Grail of future cyber insurance declinations. Do not take this task lightly.

As a further word of warning concerning the application, firms should understand that they are making representations which form the basis of a contract – the insurance policy. These representations may be held against them by the insurer following a breach. Such was the case of *Columbia Casualty Co. v. Cottage Health System.*

Cottage Health System, an operator of hospitals across southern California, purchased a "NetProtect360" cyber insurance policy from Columbia Casualty Company, a surplus lines insurer owned by CNA, a common insurer for accounting firms.[428]

While applying for coverage, Cottage was required to complete a "Risk Control Self-Assessment." As part of the application process, Cottage made the following representations in their risk assessment which will likely sound familiar to firms applying for their own cyber insurance:[429]

4. Do you check for security patches to your systems at least weekly and implement them within 30 days?   • Yes

5. Do you replace factory default settings to ensure your information security systems are securely configured?   • Yes

6. Do you re-assess your exposure to information security and privacy threats at least yearly, and enhance your risk controls in response to changes?   • Yes

11. Do you outsource your information security management to a qualified firm specializing in security or have staff responsible for and trained in information security?   • Yes

12. Whenever you entrust sensitive information to 3rd parities do you...

     a.   contractually require all such 3rd parties to protect this information with safeguards at least as good as your own
         • Yes

     b.   perform due diligence on each such 3rd party to ensure that their safeguards for protecting sensitive information meet your

         standards (e.g. conduct security/privacy audits or review findings of independent security/privacy auditors)   • Yes

     c.   Audit all such 3rd parities at least once per year to ensure that they continuously satisfy your standards for safeguarding sensitive information?   • Yes

     d.   Require them to either have sufficient liquid assets or maintain enough insurance to cover their liability arising from a breach of privacy or confidentiality.   • Yes

13. Do you have a way to detect unauthorized access or attempts to access sensitive information?   • Yes

23. Do you control and track all changes to your network to ensure it remains secure?   • Yes

Ultimately, these questions would provide the foundation of Columbia's assertions that coverage should be denied on Cottage's cyber insurance policy.

Prior to Columbia filing suit, Cottage had become the defendant in a class-action lawsuit. The plaintiffs alleged that 32,000 patients had their records disclosed on the Internet.[430] In response, Cottage's insurer, Columbia Casualty Co., had paid for the defense as well as the $4.1 million settlement. Through the process, it had reserved all rights to later deny coverage and recover all amounts that it paid on the claim. Ultimately this came to fruition as Columbia attempted to deny their claim based on the following factors.[431]

1. Columbia's policy had contained an exclusion for the "Failure to Follow Minimum Required Practices." Such a failure would exclude coverage for "[a]ny **failure of an Insured to continuously implement the procedures and risk controls identified in the Insured's application** for this Insurance and all related information submitted to the Insurer in conjunction with such application whether orally or in writing."[432]

   Columbia asserted that Cottage had failed to replace factory default setting in its servers. This failure resulted in the FTP settings on their server to allow for anonymous users accessing protected user data via an Internet search engine. Such allegations directly contradicted Cottage's representations to questions 5, 6, 13, and 23 listed in their application.[433]

2. Within the application completed by Cottage, Columbia had noted that the policy would be "**null and void if the Application contains any misrepresentation or omission**: a. made with the intent to deceive, or b. which materially affects either the acceptance of the risk or the hazard assumed by the Insurer under the Policy." [434]

Furthermore, Columbia's policy contained a condition requiring, "Minimum Required Practices" to be followed as a "condition precedent to coverage." As such, Cottage was required to, **maintain all risk controls identified in the Insured's Application** and any supplemental information provided by the Insured in conjunction with Insured's Application for this Policy."[435]

Columbia asserted that by allowing the breach to happen, Cottage's application had contained, "misrepresentations and/or omissions of material fact that were made negligently or with intent to deceive concerning Cottage's data-breach risk controls."[436]

For these reasons, Columbia asserted that they were entitled to be reimbursed by Cottage for the full $4.125 million settlement paid for the class-action claim. Furthermore, they demanded reimbursement for all related expenses, attorney's fees, and defense costs from the class-action claim.[437]

As an additional warning for firms to understand the definitions in their policy, Cottage was also denied coverage for an associated claim brought by the California Department of Justice. The California DOJ was an investigation concerning HIPAA violations stemming from the breach.[438]

Cottage's NetProtect360 policy provided coverage for "Damages and Claim Expenses resulting from any Privacy Regulation Proceeding." However, within their policy the term "Damages" was defined as, "**civil awards, settlements and judgments**... which the Insureds are legally obligated to pay **as a result of a covered Claim**." But, such payments did not include "criminal, civil, administrative or **regulatory relief, fines or penalties**."[439]

Ultimately, the court dismissed the case, but only to adhere to the policy terms requiring the use of alternative dispute resolution.[440] How such mediation or arbitration was ultimately resolved is not public record; however, even if both parties met halfway, it would still result in a +$2 million loss for Cottage. Such a loss was likely avoidable from the outset if Cottage had been duly educated on the near-impossible terms they had agreed to with their cyber policy.

Partner Action Items:

- ☐ Work with all necessary stakeholders to complete the firm's cyber insurance application;
- ☐ Ask questions regarding the meaning of terms on the application if it is unclear;
- ☐ Continuously monitor the firm to ensure compliance with the representations made on the application;
- ☐ Communicate this data to relevant stakeholders, including IT and staff;
- ☐ Update the firm's internal documents as necessary.

Researching and Understanding Coverage Offers

It is of the utmost importance that a firm contemplating the purchase or renewal of a dedicated cyber policy first undertake an in-house assessment of the potential risks they are attempting to insure. While a knowledgeable broker or competent legal counsel may assist in this area, no one will truly understand a firm like its own partners or shareholders. Failure to conduct a thorough analysis can lead to catastrophic losses that would otherwise have been insured.

Take, for example, the case of *P.F. Chang's China Bistro, Inc. v. Federal Insurance Co.* An apparent oversight by a company as large as P.F. Chang's ultimately cost them significant amounts of money that would have otherwise been covered.

P.F. Chang's had previously purchased a cybersecurity policy from Chubb Insurance through their subsidiary, Federal Insurance Company. As a warning to any firm considering the purchase of a cyber policy, the insurance company had marketed the policy purchased by P.F. Chang's as " a flexible insurance solution designed by cyber risk experts to address the full breadth of risks associated with doing business in today's technology-dependent world" that "[c]overs direct loss, legal liability, and consequential loss resulting from cyber security breaches."[441]

Of note was that P.F. Chang's had previously entered into an agreement with Bank of America Merchant Services to process the credit card payments made to the company by its customers. Under this agreement known as the Master Service Agreement, P.F. Chang's had made an agreement to compensate Bank of American Merchant Services for fines, fees, assessments and penalties that were imposed on them by the credit card associations following a breach.[442] Within a cyber policy, this is commonly referenced as PCI-DSS (Payment Card Industry Data Security Standards coverage).

Problems arose for P.F. Chang's in 2014 when it discovered that a hacker had exposed the credit card information of approximately 60,000 customers. Following the breach, Bank of America was notified by Mastercard that they were facing the following assessments:

- $50,000 Case Management Fee. This is a flat fee regarding P.F. Chang's PCI-DSS compliance;
- $163,122.72 ADC Operational Reimbursement. This charge was for the fee incurred by MasterCard to notify cardholders of the issue, reissuance, and delivery of new payment cards, new account numbers, and new security codes;
- $1,716,798.95 ADC Fraud Recovery. This was a calculation by MasterCard on the costs of fraudulent associated with the breach.[443]

In turn, Bank of America Merchant Services notified P.F. Chang's that, under their agreement, they would be responsible for those charges.[444] P.F. Chang's insurer, Federal Insurance Company, disagreed. P.F. Chang's stated that they had expected coverage for such an event under their cyber policy and brought for the following general claims:

1. The Case Management fee should be covered as the extra expenses incurred due to the impairment of operations stemming from "fraudulent access or transmissions."
2. The ADC Operational Reimbursement should be covered as a privacy notification expense which resulted from a privacy injury, as described in their policy.
3. The ADC Fraud Recovery should be covered as a this would constitute a claim made against the insured as for injury as described in their policy.[445]

In its holding, the court disagreed. Primarily, the court was unpersuaded that P.F. Chang's would have expected such coverage to exist. The court stated emphatically: "Nowhere in the record is the Court able to find supporting evidence that during the underwriting process Chang's expected that coverage would exist for Assessments following a hypothetical data breach. There is no evidence showing that Chang's insurance agent, [name omitted], asked Federal's underwriter if such Assessments would be covered during their correspondence. The cybersecurity policy application and related underwriting files are similarly devoid of any supporting evidence."[446]

In the final blow to P.F. Chang's case, the judge stated: "Chang's merely attempts to cobble together such an expectation after the fact when in reality no expectation existed at the time it purchased the Policy. There is no evidence that Chang's bargained for coverage for potential Assessments, which it certainly could have done. Chang's and Federal are both sophisticated parties well versed in negotiating contractual claims, leading the Court to believe that they included in the Policy the terms they intended."[447]

P.F. Chang's was forced to pay the combined $1,929,921.57 out of pocket, all for a risk that they reasonably should have anticipated and insured against.

Such a case should serve as a stark warning to firms nationwide. Firms should heavily scrutinize their cyber policy coverage features. To do so, they must not only understand what exposures exist within their own firm but also how such exposures are treated by the policy. Attempting to "cobble together" coverage after a breach could be an unnecessarily expensive and time-consuming endeavor when such coverage could have been obtained from the outset with a little foresight.

Partner Action Items:

- ☐ Research and understand what coverage offers are available and how that compares to the needs of the firm;
- ☐ Consult with legal counsel and a knowledgeable broker if you are ever in doubt;
- ☐ Communicate this data to relevant stakeholders, including IT and staff;
- ☐ If certain coverage features are unavailable in a dedicated cyber policy, determine if those coverages may be available in the firm's other insurance policies;
- ☐ Update the firm's incident response plan and other internal documents as necessary.

Large Losses May Lead to Novel Policy Interpretations by Insurers

While the case of *P.F. Chang's China Bistro, Inc. v. Federal Insurance Co.* was a blatant example of failing to obtain proper coverage, firms should understand that even obtaining a suitable policy could still prove hazardous. Due to the relatively new nature of insuring for cyber risks without market-standard language, plenty of litigation is still occurring that could set unforeseen precedents leading to a declination of coverage. Such is the potential in the case of *Mondalez International, Inc. v. Zurich American Insurance Company.*

Mondalez is one of the largest snack companies in the world, manufacturing beverages and snack foods for consumers in roughly 165 countries. Zurich is primarily an insurance company with approximately 55,000 employees and $60 billion in yearly revenue. Both parties are sophisticated entities with in-house legal counsel.[448]

Mondalez had purchased a property insurance policy from Zurich for "all risks of physical loss or damage" to Mondalez's property. Specific to this discussion, the policy included "physical loss or damage to electronic data, programs, or software, including physical loss or damage caused by the malicious introduction of a machine code or instruction..."[449]

Further coverage was provided for: "Actual Loss Sustained and extra expenses incurred by the Insured during the period of interruption directly resulting from the failure of the Insured's **electronic data processing equipment or media** to operate."[450]

Trouble arose in June of 2017 when Mondalez became a victim of malware which was later referred to as the "NotPetya" virus. Initially, the virus infected two of their servers in different geographic locations. Then, the virus then spread across the entire Mondalez network to allegedly render inoperable 1,700 servers and 24,000 laptops owned by Mondalez. According to Mondalez, this resulted in, "property damage, commercial supply and distribution disruptions, unfulfilled customer orders, reduced margins, and other covered losses" exceeding $100,000,000.[451]

Mondalez alleged that they promptly filed a claim and provided Zurich will all manner of assistance to satisfy a proof of loss. Regardless, approximately a year after the malware incident, Zurich sent Mondalez a letter denying coverage.[452]

The basis for Zurich's denial of coverage is not based upon a complex combination of policy elements, but rather a single exclusion in Mondalez's policy:

"B. This Policy excludes loss or damage directly or indirectly caused by or resulting from any of the following regardless of any other cause or event, whether or not insured under this Policy, contributing concurrently or in any other sequence to the loss: ...

2) a) hostile or warlike action in time of peace or war, including action in hindering, combating or defending against an actual, impending or expected attack by any:

(i) government or sovereign power (de jure or de facto);

(ii) military, naval, or air force; or

(iii) agent or authority of any party specified in i or ii above."[453]

In short, Zurich asserted that the "NotPetya" virus fell under the common war exclusion clause. Mondalez sued, alleging that their grounds for exclusion was unprecedented among other common claims such as unreasonable conduct and breach of contract. They assert that it would be the first coverage declination for a cyber policy under this decades-old exclusion for anything other than cases of conventional warfare.[454]

Given their declination of coverage, the burden rested on Zurich to prove that the exclusion did indeed apply to this case.[455] Yet, cyber-attacks are, by their very nature, difficult to attribute to any one person, organization, or country. On what grounds is Zurich likely to make their case?

While the defense of Zurich is only speculative at this point, they can refer to numerous official statements made by governments in the West alleging that NotPetya was directed by Russia against Ukraine.

For example, in the United States where the case is being heard, the White House Press Secretary released the following statement: "In June 2017, the Russian military launched the most destructive and costly cyber-attack in history. The attack, dubbed NotPetya, quickly spread worldwide, causing billions of dollars in damage across Europe, Asia, and the Americas. It was part of the Kremlin's ongoing effort to destabilize Ukraine and demonstrates ever more clearly Russia's involvement in the ongoing conflict. This was also a reckless and indiscriminate cyber-attack that will be met with international consequences."[456]

Whether such statements will be considered evidence worthy to justify a declination of coverage is yet to been seen in court. Outside of the assertions by various governments and intelligence bureaus, no definitive proof has yet been offered that explicitly and undeniable ties NotPetya to the Russian government. Any evidence of such assertions is likely highly classified and thus unavailable for scrutiny.

Ultimately, the decision may rest on the court in interpreting the nature of "hostile or warlike actions." Reconsidering such language as vague and in need of interpretation by the court could alter the meaning of a standard insurance clause which has been apparent in insurance contracts for decades.

The cyber insurance industry waits anxiously for answers to these questions.

Firms carrying large limit policies should ready themselves for possible declinations out of an abundance of caution. When large dollar amounts are on the line, insurers may look to find novel ways to deny coverage. Even if an insurer knows that they may be ultimately unsuccessful in court, they can attempt to deny coverage for as long as possible with protracted litigation. Doing so can allow them to retain the investment gains from invested premiums that would otherwise be immediately lost.

Self-Insurance for Cyber Losses

Reviewing the declinations of coverage found in the cases previously noted, firms should consider how such declinations would impact them, and whether worst-case scenarios include a partial or full declination and have funds set aside specifically to cover such an event is even worth consideration.

In addition, not every cost associated with a breach may be insurable under a cyber policy. For example, a policy may reimburse the firm for losses experienced due to a business interruption, but the reimbursement may come with various conditions. Employee overtime salary costs necessary to recover from interruption may not be covered and would need to funded by the firm. This is just one example of many unforeseen costs that could befall a firm following a breach.

Support for some cash reserves was given credence by an insurer in the Cybersecurity Insurance Workshop Readout Report from the National Protection and Programs Directorate, U.S. Department of Homeland Security. Noting, "[S]elf-insurance should not be discounted as a reasonable risk management strategy… That approach, he emphasized, is not the same thing as ignoring risk."[457]

A "rainy day" fund for full cyber losses is likely untenable for most firms due to tax implications and cash flow limitations. However, funding deemed reasonable by the firm's partners or shareholders can provide a modicum of interim risk-management comfort if the firm is declined coverage, or if certain costs are uninsurable.

Partner Action Items:

☐ Work with legal counsel and a knowledgeable insurance broker to determine if it would be advantageous to self-insure for certain amounts if a claim is partially or fully denied;

☐ Communicate this data to relevant stakeholders, including IT and staff;

☐ Update the firm's incident response plan and other internal documents as necessary.

Understanding "Named Insured"

It is imperative that firms take note of which entities are listed as being covered by the policy. How this achieved depends, as usual, on the policy provided by the insurance carrier. Subsidiary entities, entities acquired mid-policy period, or those other entities that the firm needs to be covered under the cyber policy, are often, but not always, disclosed on the application.

Certain carriers may automatically cover such entities. For example, one insurer noted the following under "Who is an insured": "… **insured means a named insured, subsidiary, employee, or acquired entity**."[458]

However, there is a caveat to the coverage of an acquired entity. As the same insurer noted: "**With respect to an acquired entity whose revenues exceed 10% of the annual revenues of the named insured** at the time of its creation or acquisition, **any coverage under this policy will expire 90 days after the effective date of its creation or acquisition unless, within such 90 day period: 1. the named insured provides us with written notice of such creation or acquisition; … 4. we agree by written endorsement to provide such coverage….**"[459]

A different insurer was direct in stating that anyone other than the named insured under the policy would not be covered, noting: "The Company is not obligated to pay any amounts for Claims if brought or maintained by, on behalf of, or in the right of: Any entity which is a parent, affiliate, Subsidiary, joint-venturer or co-venturer of any Insured, or other entity in which any Insured is a partner, and including any entity directly or indirectly controlled, operated or managed by such an entity… however, that this exclusion shall not apply to Claims brought or maintained by or on behalf of or in the right of any Additional Insured."[460]

The insurer goes on to state that if the subsidiary's gross revenue exceeds 15% of the named insured annual revenue, then that subsidiary is only covered for 90 days. The firm may provide written notice within that 90 days to request coverage under the cyber policy may be extended to the subsidiary.[461]

Depending on the policy, there may also be coverage, exclusions for contractors, seasonal workers, part-time employees, or similar working arrangements. If the specimen policy does not provide coverage for this type of worker, firms may be afforded coverage with an endorsement if requested.

Firms should perform their due diligence to check that any additional entities are properly covered their cyber policy. Additional research should be undertaken to understand what, if any, notifications provisions are necessary to the cyber insurance carrier when dealing with new entities that the firm needs covered. Failure to understand which parts of the firm's organization are covered could lead to partial, or full, declinations of coverage depending on the scenario.

Partner Action Items:

- ☐ Determine if the firm's cyber insurance policy names the appropriate parties that require coverage;
- ☐ Continuously monitor the firm's policies for any changes;
- ☐ Communicate this data to relevant stakeholders;
- ☐ Update the firm's incident response plan and other internal documents as necessary;
- ☐ Depending on ownership/legal structure, the firm may require additional dedicated cyber policies, or they will need to self-insure for the losses.

Defense Arrangements

Most cyber insurance policies are written with the insurer having the duty and right to defend. In practice, this means that the insurer will provide the counsel necessary to navigate the claim. This would also mean that they have the right to control the defense strategy of any claim.[462]

For most insureds, this will not be an issue, and indeed, they will welcome having experienced counsel assist them. Cyber-related claims are complex, and the average attorney is unlikely to have the depth of knowledge necessary to guide an insured through the litany of laws necessary following a breach.[463]

For the largest firms – generally those with full time in-house legal counsel – such a provision may not be wanted. In that case, an indemnification policy, or more specifically an endorsement to select legal counsel, may be requested. Whether the insurer will agree to this arrangement is situationally dependent. Furthermore, such an arrangement will need to be agreed to by the insurer before the policy is bound to avoid potentially costly time delays. Firms pursuing this option must be diligent regarding their choice of counsel.

Also, firms will generally be limited to a pre-selected series of vendors as offered by the insurer. In practice, most, if not all vendors dealing with first-party costs have been previously vetted by the insurer. This should allow for seasoned specialists in their particular fields to assist the firm at costs lower than those that would otherwise be offered on the open market and with a greater level of expertise. The same rules for negotiating with specific vendors apply to negotiating legal counsel. If a firm wishes to have specific vendors, those vendors should be vetted and agreed to in the policy before the policy is bound. These agreements are likewise situationally dependent. Once again, if firms choose to utilize non-standard vendors, they should be diligent regarding their choices.

Partner Action Items:

- ☐ Determine if the policy is a, "claims made and defended" policy, or an indemnification policy. Generally, only very large businesses may consider an indemnification policy;
- ☐ Consider pre-selecting vendors to minimize unnecessary time delays following a breach;
- ☐ Continuously monitor the firm's policies for any changes;
- ☐ Communicate this data to relevant stakeholders;
- ☐ Update the firm's incident response plan and other internal documents as necessary.

Tail Policy Coverage

Each policy should contain a provision for an extended reporting period, also known as a "tail policy." Given the current climate of mergers and acquisitions, it is important to understand the tail policy provisions in a policy.

Most policies contain automatic coverage for claims reported – in this case the report of a breach or other covered scenario – for anywhere between 30 to 60 days after the policy lapses due to non-renewal. However, the recent 2018 Cost of a Data Breach Study: Global Overview by IBM and the Ponemon Institute, the mean time to identify (MTTI) a data breach was 201 days in the United States. Thus, tail policies provisions are much more relevant and necessary than most firms understand.

Each policy should contain a provision to purchase a tail policy. Broadly speaking, this tail policy would provide coverage for a covered claim that results from an act that occurred while the policy was active. However, the length available for purchase varies by insurance provider.

For example, one carrier only offers a 12-month tail policy for an additional 100% of the annual policy premium.[464] Another carrier offered up to a three-year tail for 225% of the annual policy premium.[465] Considering that it took 201 days as the <u>mean time</u> to detect a breach, half of all incidents took longer to detect.[466] Therefore, if firms are reviewing tail policy terms, they should heavily consider the longest policy tail policy options.

Firms should further investigate any additional exclusions that may come with the purchase of a tail policy. Specific policies may exclude coverage elements such as business interruption, or crisis management and public relations assistance, as a condition of purchasing a tail policy.

243

Failure to purchase an appropriate tail policy can result in a declination of coverage. Not only would a firm be required to pay open market rates for all services out of their own funds, but they would also be required to organize and steer the entire process themselves which is no small undertaking. Given an M&A scenario, this could result in significant hardship on both sides of the purchase agreement.

Partner Action Items:

- ☐ Determine what length of time is offered on the cyber insurance tail policy. The longer, the better;
- ☐ Continuously monitor the firm's policies for any changes;
- ☐ Communicate this data to relevant stakeholders.

Understanding the Difference Between 1st- And 3rd-Party Cyber Insurance Coverage

Before contemplating any cyber coverage, it is imperative that a firm understands the difference between third-party coverage and first-party coverage as found within cyber policies.

It is most helpful to broadly understand who the "parties" in any insurance policy generally refer to. "First Party" is considered the insured, in this case the accounting firm. The "Second Party," though a rarely used term, is the insurance company. "Third Parties" would be those who were owed a duty of care by the firm, i.e. the First Party. These distinctions will assist the firm in understanding how policies are structured and what limits are available in various scenarios.

First-party costs in a cyber insurance policy are those costs to a firm following a covered event that they would otherwise be responsible for without a cyber insurance policy. For example, this could include business interruption costs, restoration of data, and providing breach notifications to impacted clients.

Third-party costs in a cyber insurance policy are those costs which a firm would incur responding, defending, and paying for a breach-related claim. For example, this could include, loss of client funds, regulatory fines and penalties, and private rights of action brought by clients against a firm.

Firms should be aware that cyber policies generally lack any level of conformity in structure or wording. Policies from different insurers can name the same coverage component name, but in practice, will respond in drastically different ways depending on how those terms are defined. Furthermore, some insurers offer third-party-only cyber-risk policies, others, first-party-only cyber-risk. Many contain a combination of the two.

When firms are brainstorming on the needs for various coverages, they should keep in mind how the definitions of certain coverage terms could result in coverage ranging from full, to none at all.

For example, the firm wants to insure against their bookkeeper wiring money. As such, the firm would need to consider at least the following three scenarios:

1   Could the bookkeeper misappropriate client funds for their own purpose?

2   Could the bookkeeper be fooled into transferring client's funds to a hacker?

3   Could the bookkeeper be fooled into transferring firm's funds to a hacker?

Depending on the scenario, coverage could be considered either a first-party loss or a third-party loss. Insurance coverage for these scenarios may be found in one policy, no policy, or multiple policies.

An illustrative example of the need to understand the difference between these two coverage types is found in the case of *Camp's Grocery, Inc. v. State Farm Fire & Cas. Co.*

Trouble began for Camp's when three credit unions brought a claim against them for an alleged breach of their computer system. The credit unions noted that the hack allegedly compromised confidential customer data, including card information. Due to the alleged breach, the credit unions suffered losses on "their cardholder accounts, including for the reissuance of cards, reimbursement of their customers for fraud losses, lost interest and transaction fees, lost customers, diminished goodwill, and administrative expenses associated with investigating, correcting, and preventing fraud."[467]

The credit unions asserted that Camp's was liable due to their failure to adequately train employees and their oversight in implementing reasonable cybersecurity controls such as intrusion detection systems and encryption.[468]

In turn, Camp's sought a declaratory judgment against State Farm for the insurer to defend and indemnify them under their general liability insurance policy for the case brought by the credit unions.[469]

Camp's right to coverage for the claim by the credit unions ultimately hinged upon the differences between first- and third-party coverage in an insurance policy. In its holding, the court noted: "Insurance contracts generally are assigned to one of two classes: either 'first-party coverage' or 'third-party coverage'....'First-party coverage' pertains to loss or damage sustained by an insured to its property; the insured receives the proceeds when the damage occurs. ... In contrast, if the insurer's duty to defend and pay runs to a third-party claimant who is paid according to a judgment or settlement against the insured, then the insurance is classified as 'third-party insurance'. ...Thus, wholly different interests are protected by first-party coverage and third-party coverage."[470]

Going on to note: "[T]here is no language in [the policy] whereby State Farm promises to 'defend' or 'indemnify' the insured whether in regard to claims involving computer equipment, electronic data, or anything else, for that matter."[471] In short, Camp's had no coverage for third-party cyber-related claims.

Partner Action Items:

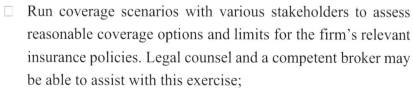

- ☐ Understand the difference between first- and third-party coverages in cyber insurance policies;
- ☐ Run coverage scenarios with various stakeholders to assess reasonable coverage options and limits for the firm's relevant insurance policies. Legal counsel and a competent broker may be able to assist with this exercise;

☐ Update the firm's incident response plan and other internal
documents as necessary to reflect the coverages found in the
firm's cyber policy.

Deductible/Retention Options

Unsurprisingly, increasing the deductible or retention will often lower the cost of the premium. While this makes the premium more immediately palatable, it does have potentially negative consequences.

Foremost among these is the issue of the sublimits within the policy. Excessively high deductibles or retentions could render various sublimits effectively useless within the policy. For example, if the firm elects to have a $50,000 deductible, a $50,000 sublimit for cybercrime could be effectively useless for most firms that are only wiring small amounts of money.

Also, consider that a firm could be subjected to multiple, unrelated data-breach events covered under their cyber policy in a given policy period. Thus, excessively high deductibles could result in a severe financial burden if those deductibles or retentions must be paid out for every cyber claim reported to the insurer.

Ultimately, cyber insurance is still relatively inexpensive when compared to other lines of insurance. Holding unnecessarily high deductibles or retentions could lead to a, "penny wise, pound foolish" scenario. Firms should take the above factors into consideration when weighing deductible or retention options. Practically speaking, firms are often better served by considering deductibles or retentions that are lower than those they would find on their other insurance policies.

Partner Action Items:

☐ Consider obtaining the lowest possible deductible/retention available given financial constraints;

☐ Understand how the deductible/retention works in the policy.

☐ Communicate this data to relevant stakeholders, so they understand the immediate costs of a breach.

Sublimits, Policy Structure, and Appropriate Limits

Due to the general lack of expertise in the market concerning placing appropriate cyber insurance, firms will need to investigate any and all sublimits within their policy. Often these sublimits may cover aspects that would be crucial to the firm given an internal breach or a breach at a crucial vendor. Policies offered across the market vary greatly in their structure, available sublimits, and policy language. Certain sublimits may not have a deductible, or the sublimit applies after the deductible is met.

Should firms fail to fully investigate a cyber insurance policy in light of their own unique circumstances, they could find themselves woefully underinsured, or not insured at all, for the presented risk. Even insurance brokers, or wholesalers, that market themselves as "cyber insurance experts" may not have the technical knowledge or inherent knowledge of the firm's risks to place an appropriate policy. Consider the following allegations made by Hotel Monteleone in the case of *New Hotel Monteleone, LLC. v. Certain Underwriters at Lloyd's of London and Eustis Insurance, Inc.*

In 2013, Monteleone experienced a breach that resulted in the loss of payment card numbers. Following the breach, Monteleone was assessed $471,000 and $377,000 by Mastercard and Visa for initial fraud recovery and operational reimbursement costs. At the time, they had no insurance policy in place that would cover these losses. [472]

Following the breach, Hotel Monteleone reached out to Eustis Insurance, Inc., an independent insurance agency. The hotel requested a cyber insurance policy that would provide coverage for similar expenses should a breach occur in the future. [473]

As stated by Hotel Monteleone in the court documents, Eustis had no expertise with procuring or placing cyber insurance policies. As such, Eustis reached out to R-T Specialty, a wholesale insurance broker to assist in the placement. [474]

At the time, R-T Specialty's website included a paragraph on their cyber insurance expertise by stating the following:

"It's particularly important for insurance professionals to help their clients identify potential cyber exposures and to select the appropriate cyber liability product to fit their client's needs. ... [W]e understand the importance of cyber liability products for our clients, and have assembled a cyber "team" of brokers whose primary focus is Cyber Liability and Technology Errors & Omissions coverage. Members of our cyber team are constantly evaluating new cyber insurance products and will work together with retail partners to find the best fit for each client." [475]

Ultimately, Hotel Monteleone purchased an Ascent CyberPro Insurance Policy with $3 million limits for approximately $20,277. Within their policy, Ascent had added an endorsement titled, "Payment Card Industry Fines, or Penalties Endorsement." Crucial to that endorsement was the following language: [476]

27.   The 2014 CyberPro Insurance Policy provides:

> We shall pay on **your** behalf **Payment Card Industry fines or penalties** in excess of **your** deductible as stated within item 4 of the Declarations, which **you** become legally obligated to pay as a result of any **claim** first made against **you** and notified by **you** to us in writing, in accordance with Section XI of this policy, during the **policy period** or any **extended reporting period**, if applicable, arising solely from a **privacy event**, or **security event**.
>
> It is agreed that Section **VII. DEFINITIONS**, is amended to include the following additional definitions:
>
>> **Payment Card Industry fines or penalties** means a written demand received by **you** by a **credit card association** for a monetary fine or penalty because of **your** non-compliance with **Payment Card Industry Data Security Standards**.
>>
>> **Credit card association** means Visa, MasterCard, American Express, Discover, or JCB.
>>
>> **Payment Card Industry Data Security Standards** means published and generally accepted security standards for the Payment Card Industry.

Unfortunately for the hotel, they would suffer another security breach shortly thereafter that allegedly compromised payment card numbers. [477]

Within the policy, the suit alleges that the endorsement only provided $200,000 in total coverage. This amount was insufficient to cover the total losses anticipated by the hotel with their new breach. Furthermore, the endorsement did not apply to reimbursements, fraud recoveries, or assessments owed to the payment card processors.

As stated in their claim, these were the costs that the hotel had specifically requested be covered in the event that another breach of their payment system occurred. According to Hotel Monteleone, Eustis had "told [them] that the 2014 CyberPro Insurance Policy would provide full coverage for losses in the form of fraud recovery, operational reimbursement, and case management fees."[478]

The hotel made various claims in their suit to have coverage afforded by other elements of the policy. Whether these claims would have been successful is speculative. The court ordered that the claims made by Hotel Monteleone against Eustis were stayed while the hotel and the insurance company arbitrated their dispute.[479]

Regardless, firms need to be diligent regarding the investigation of their own sublimits and coverage offerings. While courts will generally construe ambiguous language in favor of the insured, a "plain language" reading of the policy terms will often favor the insurer. When hundreds of thousands, or millions, of dollars are on the line, firms should be very wary of placing their financial wellbeing in the hands of any self-described "cyber insurance expert."

Partner Action Items:

- ☐ Understand how the policy is structured and what sublimits are available;
- ☐ Work with a competent broker and legal counsel to ensure that coverage is afforded for the risks facing the firm. Never assume anything is covered unless you have confirmed the coverage in writing;
- ☐ Communicate this coverage data to relevant stakeholders;
- ☐ Update the firm's incident response plan and other internal documents as necessary.

Choice of Law Provisions

If a firm finds itself in a dispute with the insurer, those disputes are generally governed by state law. Firms should be aware state laws can vary greatly with some state laws being more "friendly" to the insured than the insurer. These seemingly minor differences can mean the difference in a firm being afforded or denied coverage.

For example, in Texas an insurer is not generally required to show prejudice from a late notice involving a claims-made policy.[480] By comparison, under most jurisdictions, a late notice of a claim does not absolve the insurer of its duties unless the insurer can prove that they were somehow prejudiced as a result of that late notice.[481]

Thus, firms should understand what state laws would apply given a coverage dispute with their insurer. Some firms may be able to negotiate the dispute venue, but practically speaking, such policy changes will often be based on the premium available to the insurer and the risk profile of the insured. If a firm is considering a change to the venue where a dispute would be litigated, they should work closely with legal counsel to determine which state is most appropriate.[482]

Partner Action Items:

- ☐ Determine if the choice of law provisions and venues are appropriate for the firm;
- ☐ Communicate this data to relevant stakeholders;
- ☐ If in doubt, work with legal counsel to determine an appropriate dispute venue and work with your broker to determine if the insurer will change the venue.

Selecting Limits

Outside of selecting the correct coverage options and policy language, the most daunting task for most firms is deciding policy limits. The most common threats to firms are, in order, being underinsured in total, underinsured in part, uninsured in part, or not insured at all.

Being over-insured is generally not a concern at the moment. This is because the term "over-insured" generally refers to excessive insurance limits, which are discoverable to a plaintiff when a claim occurs. As discussed previously, the threat of a third-party data-breach-related claim is rare. The only exception to this rule could be the third-party liability found in a PCI-DSS-related claim, though usually firms can get a sublimit for this exposure negating the concern. Therefore, firms should generally look at understanding their total first-party costs when considering cyber insurance limits.

A passing glance at the common statistics being thrown around most websites and conferences is unhelpful. Frequently, firms will hear the Ponemon Institute statistics stating that the average cost of a data breach was $3.86 million, and the average cost per lost or stolen record was $148. Logically, this is absurd. Averages are not applicable to any half of a population set. Furthermore, those averages are based upon breaches of large, global companies across different industries who hold different types of information.[483] This does not invalidate the study but is meant to suggest that such a sample set is inappropriate for all but the largest firms.

Armed with the information presented in this book, accounting firms should consider the following, minimum elements when determining their insurance needs:

- Determine the number of unique records containing PII/PHI/PCI. Firms often overlook payroll services, dependents, and pass-through entities when making this calculation. Understand that a "record" in insurance parlance can roughly be translated to how many breach notification letters might go out the door following a breach. If you performed a tax return for a single individual for 10 years and his social security and driver's license were stolen, that could count as one record. If that same individual were to have a wife and two children, and their PII was likewise stolen, that could count as four records.

- Determine what possible third-party exposure may exist within the firms. As stated previously, it is unlikely that most firms will be subject to a private right of action or a class-action claim following a data breach. However, they may face state and/or federal regulatory inquiries, demands arising from their merchant services agreement (MSA) following a breach, or any other unique exposure that is firm-dependent.

- Determine how crucial first- and third-party exposures are limited or sub-limited in the policy. Make certain that the limits and sublimits are appropriate for the exposures the firm could reasonably face.

- What is the firm's network architecture?

- Are vendors contractually obligated to indemnify the firm following a breach?

- What regulatory regimes does the firm fall under?

- Does the firm have access to client funds?

- What are the terms of the firm's MSA and maximum exposure therein?

Benchmarking insurance limits against firms with similar revenue will not necessarily provide adequate protection as each firm has its own unique exposures. For example, a $50-million-grossing firm in Washington D.C. that specializes in non-profit audits has a very different exposure when compared to a $50-million-grossing firm in New York City that focuses heavily on individual and business tax returns.

When calculating appropriate limits, the D.C. firm is more likely to consider business interruption and client loss to be a leading driver of limit adequacy, followed by state/federal regulatory inquiries. The NYC firm is more likely to consider notification costs and possible state regulatory inquiries to be the leading driver of limit adequacy.

The cost of a breach varies greatly, and often for reasons that are entirely outside the control of the firm. In addition, new exposures may arise that are outside the purview of firms not keeping the pulse of the ever-changing cybersecurity law and insurance landscape. For these reasons, firms are advised to work with a knowledgeable broker, if available, and competent legal counsel to adequately insure for their exposures.

Partner Action Items:

☐ Determine what information the firm is responsible for given a breach; PII/PHI/PCI, etc.;

☐ Estimate the unique number of records that could be breached for each category;

☐ Work with a knowledgeable broker and competent legal counsel to review necessary limits and sublimits;

☐ Reference numerous sources that benchmark data-breach costs including, but not limited to NetDiligence, The Ponemon Institute, Verizon;

☐ Communicate this data to relevant stakeholders;

☐ Update the firm's incident response plan and other internal documents as necessary;

☐ Stay abreast of any new exposures that may arise as the legal landscape changes;

☐ Review the firm's cyber insurance offerings each year to determine if it still adequately covers the risks identified by the firm to the dollar amount necessary;

☐ When in doubt, consider selecting higher limits and sublimits.

Common Coverage Options

First-Party Coverage Options

As mentioned previously, first-party costs would be those costs that a firm would otherwise directly incur as a result of a covered event. Firms should note that the following is a list of features that are commonly found across multiple, cyber insurance policies. Not all cyber policies will carry every feature listed below, nor are they all necessarily relevant for each firm. Furthermore, policy nomenclature will vary – similar coverages across different policies may be referred to by different names. Even policies utilizing similar nomenclature may provide radically different coverages. Firms will also need to check any exclusions, carve-backs, or other policy language elements to make a reasonable internal coverage assessment.

Business Interruption: This category of coverage is generally meant to cover the income loss and extra expenses incurred by the firm during a breach of their computer system. Income losses are generally understood to mean the net losses that would not have occurred but for the event. Extra expenses are generally understood to mean the additional costs a firm would incur to utilize alternative sources to meet contractual obligations as well as the additional cost of employee labor during the event.

Policies will often contain a number of exclusions related to the business interruption, and those these exclusions vary greatly by policy. Additionally, most policies will contain a waiting period, a loss-of-use threshold, and a retention/deductible before the business interruption sublimit reimbursement clause will become effective.

For example, a policy may state that the $500,000 business interruption sublimit will not be available until the firm has greater than 25% of its computer systems inoperable for more than eight hours. After which, the $500,000 business interruption sublimit will be made available subject to the $5,000 retention to be paid by the firm. Often a policy will specify how many days a firm can be reimbursed.

Most policies covering business interruption reimbursement will stipulate that the waiting period will begin when the matter is first reported to the insurance company. Certain policies may contain an appraisal clause allowing for an independent, third-party appraiser to provide a reasonable loss estimate to both parties. Seasonal work may or may not be considered for reimbursement.

Cryptojacking: This coverage comes into play when a firm has had their computer systems accessed by a third party to mine for digital currency. As a result of this intrusion, the firm may experience additional costs from their electricity, natural gas, oil, or Internet providers. If a cryptojacking event were to befall a firm, this sublimit would reimburse for those additional billing costs.

Coverage for cryptojacking claims will likely need to be specifically named in the policy for coverage for apply, though coverage may circumstantially be found in a utility-fraud-type coverage.

Push Payment Fraud: Such as coverage would allow the firm to be reimbursed for the various costs surrounding push payments. This could include the cost of advising clients of the fraud, reimbursing clients for the financial losses incurred, or income losses sustained by the business because of the fraud.

Dependent Business Interruption: This coverage would generally reimburse a firm for lost revenue if one of their service providers experiences a breach event or service interruption event that leads to a loss of revenue for the firm. A service interruption is often defined as an unplanned outage due to a software or hardware error. Typically, service providers are limited to "cloud providers," IT-service providers, or supporting operations such as a fulfillment center. On many policies, these entities must be specifically named for coverage to apply.

Generally, insurance companies are unaware of the security or business practices of these third parties. Thus, dependent business interruption coverage often comes with smaller sublimits that are subject to a deductible or retention. There may also be a long list of exclusions that apply to this coverage.

An example of when this coverage may be necessary for a firm would be if their tax software provider experiences a crashed server, and this crash results in the firm being unable to process tax returns, and revenue is impacted.

System Failure Business Interruption: Whereas the previous coverage dealt with service providers, this coverage deals with a system failure within the firm proper. Generally, this coverage would provide coverage for an unintentional interruption of the firm's computer systems due to an internal error. It does not cover the business interruption costs due to a breach-like event.

Despite the best intentions of software vendors, their updates and patches do not always integrate seamlessly. There is a possibility with any changes to a functioning system that the system will be negatively impacted in a way that was totally unforeseen. This could also happen after otherwise well-meaning internal tech staff alter settings that crash the network and make recovery time-consuming.

Utility Fraud: This policy element would allow the firm to be insured against the increased expenses for various utility payments. Generally, these increased expenses must come as a result of some unauthorized access to the firm's computer system to include cryptojacking and telephone-toll fraud.

Legal Costs: This allows for the payment of the assigned attorney to perform most or all of the necessary functions when responding to a breach. Such functions could include providing advice regarding the breach investigation, assisting with notifications of regulators and affected individuals, as well as pursuing indemnification rights under a written agreement with a third party. The legal costs to advise the firm in compliance with a PCI DSS-related matter may also be covered.

Computer Forensics Costs: This assists in paying for the computer forensic contractor to determine the scope and nature of the breach. It may also cover the costs to stop the further propagation of malware. The forensics report will often be necessary for determining what individuals require breach notification letters, as well as for reports to local, state, and federal law enforcement, if necessary. Generally, this coverage is limited to a breach of the firm's system so would not necessarily be activated if, for example, a staff member fell victim to a social engineering scheme and wired money due a fraudulent phone call.

Customers' Accounts / Invoice Manipulation Coverage: This type of coverage would be afforded if the firm's computer system was intentionally used by an unauthorized third party to deceive a client or vendor into transferring money intended for the firm to a different entity.

Notification Costs: This pays for the breach notification letter to be drafted and sent to the affected parties as required by the various breach notification laws previously discussed. It should also cover the costs for alternative notification methods such as notice on a website or via news outlets to be utilized if warranted. Certain policies will also allow for voluntary notification under certain circumstances, such as the firm displaying that such action would mitigate a significant risk to those affected.

Identity Protection Services: Generally, this provides up to one year of credit- or identity-monitoring programs to those affected by the breach. Certain states may require greater than one year of services to be provided so firms will want to check the policy for this possibility. Additionally, this coverage may also provide for clients to access identity protection training services.

Firms should be aware that offering identity protection or remediation services such as credit monitoring, fraud assistance, and identity theft insurance is not without risks.

In the case of *Remijas v. Neiman Marcus Group, LLC*, the US Court of Appeals for the Seventh Circuit noted that the offer of free credit monitoring following a breach was an admission of possible harm to the plaintiffs. Thus, it supported the plaintiff's standing in their lawsuit.[484]

Conversely, the US Court of Appeals for the Fourth Circuit refused to follow the Seventh Circuit's holding in the case of *Beck v. McDonald*. This court held that adopting a standard where the offer of free credit monitoring inferred a substantial risk of future harm would unduly discourage companies from offering credit monitoring services in the future.[485]

The general consensus following a breach is to provide credit monitoring as a gesture of goodwill on behalf of the breached firm, but make sure you consult with legal counsel first.

Crisis Management Services: Crisis managers would assist with the cost for consultants to assist the firm following a breach. Typical duties would include reducing the likelihood of a claim, reestablishing the firm's reputation, attempting to identify the hacker, and assistance with identifying future security improvements.

Public Relations Services: Often working alongside the crisis managers, the public relations providers assist firms when there is a current or imminent publication of a covered event. Often this could be report of the breach in local, regional, or national news. The public relations expert can assist the firm in dealing with press releases and inquiries from the media to lessen reputational harm and potentially limit further liability.

Damage and Data Restoration: Should malware infect, corrupt, or damage your files or computer system, those items may need to be restored or corrected. Generally, this coverage allows for the reasonable costs and expenses necessary to regain access to the data, as well as the costs to replace, restore, or restore data to the state it was prior to the event. Often this will be done with backups or original sources, so firms should check on their own backups' periodicity and security to determine whether the required backups are truly secure and available.

Call Center: Often overlooked by firms is the need for a call center following a breach. The call center can be provided as a point of contact for clients who receive breach notification letters. Such a service can greatly assist firms who would be unlikely to have the resources to handle thousands of clients demanding to speak with a representative of the firm's management in the space of a few days.

Rogue Employees: Many cyber insurance policies will deny coverage if an extortion event was perpetrated by anyone insured under the policy. Coverage for rogue employees can cover the firm if an employee unilaterally threatens to attack the firm's computer system, disclose secret corporate information, or disclose PII unless a ransom is paid.

Cyber Extortion Costs: An extortion threat would most commonly be seen in a ransomware event. However, it can generally be any threat from a third party to disclose confidential client information if money is not paid to the third party. Some policies will also reimburse the firm for the ransom paid to the hacker and any reasonable expenses incurred by a representative appointed by the insurance company to assist with the process. For example, a digital currency paid to the hacker with the promise that they will give you the key to unencrypt their data.

When contemplating cyber extortion, firms should check the definition of a hacker in its relation to an extortion event. Some insurers will amend policy language to include extortion attempts from rogue employees; others will specifically exclude it. Given the damaging nature of insider threats and the vast amounts of PII at their disposal, such a threat should be considered when investigating insurance coverage.

Media Liability: This often-overlooked coverage should warrant consideration for any firm operating a website or various social media accounts. Media liability coverage can roughly be understood to cover claims of libel, slander, or defamation claims that result from content published on a firm's websites or social media accounts. Certain policies may also cover plagiarism, copyright infringement, trademark infringement, breach of license, and negligent publication.

Cyber Crime and Social Engineering: Of all the coverages to be assessed by a firm, this coverage is the most likely to bring confusion. Depending on the policy, coverage may or may not be afforded to losses incurred by the firm's own accounts, or to clients' accounts. Whether there is coverage for a social engineering scam or if the firm's computer must have been compromised also varies by policy.

In certain policies, coverage may only be afforded to losses that are attributed to the staff member who was authorized to transfer funds. Other policies may include coverage only for funds lost from a firm's transfer account. Some policies make no such distinctions and thus are open to interpretation by the insurer. Due to such wild variations in coverage, firms are encouraged to read the relevant policy language in detail. Utilizing the "wargaming" scenarios found later in this book may also be useful.

Reputation Loss / Reputation Harm: Following a breach, there is a chance that the firm's breach may be featured in an adverse publication. Certain policies will reimburse the firm for net losses in revenue incurred by the publication of the breach. Firms should note that the policies offering this coverage have lengthy requirements on how the reimbursement will be calculated, as well as various waiting periods before the coverage will come into play.

Bricking: "Bricking" occurs when a piece of hardware is rendered unusable by re-writing or overwriting the firmware of the device. In effect, this makes the device inaccessible at the most fundamental levels. Such an event could result in untold monetary damage to the firm. This coverage would rebuild, repair, or replace the hardware to the same level as before the event if a bricking incident were to occur. Conceivably, a hacker could brick the hardware of a firm if, for example, they were using that hardware for identity theft or cryptojacking.

Coverage for bricking is currently rare but may be found as a distinct coverage or may be included under the system-failure coverage feature.

Customer Accounts and Invoice Manipulation: If the firm's computer system was used to deceive a client or vendor into transferring money to a fraudulent account, this coverage may apply. This could come into play if a firm's system was compromised and clients were directed to pay money to a fake account purportedly owned by the firm. This coverage is often strictly sub limited.

Extra Expenses: When a breach occurs, it may be necessary for the firm to pay staff overtime to return to normal operation, employ contract staff, or source products or services from a different vendor to meet various contractual obligations. The extra-expenses coverage can help reimburse the firm for those costs.

Voluntary Shutdown Coverage: At its core, this is a type of business interruption reimbursement coverage. When malware attacks the firm, one of the suggested courses of immediate action may be to shut the system down to limit how far it can spread. In certain circumstances, law enforcement authorities may also request the business shut down their computer system to limit collateral damage. By shutting down the system, this could halt part, or all, of the firm from generating revenue. This business-interruption reimbursement coverage is also often sub-limited.

TRIA/TRIPRA: The Terrorism Risk Insurance Act (TRIA), later reauthorized under the Terrorism Risk Insurance Program Reauthorization Act (TRIPRA) of 2015, extends coverage for insurance related to certified acts of terror. For this coverage to apply, the act of terrorism must be certified by the Secretary of the Treasury, in concurrence with the Secretary of State and the Attorney General. Following certification, and assuming the act is covered under the policy, the government may reimburse the insurance company for losses paid to the firm under a federally mandated formula. Most insurers will add this coverage automatically unless the firm declines the coverage via an attached form.

As firms investigate the various first-party coverage options, they should understand exactly what the policy language would reasonably cover, and what it would not. Depending on the insurer, some of the above coverages may overlap into single coverage elements or may not be included at all. Failure to investigate and understand coverage features can lead to an easy declination by the insurer. Be educated and prepared.

Third-Party Coverage Options

PCI DSS: Following a breach of a firm's payment card system, there is a litany of mandatory fees that may apply on behalf of the firm. Generally, PCI DSS coverage would pay those amounts which the firms are legally obligated to pay under their merchant services agreement (MSA). This could include, penalties for non-compliance, monetary expenses, and the cost of an audit to display PCI DSS compliance before payment cards can again be used.

Private Rights of Action: Many policies will also cover the defense and claim expenses if an affected individual party were to bring a claim against the firm following a covered breach.

Regulatory Proceedings Fines and Penalties: This feature would cover the request for information, civil demand, or civil proceedings brought by a federal, state, or local government entity. Depending on the policy, foreign governmental entities may or may not be covered. Generally, the cyber policy will be a duty and right to defend. Many policies will also cover the fines, penalties, and assessments levied against the firm following regulatory proceedings.

GDPR: This is a relatively new coverage that deals with the European Union's General Data Privacy Regulation (2016/679). This policy provision can cover the defense costs from responding to a GDPR violation and possibly fines, penalties, and assessments that may arise as a result of such actions. If GDPR coverage is required by the firm but not explicitly mentioned by the policy, firms should consult the definitions and exclusions dealing with regulatory bodies. Often those definitions will only cover U.S.-based regulators.

Criminal Reward Payments: Included in some policies is a small sublimit to encourage the arrest and conviction of the hacker that infiltrated the firm's system. For this coverage to apply, the information leading to the arrest and conviction must not have come from information provided by the firm or the firm's auditors or other hired individuals.

Partner Action Items:

- ☐ Determine if the coverage options are appropriate for the firm.
- ☐ Seek competent legal assistance to assist with any questions.
- ☐ Stay abreast of additional coverage features afforded in the marketplace that may prove beneficial to the firm.
- ☐ Communicate this data to relevant stakeholders, including IT and staff;
- ☐ Update the firm's incident response plan and other internal documents as necessary.

Common Coverage Exclusions

Exclusions serve the purpose of limiting or clarifying the coverage afforded elsewhere in the policy. Generally, exclusions listed will be those not directly related to cyber-type or data-breach losses. They can also include first-party coverages found in other insurer's policies, but not those found in the policy being reviewed. Firms should be advised when comparing policy exclusions that doing so will be a tedious process. As one study of over 130 different cyber insurance policies noted: "[p]arsing out the nuances in the policies can be a challenge: exclusions include exceptions that have their own exceptions buried in them."[486]

Intentional Misconduct: Naturally, firms are not going to be covered for intentionally committing criminal or fraudulent acts. However, there could be a circumstance where a staff member intentionally exposes covered data for nefarious purposes. In a circumstance such as this, many policies generally allow for coverage until an adjudication of some type has concluded that the conduct was intentional. Many policies also contain an innocent-insured type provision where those who did not personally commit or know about the act would still be covered under the policy. How coverage will ultimately be decided may be settled on a case-by-case basis and dependent on policy language.[487]

Bodily Injury or Property Damage: Cyber policies tend to exclude coverage based upon any allegation of bodily injury or property damage. This is logical in that those types of claims should generally fall under a general liability policy. As such an exclusion would pertain to a common trip-and-fall accident, this is understandable. However, in industries where a computer error could lead to bodily injury or property damage, such as for a manufacturer, clarification on the exclusion, as well as the need for a potential manuscript endorsement to cover such potential claims, may be warranted.

Employment-Related Claims: Generally, this exclusion would cover claims that would otherwise be covered under an employment practices liability insurance policy. Examples would include sexual harassment, failure to promote, wrongful termination, and various labor law violations.

Portable Electronic Devices: Some policies may contain an exclusion for any claim that arises as a result of a lost portable electronic device, often a laptop or tablet. Given the large amount of losses that occur from portable electronic devices, firms should be wary of this exclusion.

Patent, Software, or Copyright Infringement: These types of claims would generally be covered under intellectual property (IP) insurance policy. The exclusion broadly covers the misuse or infringement of patented or copyrighted material. Additionally, this exclusion would bar coverage for the theft or misappropriation of ideas and trade secrets by the insured.

Failure to Follow Required Security Practices: Though becoming rarer, this exclusion denies coverage if a breach results from a failure to adhere to required security practices. Such clauses can still be found on many legacy cyber policies and should be avoided.

Failure to Follow Reasonable Security Measures: Also becoming rare, but this exclusion can eliminate coverage for a firm if a loss resulted in a shortcoming in security that they should have known about. Such a broad exclusion can be extremely detrimental to a firm's ability to rely on its cyber insurance policy following a breach. It would be too easy for an insurer to argue that a firm should have enacted and monitored any number of security measures that could have prevented a breach. Such clauses should be avoided.

Material Misrepresentations: This is not an exclusion, per se, but rather a policy condition. If the firm committed fraud or state material misrepresentations in their application, the insurer could have grounds to cancel coverage.

Violations of Specified Laws: Often, these laws will be specifically listed. Frequently included would be violations of the Securities Act of 1933, SEC Act of 1934, state or "blue sky" security laws, Employee Retirement Income Security Act of 1974, Racketeer Influenced and Corrupt Organizations Act, and other similar laws.

Payment Cards: Cyber policies generally do not cover the losses from the use of credit or debit cards. If fraud occurs on a personal payment card, consumer protections may be available. Whether fraud occurring on a business credit card is covered may be situationally and policy dependent. Therefore, it should be investigated by the firm in conjunction with their payment card provider.

Acts of God: Damages arising from fires, floods, earthquakes, volcanic eruptions, hail, wind, landslides, and similar disasters would not be covered.

Acts of War: Invasions, war, warlike hostilities, operations, rebellions, civil war, insurrections, terrorism, and the like, will not be covered. However, this exclusion can be modified to carve back coverage for general cyber-terrorism-related acts.

Pollution: Any claims dealing with the discharge of pollutants, or costs associated with the cleanup of those pollutants will not be covered.

Ultimately, firms need to investigate the exclusions within their own current or proposed policy(s). The lists of exclusion – often with their own internal exclusion – can frequently run for a dozen pages or more. While the above were general exclusions found in many policies, each insurer has its own unique policy language that can further be affected by various endorsements to the policy.

Partner Action Items:

☐ Understand what policy exclusions are present and how they may impact the business decisions and internal controls of the firm;

☐ If in doubt, work with competent legal counsel to make reasonable determinations of policy language;

☐ Communicate this data to relevant stakeholders, including IT and staff;

☐ Update the firm's incident response plan and other internal documents as necessary.

Simplifying Coverage Assessments with Wargaming

Due to the non-standard nature of cyber policy coverage, it may be best for a firm to "wargame" scenarios when assessing coverage. When doing so, it is best that all stakeholders, including partners, shareholders, brokers/agents, IT, legal, and HR are present. This would better allow the firm to make a reasonable assessment of coverage before the policy is needed. Below are examples that can aid as a starting point for discussing coverage. Firms should create their own series of questions tailored to their own needs taking note of all relevant policy coverages and exclusions. As discussed in previous chapters, depending on the scenario, coverage may be found in multiple policies, single policies, or is uninsured or uninsurable.

General Questions

- What the retroactive date of this policy?
- Does the policy cover the necessary-named insureds including seasonal workers, temporary employees, and subcontractors, if necessary?
- Is the policy admitted or surplus lines?
- How adept is my broker in assisting with my cyber-related questions?
- How adept in the insurer in dealing with cyber-related claims?
- Who are the vendors that must be used following a covered event, and how experienced are they in dealing with covered events?
- Has the firm assessed and confirmed the contracts of vendors before a breach has occurred?
- Are there any breach mitigation services being offered by the insurance company?

- Are those breach-mitigation services being used by the appropriate parties?

Ransomware Scenarios

- Does the policy cover cyber extortion attempts?
- Who will pay the ransom?
- What if a current or former employee perpetrated the ransom?
- What are the business interruption reimbursement provisions such as sublimit, waiting period, and retention?
- Will the policy provide for a computer forensics expert to determine the scope and nature of the breach as well as assist in removing the offending malware?
- How will the policy respond if the computer system is damaged by malware?
- Will the policy provide legal counsel well-versed in cyber-related matters to assist in navigating the process as well as notifying relevant authorities?
- If some of the firm's clients leave following a publication of the breach leading to a loss of revenue, how will the policy respond?
- Does the policy provide for crisis management and public relations personnel, if necessary?
- How do I demonstrate duress, i.e., evidence of a ransomware event to the insurer?

Breach Scenarios

- Does the policy cover breaches of my computer system?
- Will the policy provide legal counsel well-versed in cyber-related matters to assist in navigating the process?

- Will the policy provide for a computer forensics expert to determine the scope and nature of the breach as well as assist in removing the offending malware?
- Will the policy assist in notifying relevant authorities?
- Will the policy cover the cost of drafting and mailing breach notification letters to those affected?
- Will the policy provide credit monitoring to those affected? For how long?
- Does the policy provide any other services, such as financial counseling, to those affected?
- How to the policy consider voluntary notifications?
- Does the policy provide for crisis management and public relations personnel, if necessary?
- Will the policy cover the cost of a call center to handle client inquiries following a breach, if necessary?
- How would the policy respond to my network being damaged as a result of the breach?
- If some of the firm's clients leave following a publication of the breach leading to a loss of revenue, how will the policy respond?
- Does the policy provide for crisis-management and public-relations personnel, if necessary?
- If the firm is investigated and fined by regulatory bodies following the breach, how will the policy respond?
- If the firm faces legal action brought by clients following a breach, how will the policy respond?
- Does the policy exclude claims arising from portable electronic devices?

PCI DSS Scenarios

- Does the policy offer coverage for PCI DSS claims?
- Would the policy pay the costs legally obligated by the firm's merchant services agreement (MSA)?
- Would the policy cover contractual fines or penalties for PCI DSS non-compliance?
- Will the policy pay for any mandatory audit following a payment card breach to prove PCI DSS compliance?
- Are PCI DSS monetary assessments, operational expenses, card-reissuance fees, fraud-recovery fees, and case-management fees covered?
- Does the policy provide for credit monitoring to those affected by a payment card breach?
- What limits are afforded by the policy regarding the above, and will those reasonably cover the firm?

Theft Scenarios

- If an employee is duped into transferring client funds, is that covered?
- If an employee is duped into transferring firm funds, is that covered?
- If a rogue employee steals client funds, would the policy cover such a scenario?
- What sublimits and deductibles/retentions are associated with these types of claims?
- Does the policy limit coverage to only those who are authorized in writing to wire funds?
- If an employee uses a company credit card to pay a fraudulent request, how is that considered under the policy?

Regulatory Scenarios

- Does the policy cover regulatory defense expenses?
- Is the policy a "right and duty to defend" policy?
- Does the policy cover regulatory fines, penalties, and assessments?
- What regulatory bodies does the firm fall under?
- What regulatory bodies are covered?
- What regulatory bodies are excluded?
- Does the policy explicitly mention GDPR? Does it provide or exclude coverage?
- Would the GDPR coverage indemnify the firm for fines, penalties, and assessments related to a GDPR regulatory action?

Other Scenarios

- If my cloud provider suffers a breach, will the policy reimburse the firm for lost revenue? If so, what are the policy provisions and sublimits?
- If my network goes down due to an error, but it is not a breach, how will the policy respond?
- Does the policy cover GDPR-related actions?
- If my computer system is used for cryptojacking, telephone fraud, or other types of utility fraud, is there coverage under this policy?
- How does the policy respond to bodily injury or property damage arising from a breach?
- If libelous, slanderous, defamatory, or copyrighted/trademarked information is published on my website or social media account, how will the policy respond?

- Does the policy provide for pre-claim or potential-claim assistance?
- How would the policy respond to a professional ethics complaint against the firm following a breach?
- How does the policy respond to regulatory proceedings unique to my firm's circumstances? (FTC, SEC, GDPR, state-level financial regulators, etc.)
- Does the policy contain coverage for certified acts of terrorism (TRIA)?

Partner Action Items:

- ☐ Conduct tabletop wargaming scenarios will all relevant stakeholders, including IT, legal, HR, and partners;
- ☐ Use this as an opportunity to understand the firm's unique insurance needs;
- ☐ Compare these scenarios to the coverage afforded under the firm's cyber policy;
- ☐ If gaps in coverage are found, work with the broker to determine if coverage is available at renewal or policy inception;
- ☐ Update the firm's incident response plan and other internal documents as necessary.

General Guidelines on Purchasing Cyber Insurance

In totality, there are guidelines that all firms reviewing a new or existing cyber policy should consider:

- Work with a knowledgeable cyber insurance broker and a reputable insurance company. Though you may have a relationship with an existing broker who is not knowledgeable in this area, consider if that relationship is worth the potential cost of an insurance declination or uncovered loss;

- Work diligently with a knowledgeable broker as your firm "wargames" your coverage requirements. Understand what risks are unique to your firm, and how to insure – if possible – for those risks.

- Firms should purchase the largest reasonable limits that are available in consideration of funding restrictions. While there are certainly "average" breach costs, they are just that – averages. The cost of a breach varies wildly, often based upon factors that are out of the control of the firm. In particular, most firms should attempt to maximize first-party coverage limits.

- Firms should purchase the broadest policy that has the most coverage features. As new attack vectors and vulnerabilities are created and exploited, firms may find themselves responding to a method of breach that they had either not considered or otherwise deemed impossible. The legal interpretation of policy language in this field is still very much in its infancy and is rapidly evolving. Any small savings in premium can be grossly outweighed by otherwise unnecessary uncovered costs.

- If a firm wants to customize coverage found in their cyber policy, they should do so carefully and in conjunction with qualified legal counsel. Cyber policies can be exceedingly complex. Even well-intentioned unique endorsements may have unforeseen negative consequences in other portions of the policy.

The Future of Cyber Insurance

1. **2020 -2025:**
   - Lack of appropriate coverage features will remain the most common reason for a firm to be denied coverage.
   - Either the firm was unaware they needed a specific coverage feature, or their broker was unaware that a coverage existed in the marketplace.
   - Most of the legal disputes involving cyber insurance will focus on a plaintiff attempting to "invent" coverage for losses that were unforeseen or unforeseeable, and thus uninsured.
   - Lawyers specializing in privacy law will remain rare due to the lack of consistent revenue.
   - The number of insurance brokers/agent self-identifying as "cyber insurance experts" will continue to grow, though there will be no justifiable reason or insurance certification for this claim.
   - Most businesses will continue to remain ignorant of the growing number of cybersecurity regulations that govern their industry.
   - The cost of cyber insurance will remain comparatively inexpensive.
   - Lawyers that can weather the drought of revenue, while building up their expertise, will be handsomely rewarded in the future as their expertise becomes increasingly needed.
   - Consumers will continue to view breaches as more of a nuisance than a real threat, limiting the client losses firms face following a breach.
2. **2025 – 2030:**
   - As coverage features become more standardized across the board and market growth slows, coverage feature declinations will no longer be as common.

- Sophisticated insureds will be more likely to strictly instruct their broker on cyber insurance coverage needs. This will eventually trickle down into the broader marketplace.
- Insurers will increasingly look towards nuances in policy language to deny coverage.
- Some large opportunistic insurers will begin to instruct a handful of younger, cyber insurance specialty brokers in-house to gain a foothold in the market.
- Most insurance brokers without the requisite technical and legal background will find explaining or reasonably interpreting policy language to be impossible. They will sell on price by default to maintain existing relationships and market share.
- As cyber-related breaches become ever more common, the price of cyber insurance will increase.
- Smaller insurers will attempt to enter the market but will be mostly unsuccessful due to unpredictable large losses.
- Contractual cybersecurity obligations for businesses become more common.
- Lawyers specializing in privacy law will become more common in assisting firms with interpreting coverage features, policy language, and contracts.
- As more consumers fall victim to identity theft, they attempt to limit the amount of personal information that businesses have on their systems.

3. **2027 and onwards:**
   - Application misrepresentations become the Holy Grail of cyber insurance declinations.
   - Privacy laws will continue to change and grow for the foreseeable future in ways that are unpredictable given the range of technological innovation and adoption.
   - Insureds will increasingly find it difficult to remain up to date with the latest laws or may find themselves subject to contradictory and vague laws.

- Cyber insurers will closely scrutinize applications in an attempt to find any oversight on behalf of the business that could have hypothetically prevented a breach.
- As high-quality cybersecurity staff become unaffordable for many businesses, they will outsource most, or all, of their cybersecurity needs. This will make technical, in-house cyber insurance application assistance impractical.
- A greater number of lawyers specializing in privacy law, with various cybersecurity certifications, will be engaged to assist medium- to large-sized firms with their cyber insurance applications.
- A very small number of highly specialized brokers with the requisite legal and technical background will be available to assist larger firms in completing their cyber insurance application.
- Cyber insurance will be seen as a "must-have" for every business, and the cost will be comparable to most professional liability policies. This will create anxiety for business owners who will struggle to balance the high probability of use with the uncertainty of coverage declination.
- Consumers will begin to demand greater privacy, and the legislature will begin to seriously consider an Electronic Bill of Rights.

4. **2030 and onwards:**
   - Unique policy declinations will regularly occur for very large losses concentrated within a small number of nationwide or multinational businesses.
   - Insurance companies who can find no reason to deny coverage based on the policy or the application will look toward the judiciary to reinterpret traditional legal standards to support their positions.
   - Cyber Insurance companies will attempt to set a legal standard with high-profile cases to create favorable future

legal conditions or deny claims for a high volume of smaller insureds.

- Avoiding these declinations will be exceedingly difficult due to their innovative legal reasoning and circumstantial nature. This will bring rise to the first powerhouse cyber-defense lawyers who will be recognized at the national level.

- More boutique law firms specializing in privacy law will be created to assist businesses with the full cyber insurance lifecycle. Insurance brokerages solely specializing in cyber insurance will arise, though their true expertise will be questionable.

- Cyber insurance will continue to remain expensive and may surpass the cost of professional liability policies.

- Consumers will become increasingly wary of cyber breaches.

5. **2035 and onwards:**

- Insurers will continue to struggle to actuarially define cyber risks with any certainty.

- As the Internet of Things (IoT) takes hold, the possible attack vectors that could be used to infiltrate a business may become insurmountable and infinite.

- Catastrophic losses will occur in specific industries forcing insurers to deny coverage for any reason possible to save their balance sheet.

- Even if insurers don't believe that their rationale will withstand the scrutiny of a courtroom with mature technology-focused laws, they will bank on the notion that most insured will not have the monetary resources for protracted legal battles.

- Smaller businesses will return to cash payments as a preferred method of purchase. Medium to large insureds will settle their declinations via alternative dispute resolution mechanisms for a fraction of their policy limits.

- This shortsightedness by cyber insurers will preserve their balance sheet but will create widespread distrust of cyber insurance across specific industries.
- Partial or full self-insurance plans for cyber losses will become more popular.
- Lawyers specializing in privacy law will bring the first large-scale cyber insurance, class-action claims.
- Privacy laws and mandatory security standards will become commonplace.

Section 8: After the Policy is Bound

Cyber Insurance, like cybersecurity, is a year-round endeavor. As such, firms should be aware of the myriad of choices, decisions, and responsibilities that await them after their cyber insurance policy is bound. Failure to understand these obligations can lead to late reporting of claims, potential declinations of coverage, and increased regulatory actions.

Policy Benefits

Certain insurers may offer additional security services as a benefit to the policy. These can include employee training through fake phishing emails and webinars, or continuous network scanning and penetration testing.

While these tools can provide convenience, firms should be cautious about investigating the depth of such services. These broadly termed benefits can range from rudimentary to quite sophisticated. Firms should not consider these services as meeting the requirements of any state or federal law without first consulting legal counsel.

Crucial to minimizing the time from breach to notification is pre-selecting vendors. Firms should consider researching available vendors and their contracts if provided by their insurer. Most likely, this will require legal counsel who is well-versed in privacy and contract law to advise the firm on contract suitability.

Partner Action Items:

- ☐ Understand what policy benefits are afforded by the insurer;
- ☐ Before assuming that these benefits fulfill legal requirements, work with legal counsel;
- ☐ Communicate this data to relevant stakeholders, including IT staff;
- ☐ Update the firm's cybersecurity framework other internal documents as necessary;

Potential Claim Reporting

One of the most overlooked components of a cyber insurance policy is the requirement to report potential claims. As technology becomes more pervasive, complex, and distributed, it is much more likely that information held may be breached. Generally, data breaches requiring potential claim reporting fall within two categories: those breaches that occurred within the firm – internal breaches, and those breaches that occurred at a third-party vendor holding the firm's information – external breaches.

Consider how one prominent cyber insurer defines the policy obligation of the insured to notify the insurer of any potential claim: "You have the option of notifying us of potential claims that may lead to a covered claim against you. In order to do so, you must give written notice to us **as soon as possible and within the policy period**, and the notice must, to the greatest extent possible, identify the details of the potential claim, including identifying the potential claimant(s), the likely basis for liability, the likely demand for relief, and any additional information about the potential claim we may reasonably request.

The benefit to you of notifying us of a potential claim is that if an actual claim arises from the same circumstances as the properly notified potential claim, then we will treat that claim as if it had first been made against you on the date you properly notified us of it as a potential claim, even if that claim is first made against you after the policy period has expired.

All potential claim notifications **must be in writing** and submitted to us via the designated email address or mailing address identified in Item 6 of the Declarations."[488]

As later defined in the same policy, a potential claim means "any acts, errors, or omissions of an insured or other circumstance reasonably likely to lead to a claim covered under this policy."[489]

Put more simply, insureds need to notify their cyber insurer of any potential claims that occur within the policy period. This is to benefit the insured in case a claim is made against the insured after the policy period has expired. Failure to do so could result in a declination of coverage. Even when the nature and extent of the potential claim are unknown, firms should take serious consideration as to whether they need to notify their insurer.

In relation to an internal breach, firms may unknowingly run afoul of their policy requirements. Although they may give notice that a cyber event has occurred, well-meaning but often unqualified internal IT staff may tell firm owners that nothing appears to have been stolen. Or, the firm may simply decide not to report the issue for fear of an increase in policy premium. If it was later determined that covered client information was stolen, coverage may be declined if the timing of that determination fell outside policy-reporting requirements. Further, failure to report potential claims could result in all manner of expensive uncovered risks.

Potential claim reporting of external breaches tends to become more onerous for the firm. As mentioned previously, service providers are generally not responsible for the client information stored by the firm on their system. To illustrate the potential dangers that could befall a firm for failing to report a potential external breach of client data, consider the recent Wolters Kluwer CCH debacle.

On May 6th, 2019, CCH experienced "network and service interruptions" that affected some of their platforms and applications. This effectively shut down, or severely restricted the business operations of, a large number of accounting firms across the country for a significant period of time.

As later reported in a May 23rd update on the company's website, their IT team had detected a zero-day exploit. For this reason, they had shut down the majority of their systems to avoid a spread of the malware.[490]

Of greater importance to this discussion was the company's notification that: "To date, we have found no evidence that customer data or systems were compromised." However, they also stated that "Our investigation of the incident is on-going." [491]

While the outcome of this event remains unknown at the time of publication, what would happen if CCH were to later notify firms that their client's information had been stolen?

Likely, it would depend on how the firm initially responded, if at all. For firms that had notified their insurer of the CCH breach as a potential claim before their policy renewed, they would most likely be afforded coverage under their policy. For firms whose cyber policy renewed before the hypothetical CCH breach notification – and had not given their cyber insurer a potential claim notice – it would be all too easy for the insurer to deny coverage. This would leave the firm scrambling to find and review appropriate vendors, manage the entire process, research and adhere to all applicable laws, and pay for the entire claim out of pocket.

Firms who feel that their cyber insurer acted in bad faith by declining coverage could attempt to litigate the issue. Regardless of the outcome, a timely potential claim notification would be exponentially cheaper and less painful.

Partner Action Items:

- ☐ Understand what requirements the policy contains regarding the reporting of potential claims;
- ☐ Communicate this data to relevant stakeholders, including IT staff;

☐ Update the firm's incident response plan and other internal documents as necessary;

☐ Conduct regular training for staff so they are aware of their obligations to report a potential cyber claim.

Claim Reporting

Many firms rightfully believe that a claim is a breach of their computer system by an unauthorized third party, but a cyber insurer may have an expanded definition. Consider the following definition from a well-known cyber insurer:

A "Claim" means:

1. a written assertion of liability or any written demand for financial compensation or injunctive relief;
2. a regulatory proceeding;
3. unintentional breach of a written contract asserted by a client;
4. contractual indemnity – breach costs, or;
5. contractual indemnity – third-party.[492]

In this example, the insurer is considering the traditional understanding of a computer system breach to be only one of five claim scenarios that would need to be reported. Regardless of what a firm's leadership believes, they should have a clear understanding of what the insurer defines as a claim. In turn, leadership should relay that information to all other relevant parties, including staff and IT professionals. These understandings should be encapsulated in the firm's incident response plan and information security policy.

Firms should understand that each insurance provider will have different definitions of what a "claim" will entail. Furthermore, different cyber policies from the same carrier may have different definitions, even for the same word or phrase. As such, it is up to the firm to keep abreast of any changes to their policy and incorporate those changes accordingly. Because firm owners are unlikely to fully immerse themselves in network architecture and sub-vendors of their primary vendors, they should ensure that their IT professionals are well-versed in understanding what constitutes a claim or potential claim.

At worst, the failure to report a claim within the policy period can lead to an otherwise unnecessary full declination of coverage. At best, a late report of a claim will make the firm ineligible for a relatively minor recoupment of funds, often from a sublimit such as one applying to a dependent-business interruption. Nonetheless, a firm should not test the limits of their policy.

When in doubt, consider reporting the matter and let the system sort it out.

Partner Action Items:

- ☐ Understand how the policy defines a claim;
- ☐ Communicate this data to relevant stakeholders, including IT staff;
- ☐ Update the firm's incident response plan and other internal documents as necessary;
- ☐ Conduct regular training for staff so they are aware of their obligations to report a cyber claim, and how to do so.

Giving Notice to the Insurer

Different policies will have different policy language requirements regarding how soon claims or potential claims should be reported to the insurer.

In regard to a claim, one insurer was succinct in their policy language: "You must notify us of claims as soon as practicable once such claim is known to any board member, trustee, director, officer, in-house counsel, risk manager, chief technology officer, chief information officer, or chief privacy officer of the insured organization, but in any event no later than: (i) the end of the policy period; or (ii) 30 days after the end of the policy period for claims made against you in the last 30 days of the policy period. Proper notification of claims must be sent in accordance with the notification details in Item 7 of the Declarations."[493]

How the term, "as soon as practicable" should be interpreted could vary based upon the controlling case law and venue where the coverage dispute is litigated.[494]

A different insurer appears to be slightly more lenient regarding the treatment of potential claims in their policy language, stating: "What you must do in the event of a circumstance which could give rise to a claim: In respect of INSURING CLAUSES 5 and 6, should a senior executive officer become aware of: a. a situation during the period of the policy that could give rise to a claim, or b. an allegation or complaint made or intimated against you during the period of the policy; then you have the option of whether to report this circumstance to us or not. However, if you choose not to report this circumstance, we will not be liable for that portion of any claim that is greater than it would have been had you reported this circumstance.

If you choose to report this circumstance you must do so no later than the end of any applicable extended reporting period for it to be

301

considered under this Policy and we will require you to provide full details of the circumstance…"[495]

Partner Action Items:

☐ Understand how to give notice to the insurer;

☐ Communicate this data to relevant stakeholders, including IT staff;

☐ Update the firm's incident response plan and other internal documents as necessary.

Material Changes

Cyber insurers will often include state-specific amendatory endorsements like those found in more traditional insurance policies. While often overlooked, there are specific cancellation provisions which require vigilance on behalf of all firms.

Take the following clause found in a cyber policy endorsement: "[W]e may cancel this policy only for one or more of the following reasons: … d. Increased hazard or material change in the risk assumed which we could not have reasonably contemplated at the time of assumption of the risk; e. Substantial breaches of contractual duties, conditions or warranties that materially affect the nature and/or insurability of the risk;"[496]

Encapsulated within the above policy language are a number of issues that firms should address.

Foremost, any material changes concerning the risk to the firm should likely be reported to the insurer. Changes could include the firm falling under new regulatory schemes not disclosed in the application, or material changes to network security and control regimes.

Second, the firm should ensure that it is staying true to the representations that it made on the application. Often the application or the policy will include a warranty statement. This statement is essentially a promise that the statements made by the firm are true and the validity of the insurance policy depends upon the firm fulfilling those promises. Failure to do so can result in a declination of coverage.[497] This was one of the elements used by the insurer to deny coverage in the case of *Columbia Casualty Co. v. Cottage Health System* discussed in a prior chapter.

Partner Action Items:

☐ Understand when material changes must be reported to the insurer;

☐ Communicate this data to relevant stakeholders, including IT staff;

☐ When in doubt, work with legal counsel to ensure policy compliance.

Section 9: Interesting Extras

The following are additional tools and resources that a firm can use to better strengthen their cybersecurity posture. In turn, this can lower premiums, minimize the potential of a breach, and lessen the possibility of an insurance declination due to oversights.

Examples of Real CPA Firm Breaches

Below are examples of recent and real breaches experienced by CPA firms all across the country. Although these breaches are public knowledge, the authors have removed identifying information. The goal is not to embarrass these firms but to allow other firms to learn from their mistakes.

Firm 1: CPA Firm 1 was performing a routine test on their data restoration procedures. The data was held by a third-party cloud provider in an offsite, separate location. While performing this routine test, the firm was notified that the data had been subject to a ransomware attack. An investigation by the firm's outside IT expert determined that there was no evidence that any information had been downloaded or copied.

Early the following year, the state's Department of Taxation and Finance notified the firm that approximately 50 tax returns were filed under the firm's electronic filing ID number for existing clients. The firm contacted the IRS which confirmed similar activity. Subsequently, the firm suspended the filing of any electronic tax returns.

In response, the firm engaged a forensics expert to provide an assessment of the network and security. At the time of notice, the forensics expert had found no indication of any vulnerability or of any previous compromise on the firm's network. Additional forensics were performed on the firm's off-site data location to determine if any prior breach had occurred at that location.

The firm conducted a full review of their security practices and systems. Credit monitoring and identity theft and resolution services were provided to affected clients.

Firm 2: CPA Firm 2 was attempting to resolve an email failure with their email-hosting service. During this action, the partner was directed to a website that instructed them to call a phone number for immediate assistance. After the phone call was placed, the technician requested to access the partner's computer to understand their email problem.

The partner on the call installed the software necessary to allow remote access. The technician began to access various IP addresses on the partner's computer and notified him that this was the reason behind the email issue. To fix the issue, the technician insisted that they allow him to install a program on the office's network server. The partner resisted and told the technician that his local IT provider would contact him to resolve the issue. At this point, the technician on the phone stated that only a Microsoft technician could solve the issue. At this point, the partner realized that he was not speaking with his email-hosting service and disconnected his computer from the network and uninstalled the remote-access software. The interaction was stated as lasting less than eight minutes.

The partner contacted his IT provider and was notified that he had fallen victim to a scam. The remote-access software was meant to copy information on the local computer. On the partner's desktop was a "My Documents" folder that kept items which had been emailed in the past and included tax returns and other documents. Also, on his computer were previous years of their tax program which were not encrypted.

Upon examination, it was discovered that the computer was infected with a virus that was immune to "normal" virus-protection software. Virus scans were performed on all computers, and the virus software was upgraded. Physical controls were updated to ensure that all client data was stored in encrypted form.

Firm 3: CPA Firm 3 fell victim to a social engineering scam that allowed an unauthorized party to gain access to a staff member's email account. Upon discovery of the intrusion, email access was shut down for all accounts.

Firm clients were warned that unwanted email requests looking similar to the firm's normal emails might be made, but those requests should be immediately disregarded. Clients were encouraged to continue using the client portal provided by the firm to transfer any sensitive documents.

Firm 3 indicated that they engaged their IT experts to conduct a review of their email security practices and systems to ensure that appropriate security measures were in place moving forward. It was not reported how many clients received notification letters and credit monitoring.

Firm 4: CPA Firm 4 became aware of a breach when they were notified that their clients' accounts were experiencing attempts to have funds withdrawn. Their clients also experienced multiple attempts to have fraudulent credit cards opened in their names.

Upon learning of the breach, Firm 4 retained a computer forensics firm to determine the scope and nature of the breach. The forensics team discovered that one computer was compromised and had been accessed over a period of two days. The unauthorized party may have accessed clients' personal information, names, home addresses, social security numbers, tax returns, and financial account numbers.

The firm contacted the IRS and the FBI to conduct investigations and corrected the vulnerability in their computer system. Additionally, they reviewed their internal policies on data management protocols and implemented further security measures. Ultimately 1,856 of the firm's clients received notification letters and credit monitoring services.

Partner Action Items:

☐ A continuously updated list of breaches can be found at www.idtheftcenter.org. The list can be searched for CPA firms.

☐ Consider using these breaches as training aids and warnings for staff.

☐ Every breached firm indicated that they performed some sort of update to security systems and/or their computer-use policies. Take this as a warning and become proactive, not reactive.

Tips on Passwords from NIST

Nearly all firms, and for that matter all businesses, nationwide adhere to the same minimum password requirements. Generally, at least eight characters long, one uppercase letter, one number, one lowercase letter, one special character, and so forth. Passwords must be changed at periodic intervals, such as every 90 days. However, such long-standing and ubiquitous practices are now being recommended for change by the National Institute of Science and Technology (NIST).

NIST is a non-regulatory federal agency within the Department of Commerce. This organization creates and develops the Federal Information Processing Standards which creates compulsory standards for all federal agencies. Through their Special Publication (SP) 800-series, they often set cybersecurity best practices across the industry.

In early 2019, NIST published revised guidance on security best practices in NIST Special Publication 800-63B Digital Identity Guidelines: Authentication and Lifecycle Management. NIST refers to what is colloquially known as a "password," with the fittingly a cryptic "Memorized Secret Verifiers." While their purely technical recommendations are beyond the scope of this book, their updated password recommendations are as follows:

- When a user establishes or changes a password, that password should be screened against a list of commonly used or previously compromised passwords. Other examples of improper passwords include dictionary words, context-specific words such as the name of the firm or derivates, and repetitious or sequential characters such as "123456" or "abc123."

- Passwords should not be changed at periodic intervals. For example, no more new passwords every 90 days. Changes should only be forced when there is evidence of compromise.
- The traditional composition rules requiring the mixture of special, uppercase, and lowercase letters, in combination with a number, known as 'composition rules," are no longer necessary.
- Passwords should be between 8 and 64 characters.
- NIST encourages users to utilize passwords managers which they say may "increase the likelihood that users will choose stronger memorized secrets." 498

Beyond this shortlist, there are numerous other recommendations which are worth consideration in conjunction with the firm's IT and cybersecurity professionals. NIST's *Special Publication 800-63B; Digital Identity Guidelines: Authentication and Lifecycle Management* is available free to the public at: https://doi.org/10.6028/NIST.SP.800-63b.

Useful NIST Special Publication (SP) Resources

- *SP 800-12 Rev. 1, An Introduction to Information security*
- *SP 800-16, Information Technology Security Training Requirements: A Role and Performance Based Model*
- *SP 800-50, Building an Information Technology Security Awareness and Training Program*
- *SP 800-61 Rev. 2, Computer Security Incident Handling Guide*
- *SP 83 Rev. 1, Guide to Malware Incident Prevention and Handling for Desktops and Laptops*
- *SP 800-100, Information security Handbook: A Guide for Managers*
- *SP 800-111, Guide to Storage Encryption Technologies for End User Devices*
- *SP 800-115, Technical Guide to Information security Testing and Assessment*

The above is but a small sample of useful special publications offered by NIST.

Firms should visit: https://csrc.nist.gov/publications/sp for a full listing of all NIST Special Publications.

Common Signs of a Breach

Below are common signs that a firm may be experiencing, or has experienced, a breach:

- Inability to login to your computer system;
- Strange computer behaviors such as popups, new toolbars, anti-virus warnings, or unexplained movement of your cursor;
- Slow computer speeds, often across multiple computers or the entire network;
- Unusual login activity reported by system administrators, often from unexpected and varied geographical locations;
- Abnormal outbound traffic detected on the network;
- Changes or additions to administrator login permissions;
- Off-cycle or unusual requests for money to be transferred to new accounts;
- Urgent requests that money be transferred to established clients or vendors using new payment methods in conflict stated firm protocol and verification methods;
- Emails in the staff member's outbox that are unexplained;
- Abnormal request to change usernames or passwords, often seemingly from trusted sources;
- Lengthy and/or cryptic file extensions;
- Unsolicited emails requesting the staff member download a file or open a file and enable macros;
- Unexplained loss of client or firm funds/information;
- Abnormal amount of client returns filed by your firm being rejected because their returns were already filed;
- Clients receiving refunds before filing their returns;
- Clients receiving IRS authentication letters from the IRS before they've filed;

- Clients receiving notice from the IRS that their account has been disabled, locked, accessed, or one has been inexplicably created for them;
- Clients reporting emails from the firm that were never sent by the firm;
- The number of returns filed with under the EFIN exceeds the number of relevant clients;
- Notification from state or federal agencies that a breach is likely to have occurred;
- <u>Any other indication that the firm reasonably believes may indicate a breach</u>.

What is an Incident Response Plan?

In a recent Ponemon Cost of Data Breach Study (2017), the authors looked at the impact of 20 different factors on the cost of a breach. Most notably, the greatest reduction in the per capita cost of a breach was through the use of an incident response team (IRT).[499] Simply put, an IRT is responsible for creating, practicing, refining, and implementing an Incident Response Plan (IRP). Eventually the firm will be breached. With a little forethought and planning, firms can lower the cost of a breach, lessen disruption of business activities, and avoid embarrassing or costly mistakes.

In light of this information, many firms commit the following errors:

- They do not have a plan. When a breach occurs, this often results in a number of easily preventable and frustrating errors. Because responsibilities were not delineated before the event, egos often clash in the partner group. This can lead to necessary steps being skipped and redundant tasking. It also tends to prolong the response times, which are subject to various state and federal limitations. Contemplating if the firm should respond to reporter's phone call immediately after a breach is no time to make a judgment call. Have a plan.

- Firms have a plan, but they've never rehearsed it. Often this occurs when a single member of the firm is tasked with creating the plan. While the "box has been checked," it is of no use if the firm has never taken the time to educate stakeholders and staff on how it is to be used. This often leads to increased breach detection times by firm owners, increased time to potential client notification, and an unnecessary increase in business disruption length. In addition, this can have major insurance implications such as decreased

317

recoupments of various sublimits or outright declination of coverage.

- Firms have a plan, but it was saved on their now-inaccessible computer system.
- Firms don't update their plan. Threats change. Key members of the team come and go. Before a firm knows it, their plan is obsolete. Make certain the plan stays updated, and key members have been educated and rehearsed their roles. Staff should also understand how to identify a potential security incident and who should receive reports of those incidents.

Incident Response Plans can become very complex, but for most firms, they should be relatively straightforward. Firms should begin by understanding the basic functions of an IRT. At its most basic, an IRT should minimize the harm done to the business and respond to the incident in a calm and coordinated manner.

Firms should begin by identifying their IRT.

The IRT should be compromised of at least one member from each of the firm's functional groups. This could include A&A, Tax, HR, IT, Legal, Executive Committee, and so forth. Each group should include a staff member assigned to them so that they can take over in the event the primary member is absent. These will act as the firm's subject-matter experts and decision-makers in their respective disciplines. Each incident will be unique, so their level of engagement will be dependent on the event at hand. However, there should be an incident leader for all events that can coordinate the actions of the team. Typically, but not always, this will be the managing partner.

Once an IRT is identified, they will need to be comfortable with the following minimum tasks:

- How will the firm identify a network intrusion, privacy breach, denial of service attack, network interruption, or ransomware event?

- What is the communication plan when one of those events occurs?

- Who should be notified when an incident occurs?

- Who will be responsible for coordinating with law enforcement?

- How will the IRT communicate with software vendors, service providers, and the media?

- How will staff be trained to adhere to the policies enacted by the IRT?

- Who will the primary point of contact with the cyber insurance provider following the incident?

- Who is ultimately responsible for coordinating all the activities of the IRT?

As a word of warning, firms should not make their plans overly complex, nor should they be inflexible by hinging on a single person. Aim for the middle ground that has enough detail to enable intelligent decisions, but not so detailed that any deviation will implode the plan and result in gridlock. It would be infeasible to create a plan for every possible scenario that could befall a firm. Greater results can be derived from having members of the IRT who understand why steps are taken, as opposed to warming a chair while following a predetermined plan.

Finally, insurers are increasingly asking for firms to disclose the fundamentals of their IRP. At a minimum, the failure to have a written IRP could result in a higher premium paid by the firm. At the maximum, the failure to have a written IRP could result in terms not being offered, declination of coverage, or necessary coverage elements not being included in the policy.

Partner Action Items:

- ☐ SP 800-61 Rev. 2, Computer Security Incident Handling Guide can be found for free at: https://nvlpubs.nist.gov/nistpubs/SpecialPublications/NIST.SP.800-61r2.pdf;

- ☐ The firm's cyber insurer will likely have a template the firm can utilize to create a formal IRP.

What is a Cybersecurity Framework?

There is no shortage of cybersecurity vendors that promise to solve all the security woes your firm is experiencing. Conversely, it is common for your IT department always to be asking for a larger budget, new tools, and they often use terms that are alien to anyone outside their field. Meanwhile, there is the threat of hackers penetrating the computer system, and regulators playing "Monday-morning quarterback" after an event. How should your firm balance all of these competing interests without information overload?

Thankfully, there is a solution to these problems, and it is called a cybersecurity framework. If you don't have one – get one. If you have one – use it. When you use it – update it.

A cybersecurity framework can best be described as a guide to managing your cybersecurity responsibilities and technology choices. Naturally, these are crucial metrics for anyone overseeing a cybersecurity program. By their very nature, a framework needs to be comprehensive enough to be used by multiple industries, adaptable enough that various business types can use it, and simple enough that all parts of an accounting firm can implement it.

Like any technology ecosystem, there are a number of different frameworks to choose from. A shortlist of frameworks includes PCI/DSS, COSO, ITIL, BiSL, COBIT, TOGAF, PBMOK, and NIST CSF. Some frameworks may be situationally mandatory, such as PCI/DSS. Others are designed for niche industries with very specific needs. Regardless of the number of frameworks available, the best fit for most accounting firms will likely be NIST CSF.

Why Choose NIST CSF?

Foremost, NIST CSF is a free tool. Given the high amount of PII stored per revenue-dollar generated for accounting firms, every

321

dollar spent towards cybersecurity is a precious commodity. NIST CSF can help management level the playing field with security vendors and in-house IT personnel to ensure that they are steered towards what will inevitably become an essential business function in the years to come.

The Recent Trends in Security Framework Adoption Survey showed that 70% of US IT and security professionals viewed NSIT CSF as a security best practice.[500] Given this finding, it is common sense to adopt a framework that the professionals view as superior. Furthermore, as an accounting firm grows or the regulatory environment becomes more burdensome, it is more likely that they will need to hire cybersecurity personnel. Having personnel that are familiar with the framework from the outset will make personnel integration faster and costly mistakes less likely.

Regulatory oversight of data security has become a hot topic as of late. Increasingly, the language seen in these oversight/regulatory actions and data security laws hinges on the notion of "reasonable" cybersecurity measures. Of concern to accounting firms are their requirements under the Gramm Leach Bliley Act, the FTC Safeguards Rule, and SEC Regulation S-P, just to name a few. In its enforcement actions, the FTC has connected consent decrees for the offending business with specific parts of the NIST CSF despite the framework still being considered voluntary.[501] Indeed, the FTC has come out with a video on their webpage which details how the NIST CSF aligns with their work on information and data security.[502] Should a U.S. regulatory body ever seek interest in an accounting firm, NSIT CSF framework provides a relatively seamless method of communication that may avoid, or help lessen, fines and penalties.

For accounting firms holding vast quantities of PII/PHI/PCI, or any firm that could be subject to a claim related to a breach of their computer system, good news is on the horizon at the state level. Ohio Senate Bill 220 provides a safe harbor to firms that have maintained and abided by a cybersecurity program. This would allow qualifying entities an affirmative defense to tort claims if they have met the following eligibility requirements:[503]

- The firm reasonably conforms to an industry-recognized cybersecurity framework, in particular, the NIST frameworks.[504]

- The cybersecurity program was designed to protect confidential client information against threats that could result in a material danger of identity theft or fraud. In this case the NIST CSF will provide guidance via the current and target profiles in conjunction with the remainder of the framework.[505]

Granted, this is not a perfect solution for firms inside of Ohio, nor would it effectively cover most firms outside of Ohio. However, it does suggest a trend of state-level legislatures attempting to entice businesses to adopt better cybersecurity hygiene with provided tort defense. Although the relative cost of compliance may not outweigh the cost of litigation for those with a cyber insurance policy, the ability for a firm to avoid or minimize bad publicity at the local and national level is priceless.

President Trump recently issued his Executive Order on Strengthening the Cybersecurity of Federal Networks and Critical Infrastructure. Effectively, this Executive Order directed all federal agencies to adopt the NIST CSF.[506] While accounting firms will not mandatorily fall under this guideline, it does point to the fact that NIST CSF will continue to be updated with industry best practices and federal support for the foreseeable future. This will enable a firm to take advantage of any updates to the framework as time and threats progress without worrying that their framework of choice may someday become antiquated.

NIST CSF is voluntary, neutral to technology, and flexible enough to scale based upon firm growth or retraction. Whether a firm is cloud-based, has a dedicated server in-house, or have a hybrid of the two, the framework can be adapted to their needs. Thus, every firm will be able to identify their own "best" cybersecurity solutions based upon their own characteristics and circumstances, saving valuable time and money. As a firm grows or contracts, the framework can be updated to best suit their current needs.

While undeniably enticing to firm leadership, a common retort to adopting a framework is the belief that it is simply too complex a task to be undertaken. It should be noted that NIST CSF is relatively straightforward if taken one piece at a time. Broadly speaking, NIST CSF is comprised of three main parts: Framework Implementation Tiers, Framework Core, and Framework Profile. Each provides a particularly useful piece of the puzzle that allows a firm to quickly assess and improve their cybersecurity posture at the most cost-effective level.

Implementation Tiers

First, a firm can utilize the Framework Implementation Tiers to "provide context on how an organization views cybersecurity risk and the processes in place to manage that risk."[507] Notably, implementation tiers create a high-level overview for other stakeholders that may allocate funding but do not have an understanding of the specific cybersecurity program in place. While partners at accounting firms often believe they are meeting industry best practices for security, once confronted with the objective criteria in the Implementation Tiers, they often fall to the lowest tier.

Four tier levels exist within the NIST CSF. They exhibit the following general criteria:

Tier 1 (Partial): Risk management practices are not formalized. Implementation of risk management for cyber threats is not objectively measured and recorded. Processes to facilitate sharing of cybersecurity information within the firm is limited. The firm does not fully appreciate its standing within the cybersecurity hierarchy in relation to its dependents and dependencies, nor does it receive or share threat information with the broader market.[508]

Due to the novel and complicated nature of cybersecurity, most small- to medium-sized firms without a formalized cybersecurity framework will fall within this tier.

Tier 2 (Risk Informed): Management has approved risk management practices, but this may not lead to a policy at the organizational level. While there is an awareness at the organizational level of cybersecurity risks, these risks are shared at an informal level. Information on risks may not be shared with others. [509]

While this may sound like low-hanging fruit, it will be a worthwhile goal for most local and mid-sized accounting firms.

Tier 3 (Repeatable): Risk management practices are formally enshrined in an organization-wide policy that is continuously updated. The organization has both cybersecurity and non-cybersecurity executives that communicate frequently on risks. Continuous monitoring of key organizational assets exists. External participation with the broader community exists as a priority and frequently occurs.[510]

Regional-sized accounting firms may be able to reach this level with prolonged commitment from upper management. It will likely take a dedicated IT department and robust planning with oversight.

Tier 4 (Adaptive): The organization uses predictive indicators and updates policies with any lessons learned. As threats and technology changes, the organization purposefully adapts to the changing threats quickly. The interplay between organizational objectives and cyber-associated risks are considered when decisions are made. Contemplations of cybersecurity risks are ingrained within the culture of the organization. External participation occurs in near real-time with the broader community. [511]

Due to the time and cost-intensive nature of this tier, most accounting firms – outside of the largest accounting firms – will lack the financial resources to reach this level. Reaching such a tier will likely require full-time IT and cybersecurity staff that are supported and prioritized by both management and staff.

Framework Core

Per NIST, "The Framework Core" is designed to be intuitive and to act as a translation layer to enable communication between multi-disciplinary teams by using simplistic and non-technical language."[512] The Core is broken down into three component parts; functions, categories, and informative references for further guidance. With 23 categories split across five functions, the Framework Core encompasses the totality of cybersecurity goals for a firm.

While this may appear abstract at first glance, these functions and categories serve an immediately useful purpose. When a firm looks to understand the cornucopia of cybersecurity products available for purchase, each product should address at least one of the firm's necessary Core Functions and categories.

The five listed functions of the Framework Core are Identify, Protect, Detect, Respond, and Recover. Each is a crucial competent to maximize probabilities of cybersecurity success. Each function is described below:

Identify: This function can be understood as the asset management, business environment, and risk management strategies necessary for a firm to operate in their current environment. Steps ranging from identifying key devices and systems required to meet business objectives and to understanding regulatory and legal requirements are addressed. For an accounting firm, this could include understanding their obligations under the Gramm-Leach-Bliley Act to enforcing a computer use policy.

Protect: Included within this function are awareness and training, data security, protective technology, maintenance, and protection policies or procedures.[513] It is convenient to think of this function as a method of implementing appropriate safeguards to protect your defined assets. This can include monthly employee training on best practices, firewalls, intrusion prevention systems, and your document retention policy.

Detect: This function helps a firm identify anomalous events, anticipate cyber events, and utilize continuous network monitoring and threat hunting to both analyze and minimize breaches. Common detective controls include antivirus, antimalware, and intrusion detection systems.

Respond: This is the immediate function which comes into play when the previous functions have failed. It covers response planning, communications with internal and external resources such as law enforcement, analysis, mitigation techniques, and incorporation of future responses with the lessons learned.[514] A common example which would cover this key function is a breach/incident response plan that is well-rehearsed and understood by all participants.

Recover: When a firm's operations have been halted, this function will help develop and implement a recovery plan to minimize disruptions and return to normal operations. This function encompasses public relations, implementation of the recovery plan, and ultimately updating recovery strategies.[515] Common elements of this function include hot failover sites, hard drive or server redundancy, and reputation restoration.

Within each function are categories, subcategories, and informative references. An example is as follows:[516]

Function: Detect

    Category: Security Continuous Monitoring (DE.CM) – "The information system and assets are monitored to identify cybersecurity events and verify the effectiveness of protective measures."

    Subcategory: (DE.CM-8) – "Vulnerability scans are performed."

    Informative Reference: CIS CSC 4, 20.

    The hierarchical system provides a meaningful way for a partner to oversee the firm's cybersecurity without necessitating a broad mastery of the entire spectrum of knowledge comprising cybersecurity and information technology. This format links common vernacular, via the Function and Category, with the specific action, via the Subcategory to the informative reference.

Furthermore, this structure allows a busy partner who is tasked with oversite of the firm's cybersecurity to devote various levels of effort and study into higher risk areas while also allowing them to briefly cover areas where they feel more comfortable or knowledgeable. Any specific questions can be immediately addressed with informative references.

If a question is beyond the ability of in-house personnel, the category, subcategory, and informative reference can provide a meaningful point of discussion with contracted, outside experts. Ideally, this would enable the firm to avoid incurring the undue cost of asking for blanket cybersecurity assistance. Given the ubiquitous nature of the NIST CSF framework, most outside cybersecurity experts should be able to quickly assist the firm as they will already share a common knowledge base.

Framework Profile

Once a firm has detailed its current needs, requirements, and resources with the Framework Tiers and Framework Cores, they can create their Framework Profile. This initial Framework Profile can be compared with a firm's Target Framework Profile to display gaps in cybersecurity. These gaps can be rank-ordered in terms of size, corrective cost, and implementation priority. As a living document, this will allow a firm to make an educated decision each year on their cybersecurity status and budgetary needs.

As addressed specifically within NIST CSF: "Once a product or service is purchased, the Profile can be used to track and address residual cybersecurity risk. For example, if the service or product purchased did not meet all the objectives described in the Target Profile, the organization can address the residual risk through other management actions. The Profile also provides the organization a method for assessing if the product meets cybersecurity outcomes through periodic review and testing mechanisms."[517]

In total, the above may appear to be a monumental undertaking. However, when taken one step at a time, it can be implemented effectively. The framework will ultimately best position a firm to adhere to regulatory requirements, track necessary cybersecurity controls, and most effectively utilize their budget. If a firm falls under multiple regulatory regimes such as PCI DSS, HIPAA, DFARS, and so on, there are numerous "crosswalks" which allows a firm to map how NIST will demonstrate reasonable cybersecurity measures needed in those other regimes. Failure to do so could later result in unnecessary breaches of client data and the potential for unwelcome regulatory scrutiny.

Partner Action Items:

- ☐ The NIST Cybersecurity framework can be found for free at: https://www.nist.gov/cyberframework.
- ☐ Smaller businesses should also consider:
     https://www.nist.gov/itl/smallbusinesscyber/planning-guides.

Assessing the Security of Cloud Providers

For practical purposes, firms will continue to look towards the cloud to host data and applications. For many, this will be an act of necessity as internal IT and cybersecurity staff become too rare and expensive to hire. For others, it will be a practical decision based on convenience, geographic dispersion, cost, or any number of other factors. Some may elect to maintain a hybrid system where certain information is stored on-site in a server while other information is stored in the cloud. Many companies will be forced into some cloud service as locally hosted applications become impossible.

Regardless, here is the most important consideration: There is no cloud. It's just someone else's computer. It should be unsurprising that a recent report listed 11% of breaches originating from vendors.[518] As such, firms will want to assess the security of their cloud provider. This could be for practical reasons, such as regulatory requirements listed earlier in this book, or for insurance reasons. Firms may be able to transfer the responsibility to keep the data available and secure, but they will not be able to transfer legal accountability. Ideally, earlier examples provided in this book prove the point.

Yet, with thousands of potential cloud providers available, how is firm to reasonably assess the security of a cloud provider? Unfortunately, it is not as easy as going with the largest provider or the one with the largest marketing budget.

Consider recent allegations in the class-action case of *Howard v. Citrix Systems*.

Lindsey Howard ("Howard") is a former employee of Citrix Systems, Inc. ("Citrix") bringing a class-action claim against her former employer. Citrix is an American multi-billion-dollar grossing, multinational, software company that employs over 8,000 people worldwide.[519] They provide, among other offerings, software as a service and cloud services. Many accounting firms rely on Citrix ShareFile to allow secure communications between the firm and their clients.

In late April of 2019, Citrix sent out a breach notification letter to numerous parties. According to Citrix, in early March of that year, the FBI informed Citrix they had reason to believe that international hackers had gained access to Citrix's internal network. Citrix believes that the hackers had intermittent access from roughly mid-October until two days following the FBI's notification.[520]

Information that may have been potentially stolen included information on current and former employees, and potentially the information of their beneficiaries and/or dependents. This may have included names, social security numbers, and certain financial information.[521]

According to the claim, this breach occurred when the hackers attacked using "password spraying," a well-known breach method.[522] By way of background, password spraying is a well-known attack that attempts to access large numbers of accounts by using a few commonly used passwords such as "Password," "Password123," and the like. This technique is used across many accounts in succession to avoid any one account from being locked-out and notifying the user.[523]

Howard alleges that this type of attack is well known and could have been prevented. She further alleges that "the deficiencies in Citrix's data security were so significant that the intrusion by the hackers remained undetected for months and was only revealed to Citrix when it was informed by the FBI." Ultimately the hacker absconded with six terabytes of information.[524] To put that in perspective, it would take roughly 9,000 CDs to hold that much information.

While those allegations are bad enough, Howard further alleges that Citrix had faced previous breaches but failed to react appropriately to the threats presented.

According to the claim, in 2016, a Russian hacker known as "w0rm" published a blog post where he claimed that he was able to gain access to Citrix's content-management system with an unsecure password.[525]

Cyberint, an Israeli cybersecurity intelligence company, claimed that it had identified the breach in October of 2015. Cyberint allegedly made multiple efforts to notify Citrix of the incident but never received a response. That same month, "w0rm" supposedly tweeted a link of his blog post detailing the breach to Citrix but received no response. [526]

In 2016, Critix's popular remote-desktop-software company, GoToMyPC, forced all users to reset their passwords after they were "targeted by a very sophisticated password attack." [527]

In December of 2018, Citrix forced password resets to protect against "credential stuffing." This is where credentials such as usernames and passwords from other hacks are used to gain access to unaffiliated systems. [528]

In response to the 2019 breach, Citrix's chief digital risk officer stated, "Certainly the incident that happened, if anything, made us more focused on the topic, and made us look even deeper at everything what we do[.]"

Regardless of the outcome of the lawsuit, firms would do well to remember that according to the various state-level breach notification laws, they are responsible for their clients' information held by third-party providers. In addition, firms may be required by regulatory requirements such as HIPAA or their cyber insurer, to assess the security of their service providers.

With that in mind, how should a firm look to assess the cybersecurity of their cloud provider?

While there are a number of different methods that could be used, perhaps the most readily available, understandable, and pertinent choice for most firms would be the Cloud Security Alliance (CSA) Cloud Controls Matrix (CCM).

CSA is a multinational organization with the stated goal of "defining and raising awareness of best practices to help ensure a secure cloud-computing environment."[529] Notably, the CCM is designed to create a shared matrix that is useful for both cloud vendors and prospective cloud customers.[530] Much like the NIST CSF discussed prior, the CCM provides a framework for firms to conduct its due diligence in understanding the controls that various cloud providers put in place to secure their data.

While not mandated as an industry standard, CCM can be used as a standardized metric within an RFP to maximize a firm's security in a cloud environment. In addition, the CCM is mapped to various other standards that a firm may be obligated to follow or are familiar with, such as HIPAA, PCI DSS, AICPA SOC, and NIST CSF. This will enable a firm to maximize the probability that its client's data will remain as secure as possible while also staying compliant within various other regulatory or contractual mandates.

CCM is categorized into the following 16 domains:
- Application and Interface Security (AIS)
- Audit Assurance and Compliance (AAC)
- Business Continuity Management and Operational Resilience (BCR)
- Change Control and Configuration Management (CCC)
- Data Security and Information Lifecycle Management (DSI)
- Datacenter Security (DCS)
- Encryption and Key Management (EKM)

- Governance and Risk Management (GRM)
- Human Resources (HRS)
- Identity and Access Management (IAM)
- Infrastructure and Virtualization Security (IVS)
- Interoperability and Portability (IPY)
- Mobile Security (MOS)
- Security Incident Management, E-Discovery, and Cloud Forensics (SEF)
- Supply Chain Management, Transparency, and Accountability (STA)
- Threat and Vulnerability Management (TVM)[531]

Within those primary domains listed above, there are roughly 130 different total controls to be considered. Thus, using a standardized metric for cloud-provider security could provide a robust method of maximizing security per dollar spent as well as maintaining compliance with various regulatory schemes.

While obviously, it is a good idea for a firm to perform due diligence in keeping client information secure, it may also be mandatory. Consider the allegations and warnings of *In the Matter of GMR Transcription Services, Inc.*

GMR is a company that takes audio recordings from customers and has them transcribed into text format. The audio and transcript files can include names, dates of birth, social security numbers, driver's license numbers, tax information, and medical information.[532]

The FTC noted the following practices, which, they alleged, did not protect the information stored by GMR.

- GMR failed to require transcriptionists to adopt and implement reasonable security measures such as installing an anti-virus application.

- GMR failed to adequately assess the security of their contractor, Fedtrans.
- GMR failed to require that Fedtrans implement appropriate security measures to safeguard GMR client information. [533]

Due to these failures, the FTC alleged that Fedtrans' internal application stored client data in readable text that was accessible to anyone and without authentication. Furthermore, a quick Internet search found the Fedtrans application and indexed thousands of sensitive client documents in their control. [534]

Under the terms of their settlement with the FTC, GMR agreed to a 20-year consent order. This includes having their information security program evaluated every two years by a certified third party. Also, GMR must establish a comprehensive information security program that ensures the information security of GMR as well as that of their service providers.[535]

The main takeaway for firms is the understanding that they may be held responsible for the security of their vendors.

For any firm with service providers that host client data, there are insurance considerations.

On the cyber insurance application, the firm may be asked if they require vendors to demonstrate various information security protections. Or, they could be asked whether the firm is auditing vendors to ensure they are meeting various security standards. If a firm fails to perform their required due diligence on their vendors, and in particular their cloud service provider, it could later result in a declination of coverage.

Partner Action Items:

☐ Assess the security of all vendors to ensure they are meeting the same security requirements of the firm;

- The Security Guidance for Critical Areas of Focus in Cloud Computing V.30 can be found for free at:
  - https://downloads.cloudsecurityalliance.org/assets/research/security-guidance/csaguide.v3.0.pdf.
- The latest version of the CSA CCM can be found for free at: https://cloudsecurityalliance.org/working-groups/cloud-controls-matrix/#_overview.

What are Written Information Security Programs & Policies?

Written Information security Program (WISP) and Information security Policies (ISPs), set the groundwork for what measures a firm will utilize to protect sensitive information. Some firms will create these documents as required by various laws such as Massachusetts' 201 CMR 17. Others will adopt them as part of demonstrating "reasonable" cybersecurity measures for various Safeguards Rule, HIPAA, or other federal-level requirements. Even without any legal requirements to do so, WISPs and ISPs are foundational for ensuring that the firm and staff understand their cybersecurity obligations.

Broadly speaking, a WISP attempts to provide overarching guidance in the following areas:

- The purpose and scope of the program. This can include how the firm defines personal information that requires specific safeguarding;
- Designation of an Information security Coordinator to implement the WISP, train users, and maintain records;
- Standardization of Risk Assessment frequency as well as actions to be taken following those assessments;
- The creation of information security policies and procedures that will be used by the firm;
- An accounting of the minimum safeguards necessary to adhere to required laws and ensure the security of personal information;
- A requirement to oversee the security of various service providers;
- The monitoring and evaluation of the program to maintain security and address any shortcomings in security;
- The establishment of an Incident Response Plan (IRP);

- Enforcement for infractions of the WISP;
- A minimum yearly review of the WISP to address any material changes.[536]

As tempting as it would be for firms to share a common WISP template, each firm's WISP should be unique. Truly, the policies prescribed to a small firm with an in-house server exposed to vast quantities of PHI will differ greatly from a large firm which is entirely cloud-based and focused on the agricultural industry. Standard templates can provide a useful starting point for developing a unique WISP, but a template is unlikely to satisfy unique firm requirements in the eyes of regulators.

Furthermore, a firm's WISP should be considered a living document. As required by the findings of ongoing risk assessments, security audits, and other internal or external findings, the WISP should be updated. Often, this can be accomplished by an IT compliance firm, or a law firm specializing in privacy law.

Concurrent with development and implementation of a WISP is the development and implementation of the firm's Information security Policy (ISP). While there will be a natural overlap between the two – an ISP is generally part of the WISP – the WISP can be thought of as a high-level document referenced by management, while the ISP is more of a document to be used by staff members.

At the heart of any ISP is the acknowledgment that technology is useful, but people will always be the weakest link. Staff may inadvertently break rules, fall victim to phishing attacks, or purposefully circumvent established controls. An ISP attempts to minimize these risks by clearly communicating firm expectations to staff.[537]

Generally, ISPs should cover the minimum following areas:

- An introduction to staff which legitimizes the necessity of the document and the rules contained therein. This can include guiding principles, scope of the policy, resources for additional questions, notes on workplace privacy and monitoring, and regulatory compliance issues.
- A section on responsibilities in the workplace.

WISPs and ISPs can either be directly or indirectly referred to on a cyber insurance application. In the direct sense, an insurance provider may ask if the firm has implemented and enforces an information security program or policy. More indirectly, the insurer may allude to such policies and programs by using alternative nomenclature, or implying compliance, typically, in questions referring to regulatory compliance. If the firm is ever in doubt, they should seek guidance from legal counsel and query the underwriter for clarification. Failure to do so could lead to a declination of coverage.

For example, an insurer may pose the following question on an application: "Does the firm comply with local, state, federal and international security and privacy laws affecting the firm's business?" If the firm had a Massachusetts resident as a client but had failed to develop a WISP in accordance with 201 CMR 17, any part of the claim involving that law, or the entire claim, could be denied by the insurer.

Partner Action Items:

- ☐ Determine if your firm is obligated to maintain a WISP.
- ☐ Work with legal counsel to meet any legal or technical requirements.
- ☐ Update the firm's incident response plan and other internal documents as necessary.

The Golden Rules of Cyber

- **Rule #1:** If it's drastically cheaper than the other guy, it's probably run out of someone's basement.
- **Rule #2:** Big words do not equal big results. If they can't explain it to you in common terms, they don't understand it. When in doubt, ask them to draw a picture explaining where it works and how it fits into your system – see Rule #3.
- **Rule #3:** Einstein couldn't drive a car, so don't be afraid to look dumb. Ask probing questions and educate yourself on the topic. We all started from scratch with technology. The Internet is your friend.
- **Rule #4:** You can outsource responsibility, but not accountability.
- **Rule #5:** Talking about geographically isolated redundant backups stored in a nuclear blast-resistant underground facility is fun. Quality employee training and free coffee will probably keep you safer.
- **Rule #6:** The cloud is someone else's computer. Act accordingly.
- **Rule #7:** Everyone will get hacked. Have a breach response plan.
- **Rule #8:** If your breach response plan is only available on the computer that just got hit with ransomware, you don't have a breach response plan.
- **Rule #9:** There are no magic bullets. Defense-in-depth is your friend – an expensive but necessary friend.
- **Rule #10:** Should you buy that new fancy cybersecurity product? Consult your cybersecurity framework.

- **Rule #11:** If you don't have a cybersecurity framework, you probably shouldn't buy it.
- **Rule #12:** If you drive a $100,000 car to work and complain about the cost of cybersecurity, you're missing the point.
- **Rule #13:** For anything cyber-related, beware the self-labeled "experts." You probably want to talk with the guy who considers himself "pretty-damn-good." The first guy will probably screw you over; the second guy will let you know when there is a legitimate problem that he can't fix.
- **Rule #14:** IT makes information easy to get to. Cybersecurity makes information harder to get to. The two require constant balance.
- **Rule #15:** "Cyber-Secure" is a journey, not a destination.

Attorneys and Cybersecurity

An often-overlooked ally for a firm needing assistance navigating the morass that is cyber insurance and cybersecurity law is a qualified attorney. As alluded to numerous times in this book, an attorney can provide invaluable assistance before, during, and after a breach.

Most cyber insurance policies should provide an attorney to assist with basic data-breach legal functions. This can include:

- Assisting in overall firm response to a ransomware or data-breach incident;
- Coordinating breach notification responses;
- Coordinating vendor responses;
- Assisting firms with computer forensic needs following a breach;
- Working with state and federal law enforcement entities;
- Short advice calls – generally, for up to one hour;
- Providing defense following government, regulatory investigations as well as for class action, or private litigation from data breaches.

There are numerous other cyber related functions that a qualified attorney can provide a firm that are not as apparent but just as crucial as those listed above. These may include the following services that are generally not provided by cyber insurance carriers, or their assigned legal counsel:

- Ongoing assessments of regulatory compliance issues in the international, federal, state, local, and industry-specific areas;
- Facilitating cybersecurity compliance, privacy, and network security audits;
- Counseling executives and the board of directors regarding risk-management strategies;
- Proactive liaising with government and state law enforcement as appropriate;

- Providing guidance regarding the cybersecurity risk of particular agreements, such as mergers and acquisitions, or corporate transactions;
- Providing contract review or negotiations of contracts as they pertain to data risks and disclosures;
- Enforcing contractual obligations against third parties;
- Assisting with cyber insurance applications to avoid material misrepresentations;
- Providing guidance regarding the policy language of various cyber insurance policies to provide the best coverage for each firm's unique exposures;
- Guiding the firm through potentially conflicting privacy or cybersecurity law issues;
- Providing further guidance on various privacy or cybersecurity law requirements not covered in this book.

While non-legal professionals may be able to provide some of the services listed above, perhaps the greatest benefit provided by an attorney is that of attorney-client privilege. This allows a company to likely keep information provided by the attorney from being disclosed to third parties such as regulators or government investigators. For this reason, many companies will retain an attorney to hire third-party cybersecurity assessors to perform their services. The findings of these assessments often disclose security flaws that may evidence a lack of compliance. For firms who believe that they could face legal issues for these flaws, keeping the findings of assessments confidential is crucial.

As laws vary by state, firms should check with local counsel to determine how attorney-client privilege applies to their unique needs and circumstances.

Finding Qualified Legal Counsel:
Boutique cybersecurity-law-focused firms or larger multi-disciplinary law firms may have the expertise to assist a firm with these additional functions as they often have a dedicated privacy and cybersecurity law

practice area. Given that these topics are such a multi-faceted, complex, and ever-changing area of the law, general counsel is unlikely to possess the resources or skills necessary to fully advise a firm on their evolving exposures. In many instances, even firms possessing in-house legal counsel may outsource their cybersecurity-law needs to a specialist. It is not advisable to rely on in-house or contracted IT staff to give legal recommendations. Insurance brokers are certainly ill-suited for this task.

When a firm is looking to engage a cybersecurity attorney, they should heavily scrutinize their credentials and experience. Like any other specialty law area, the partner overseeing these engagements will often possess additional qualifications specific to the field of cybersecurity law. This could include a Master's Degree in Cybersecurity Law, various IT or privacy law certifications, extensive practical experience – often in a government capacity, certified ABA Privacy Law Specialist, or something similar.

Regardless, due diligence should be a serious consideration for every firm when retaining a privacy- and cybersecurity-law-focused attorney.

Section 10: Other Useful Publications from the Authors

Tips on Minimizing Wire Fraud
(Adapted from True Course: The Definitive Guide for CPA Practice Insurance)

Throughout the profession, many firms have experienced losses that could have been avoided with basic countermeasures. Losses in this arena can range from small dollar amounts to millions, and the ability to recoup those funds is often circumstantial. Rather than worry about fund recovery after a breach, it is much simpler to avoid the problem altogether. As humans will always be the weakest link in any security program, it is vital that not only the appropriate internal controls are implemented, but that those controls are explained and strictly adhered to by staff and clients.

Thoroughly consider the measures below and discuss with your partners if and how they can help protect your practice. While the below list is no means a foolproof way to avoid all fraud, even basic checks can save you a lot of heartache. Remember, it's much easier for a criminal to use psychology and guile than to implement a complex and highly technical heist.

- Make an established policy to never approve the release of funds without actually speaking with your client over the phone. Consider using a pre-approved phone number. Having a client that is "too busy" to speak with you can also be a red flag to other problems that should warrant your interest.
- Avoid sending pre-filled wiring instructions. If, by circumstance, this is unavoidable, encrypt the email and send it to your client while you are already on the phone. This can help quickly confirm that they are in receipt of your instructions, and there is no ambiguity.[538]
- Use encryption for any personally identifiable information (PII). Failure to do so is not only bad practice; it may have the

SEC knocking on your door.[539] Consider this for tablets, company phones, laptops, and any other devices which can store or view this information.

- Give your employees the power to raise a red flag if something doesn't "feel" right. Make sure that they are communicating with clients via phone numbers that are registered and on file with your firm. Be very wary of sending funds to new accounts in foreign countries and new locations.
- Use multi-step authentication.[540] Consider a series of authentication questions to confirm the identity of your client. Common measures include a PIN number, codeword, and special authentication question. Pay special note to use information that cannot be readily found on a social media profile.
- Advise your clients to increase their security as well.[541] Complex passwords and two-step authentication to access email and sensitive information are a great start.

Remember that new technology can appear foolproof, but we are in a digital arms race with criminals where there is no clear advantage. As such, the human element will always be the most susceptible to fraud. Pay special heed to reinforce best practices with your employees and hold them accountable to abiding by your policies. Also, describe your security measures to new and existing clients immediately upon implementation. While no one wants to unnecessarily annoy a client, it's much easier to apologize for the inconvenience than to explain why their account is empty.

As a warning on how crucial a healthy degree of skepticism can save your firm untold amounts of money and time, consider the allegations in the case of *Ameriforge Group Inc., d/b/a AFGlobal Corp. v. Federal Insurance Co.*

According to AFGlobal's original petition, they had originally purchased a $3 million insurance policy from Federal Insurance Company, a division of Chubb Group. [542]

From May 21st, 2014 until May 27th of that same year, fraudulent emails impersonating AFGlobal's CEO, Gean Stalcup, were sent to the Director of Accounting, Glen Wurm.[543]

The imposter's email sent to Stalcup stated the following: [544]

"Glen,

I have assigned you to manage file T521.

This is a strictly confidential financial operation, to which takes priority over other tasks.

Have you already been contacted by ███████████ (attorney ██████ ?

This is very sensitive, so communicate with me through this email, in order for us not to infringe SEC regulations.

Please do not speak with anyone by email or phone regarding this.

Regards,

Gean Stalcup."

Apparently, the imposter somehow knew the normal procedures of the company and also knew that Wurm and Stalcup had a personal relationship. After approximately 30 minutes, Wurm was contacted by phone and email from the attorney that the due diligence fees associated with an acquisition in China in the amount of $480,000 were required. Wurm then instructed the cash manager and treasurer of AFGlobal to transfer the funds. [545]

Nothing further was noted until May 27 when the imposter confirmed receipt of the funds, then asked for an additional $18 million. It was then Wurm became suspicious and alerted his supervisors.[546]

Officers of AFGlobal attempted to retrieve the lost funds and attempted to recall the wire transfer from Bank of America. In addition, they alerted all of the bank involved and their security departments of the perpetrated fraud. Finally, they filed a police report. Later, they were informed that the bank account which had received the money had been zeroed out and closed. [547]

Concurrently, AFGlobal had to make their brokerage firm, Aon Risk Services, aware of the loss. By June 2, the company had filed a formal proof-of-loss to their insurance carrier.[548] They were seeking coverage under the Computer Fraud and Funds Transfer Fraud coverage elements of the policy.[549]

Approximately a month later, AFGlobal's insurer declined their claim. While their reasoning for declination is lengthy, it mainly centers around the policy definitions of "Computer Fraud" and "Funds Transfer Fraud" not being met as Wurm had knowingly authorized the transfer. [550]

Regardless of the final outcome of the case, numerous points of failure are apparent. Foremost, AFGlobal should have enforced internal controls on wire transfers. A quick phone call or a face-to-face meeting could have saved AFGlobal $480,000 plus legal costs. Assuming that no internal control is fool-proof, the risk manager should have "war-gamed" the scenario seen above and compared that to the insurance coverage offered.

Partner Action Items:

- Review internal control procedures regarding the transfer of firm or client funds;
- Review the firm's cyber insurance policy and compare to different wargame scenarios to determine if there is a reasonable belief of coverage;
- Communicate this data to relevant stakeholders.

Russian Hackers Specifically Targeting Accounting Firms

(As seen in *CPA Practice Advisor* – June 2018)

Much to the ire of businesses worldwide, hackers have ceaselessly attempted to penetrate their computer systems and abscond with valuable information. While seemingly no business sector is beyond the reach of opportunistic hackers, the financial services industry has been particularly sensitive to these intrusions due to the vast quantities of personal information stored therein. Yet, like all systems found in the business world, specialization of skills is a natural outgrowth.

Unfortunately for accounting firms nationwide, this specialization has resulted in an alarming new finding. Hackers are now specifically targeting your firm. With most firms using relatively similar software and service providers, a flaw found in one system can be easily replicated in countless others. The game of cybersecurity cat-and-mouse is quickly accelerating against your firm.

"Authors: You're most famous in the cybersecurity world for discovering some of the most high-profile breaches in history such as those at JPMorgan, Adobe, and Lexis Nexis. How did you discover that there is a gang of cybercriminals focusing on CPA firms?

Alex Holden: We monitor a number of Dark Web forums and information exchanges. In this particular case, one of the lesser-known forums was used for this type of data exchange. Fortunately for us, hackers disclosed more information than they wanted to, allowing this glimpse into their activities.

355

Authors: Do you have any indication where these criminals are located geographically?

Alex: We have no clear indication of where they are from geographically. We can only assert that one of them spoke Russian natively but communicated in broken English.

Authors: Why would this group be focusing on accounting firms specifically?

Alex: I believe that the main direction is tax fraud. Accounting firms were targeted, but also other sources of W2 information and other financial data were on the targets list.

Authors: Is there a specific avenue of attack, such as keyloggers or ransomware, that these criminals prefer?

Alex: The CPA's computer had some kind of virus allowing data-logging along with screenshots and keyboard inputs from the victim. This was non-disruptive, seamless, for the victim as likely the infection and operation of his computer.

Authors: Once the criminals have stolen data from these firms, how are they distributing the data?

Alex: The stolen data is not as useful as the hackers' ability to generate profits. This crime model deals more with tax refunds than any other abuse vector. It is unclear how if actual data was exfiltrated or was the victim's computer was used as a conduit to commit tax fraud.

Authors: In your experience, what size accounting firm are they targeting, and why?

Alex: Accounting firms are targeted not based on size but on opportunity. While larger firms may have dedicated IT and data security staff, they are also significantly attractive targets for potential profits. Yet smaller firms who operate on a one-on-one basis are easier targets because of lack of data security measures. At the end of the day, you are likely to do business with a smaller firm because of personal touch and trust, but this personal touch may come with an expensive price tag of missing a lot of critical data security safeguards.

Authors: For a small accounting firm, with a very limited cybersecurity budget, if any, what are some cost-effective ways that can lessen their odds of being compromised that are often overlooked?

Alex: Smaller firms invest in commercial-grade accounting software, yet the data security side is far below the commercial-grade or may be missing. Basics: patch your system regularly, don't miss any updates; buy anti-virus and anti-malware software and keep it up-to-date; do not use your work computer for any other purpose than work; and lastly, become more educated about email scams, viruses, hoaxes – don't get victimized yourself and endanger your clients.

Authors: For large accounting firms with a dedicated cybersecurity budget, what is one area they continually overlook, but should pay much greater attention to?

Alex: Larger firms may not have a challenge with commercial-grade security software, yet the employees are still often tasked with the upkeep of their devices as they travel and do not always connect to the corporate networks. Stricter data security policies are definitely needed. But what is usually lacking is a deeper understanding of security threats and poor password policies. End-user education around data security must be a paramount concern for larger firms and re-using or assigning weaker passwords should not be tolerated.

Authors: What is Deep Web monitoring and why would an accounting firm need such a service? Could they include this service for their own clients?

Alex: This tax season we saw tax data of tens of thousands of victims traded on the Deep and Dark Web by hackers. At the same time, exploitation of accounting firms is visibly on the rise, and this particular incident is not a unique occurrence. To see what hackers are targeting and if you are on a list of targets or victims is sometimes a quick check that may save you not only money, but reputational loss. And knowing if your clients have been already compromised, in many cases, may allow you to help them proactively as recovery from tax fraud is not an easy task at all.

Authors: Understanding that no computer system is ever 100% secure, how important is a breach response plan, and when should a company start seeking assistance in crafting and implementing such a plan?

Alex: Breach or incident response planning is essential for a company of any size. Pretty much like dealing with any kind of incident (car accident, fire, etc.) it is much better to put some or a lot of thought into your response than trying to ad-lib during a crisis. Your ability to find the right partners that will help you with the recovery process cannot be hindered by timing of a breach. Knowing who to call, what to do, and how to respond is critical. In many cases, doing things the right way and quickly can minimize the impact of an incident.

Authors: Are there any new cybersecurity tools that you are particularly excited about that firms should be aware of?

Alex: I do not want to endorse any specific vendors but rather want to highlight technologies, many not new but enhanced. Anti-phishing solutions, ransomware protection, robust anti-virus, and anti-malware solutions, and Internet traffic filters preventing computers from going out to malicious sites.

Authors: Within the next 5 years, do you expect the frequency and severity of cyber breaches to increase or decrease, and why?

Alex: I believe that the overall amount of breaches is on a slow decline as security tools are getting better. However, the severity of each new breach will become more and more devastating as hackers are getting better at their evil tasks and not caring about the devastation they leave in their path."

When asked for comment concerning the above revelations, Anthony Valach, counsel at BakerHostetler, cautioned accounting firms to consider the larger ramifications for their own clients. "It doesn't matter what time of year it is, it's always W-2 season. Remember, the main goal of these actors isn't to steal someone's identity, it's to monetize the information as quickly as possible. If they get W-2s, they will try to file fraudulent tax returns."

On a more optimistic note, he did add that many breaches he works on center around fundamental security measures that would have been easily rectified. "Yes, there are government-backed actors looking to cause chaos, but the run-of-the-mill hacker is trying to turn information into money as quickly as possible. If they can't do that easily, or at least have a reasonable chance at doing so, they will move on to the next one."

Garrett Wagner, CPA/CITP and founder of consulting firm C3 Evolution Group, emphasized the need to educate your staff. "Internally, they need to provide regular training and reminders to their staff about the various threats and email attacks currently being used." Furthermore, he noted the often-overlooked client vulnerability saying, "Externally, they need to remind their clients of the tools they have to send secure communications. Nothing is worse than having all the tools and resources to keep data secure than to have all your clients email un-encrypted emails into the firm on a regular basis."

No matter how secure you may think your computer systems may be, we are entering a new and dangerous phase for accounting firms worldwide. It is well worth the time and energy to commit to investigating new cybersecurity technologies and employee training programs. As with all things in life, the longer you wait, the more painful and costly the transition may become.

Cyber-Related Claims Without a Breach … They're Coming

A new series of cyber-related class-action claims against at least 15 law firms could have serious implications on how CPA firms, and many of their clients, manage their computer systems and view data security. The most troubling aspect of the only-publicly-available complaint centers on these new claims is that there was no actual breach of confidential client information, merely the possibility of a breach (Gabe Friedman, "Class-Action Suit Targeting Law Firm Privacy Protections Could Be Unsealed," Bloomberg Law, May 5, 2016, http://bit.ly/2Fo0ryp). To make matters worse for potential defendants, claims such as these are probably uninsurable, so they could become quite costly to firms and their clients. It is no longer enough to simply avoid a data breach. Firms and clients must become proactive and deliberate about network and data security.

Shore v. Johnson & Bell

In the above-mentioned, publicly available complaint, two former clients of the law firm Johnson & Bell alleged that confidential client information had been put at risk due to inadequate data security [*Shore v. Johnson & Bell, Case No. 16-cv-4363 (N.D. Ill. 2016)*, http://bit.ly/2osxhGr].

Namely, the complaint calls Johnson & Bell "a data breach waiting to happen" and claims that, among other computer-related issues, the "time record system could have been accessed without any username or password (or any other credentials)." The complaint further alleges that if a breach of this system were to occur, sensitive information would be easily stolen. Hackers could also obtain sensitive information from Johnson & Bell's clients by impersonating the firm's lawyers via email.

The four-count complaint alleges breach of contract (legal malpractice), negligence (legal malpractice), unjust enrichment, and breach of fiduciary duty. While the exact monetary damages are not stated, "the amount exceeds $5,000,000." In a conversation with the authors, Anthony Valach, counsel at BakerHostetler, said, "Since there was no breach, the class cannot allege out-of-pocket damages and must rely on the benefit-of-the-bargain measure of damages. Essentially, the class representatives allege that a portion of the fees paid to Johnson & Bell was to cover the administrative costs of protecting their data. Plaintiffs argue that the firm did not employ adequate measures to protect the data and are due a refund of those amounts because they did not receive the benefit of their bargain."

When asked whether this type of claim could expand to other professions such as accounting firms, Valach stated, "Absolutely. It is easy to imagine a situation where professional services firms become the target of lawsuits for failing to employ reasonable measures to secure client data. Unfortunately, I think we are still at a point where many firms don't think they are a target or don't have data hackers would want. That's a dangerous and potentially fatal attitude for a business. People don't realize that on the Internet, we all live in a bad neighborhood. Ultimately, we may see the same effect as the Dodd-Frank Act. Small firms will be forced to choose between drastically increasing their cybersecurity budget and posture, or face potential lawsuits and exposure from data breaches that can do lasting harm."

The arbitration clause between the law firm and its former clients has, for the time being, saved the defendants from having to litigate this matter in the public eye. The court recently ruled that Johnson & Bell's arbitration clause did not permit class-wide arbitration; only an individual action was permissible. As it currently stands, the plaintiffs will need to pursue individual arbitration, though their attorney, Jay Edelson, will likely appeal the decision (Derek Borchardt and Michael F. Buchanan, "Law Firm Sued for Alleged Lax Data Security Obtains

Significant Win in District Court," *Patterson Belknap Data Security Law Blog*, Mar. 8, 2017, http://bit.ly/2HGjg0L).

If Johnson & Bell wins the potential appeal, it may still need to weather two separate arbitration cases. In the meantime, the firm has filed a defamation suit against Edelson. Even if Johnson & Bell are victorious on all counts and cases, there may be irreparable reputational harm to their brand.

A quick Internet search for Johnson & Bell was telling. The first result was the firm's website, followed by two headlines that could easily scare off existing or potential clients, resulting in unquantifiable future economic losses:

- "Chicago's Johnson & Bell First U.S. Firm Publicly Named in Data Security Class Action"
- "Chicago Law Firm Accused of Lax Data Security in Lawsuit"

With data breaches constantly in the headlines, consumers are increasingly concerned about a company potentially mishandling their information. No matter how one views the merits of the case, no firm wants that type of publicity.

What if this was a CPA Firm?
It is only a matter of time until cases such as the above are brought against CPA firms. Do firms' insurance policies cover such liability? Even as brokers specializing in this area for CPA firms, the authors' research and experience leads to an uncomfortable answer: Maybe, but it is unlikely.

Professional liability and cyber-insurance carriers generally cover claims when a client demands money or services for damages due to professional services rendered. In this case, there did not seem to be any damages per se because a breach had not yet occurred. This leads to the potential for an uncovered claim where the firm may have to pay entirely out of pocket for defense and damages awarded.

The ability to perform a wholesale security scan of a firm's network is not only easy; it is free. According to Byron Patrick, managing director of the CPA Practice at Network Alliance: "Every vulnerability in this case is easily discernable from readily available online tools that are free. Port scans, vulnerability scans, penetration testing, etc., can all be conducted by a savvy 15-year-old with no formal cybersecurity training. It's unlikely the plaintiffs knocked the digital door down. All they needed to do was peek through the windows." He adds: "A disgruntled client could perform a quick Internet search, watch a few videos, and you're suddenly staring at a multimillion-dollar claim. It's terrifying for the accounting profession, and everyone should take this very seriously."

The authors reached out to the plaintiff's attorney in the case mentioned above, Jay Edelson, to gain insight into his thought process on these types of claims. When asked whether he would eventually pursue other professional services firms, such as CPAs, he replied: "We aren't specifically 'targeting' law firms, financial service firms, or any other companies. Rather, our focus is bringing cases where companies are (a) holding onto sensitive personal information, (b) likely can be the subject of cyberattacks, and (c) not using reasonable security measures. In some sense, we are going to the same places that hackers are going; our motivation is to get there first to force negligent actors to use better security measures so that a data breach never occurs. We have been very pleased with the success we have had to date and look forward to having an active role in ensuring corporate cyber-responsibility."

Taken in total, most CPA firms could easily match all three criteria mentioned. If Edelson is ultimately successful in any of his 15 class-action claims, this will embolden other attorneys to pursue similar cases against CPA firms. For partner groups that have not yet taken a proactive and sustained approach to network security, the circumstances above should give them plenty to speak about.

Partner Action Items

☐ **Engagement letters**. In the Johnson & Bell case, an arbitration clause in an engagement letter proved valuable to the defendants. Firms should consider working with their professional liability insurers to review such engagement letters and inquire about including, or updating, the arbitration or mediation clauses therein.

☐ **Vulnerability scanners**. These services attempt to identify susceptibilities in open ports, IP addresses, software, and operating systems. Once a system is scanned, a company specializing in this area can further assist with determining how much risk the firm is willing to tolerate in each component part of its computer system.

☐ **Third-party penetration testing**. This type of testing is performed by "white-hat" hackers to specifically target weaknesses and determine how vulnerable the firm is. It can be performed from both outside and inside the network, to give the firm a more robust picture of its total network security.

☐ **Warning clients**. As trusted advisors, CPA firms should ensure that clients are also aware of this new type of danger to their business. If the firm offers various IT services, this class-action claim should serve as a serious warning. Clients may ultimately need to reallocate resources, update software, and improve security processes, which may require significant time and resources.

There is no time like the present to take a proactive stance towards cybersecurity. Previously, merely avoiding a breach counted as a success, but this is no longer the case.

Use of Driver's License Numbers Raises Security Concerns

(Published March 2017 and July 2017 – *Journal of Accountancy*)

The IRS is now recommending that taxpayers use their driver's license number to provide another layer of security when electronically filing a federal tax return. A few states, notably New York, Ohio, and Alabama, are requiring a driver's license number, or an equivalent, for state returns. This sounds promising at first; another layer of verification to help prevent tax identity theft seems prudent. However, as with many other "good ideas," the unintended consequences can cause problems.

This new use for driver's license numbers should create concerns among CPA firms about data security and the potential for a cyber breach. Most CPA firm staff and clients have been trained to treat Social Security numbers (SSNs) with exceptional care, but the same has not been true necessarily with driver's license numbers (DLNs). While the reasons for that, explained below, are understandable. The increased relevance placed upon DLNs has made them a new high-value item for criminals and CPA firms alike.

Regulatory Requirements

Why do CPAs need to be concerned about the possibilities of a data breach involving driver's license numbers? The first reason is that while the 47 states' and territories' breach notification laws are different, they all qualify DLNs and SSNs as being equally important pieces of personally identifiable information (PII). And, while it's important to consult competent legal counsel to understand the breach laws pertaining to your firm, California's definition of personal information in its civil code regarding customer records (Cal. Civ.

Code §1798.82) illustrates the point. Specifically, personal information includes but is not limited to the following:

(1) An individual's first name or first initial and last name in combination with any one or more of the following data elements, when either the name or the data elements are not encrypted:

(A) Social Security number;

(B) Driver's license number or California identification card number;

(C) Account number or credit or debit card number, in combination with any required security code, access code, or password that would permit access to an individual's financial account;

(D) Medical information;

(E) Health insurance information. [Cal. Civ. Code §1798.82(h)]

As you can see, the driver's license number is given equal status with the SSN, and that's a concern because our experience indicates that a significant percentage of the population does not see DLNs as important as SSNs in the protection of personally identifiable information.

Views on Driver's License Numbers

To illustrate the types of attitudes we encounter regarding SSNs and driver's license numbers, we sent a couple of questions to 15 of our non-CPA but college-educated peers to determine how they view a lost DLN versus a lost SSN. While certainly not scientific, the answers they provided give a voice to the attitudes the authors have heard in the field.

Question #1: "What would you do if your Social Security card was lost or stolen?"

Selected answers: "Freak out," "Notify the credit
agencies," "Watch my credit score like a hawk,"
"Purchase identity theft protection."
Question #2: "What would you do if your driver's
license was lost or stolen?"
Selected answers: "Get a new one," "Ask my (spouse)
if they've seen it," "Wait a week then go to the
DMV," "Is that a big deal?"

The difference in answers is telling. Lost SSNs are generally
understood to be a serious threat to identity theft. Lost DLNs are
perceived as a mere inconvenience.

To gain insight into how CPA firms view this exposure, the
authors conducted an anonymous survey with 29 respondents.
Respondents came from varying levels of seniority, firm size, and
geographic location. Again, the results are not scientific but are
interesting:

We found that 55% of respondents said they are collecting DLNs,
but 35% didn't know DLNs are considered PII. Contradictorily,
nearly half were using unsecure methods of collecting DLNs from
their clients.

When asked if their clients knew DLNs were PII, 72% responded
either "No," or "Not sure."

The Risk

Now that driver's license numbers are being used as a form of
identification verification for tax return filing, it's easy to see them
becoming a high-value target for hackers and other cybercriminals.
And, if accounting firms and their clients don't take care in protecting
DLNs and other personally identifiable information, the results can be
costly.

The Ponemon Institute's 2016 "Cost of a Data Breach" study illustrates how costly a security breach can be. The average total cost of a data breach for the nearly 400 companies studied came to $4 million, or $158 per each lost or stolen record. The costs were even higher in highly regulated industries, with an average cost of $221 per stolen or lost record in the financial services section. Adding insult to injury, adverse media attention could further result lost business opportunities and revenue for years to come.

Insurance can offer some protection, but not as much as you might expect. CPA firms can find insurance for a number of items including credit monitoring for clients, forensic analysis of computer systems, removal of malware and system restoration, among others, but the Ponemon study found that insurance protection reduced the cost of a data breach by a mere $5 per record.

CPA firms also have to be concerned that improper breach notification to a client could be a violation of rule 1.700, Confidential Information, in the AICPA Code of Professional Conduct and also lead to problems with various regulatory bodies and state attorneys general. While the penalties vary, in several states, fines can easily reach more than $100,000, and violation of Internal Revenue Code Sec. 7216 can result in possible conviction for a misdemeanor with a fine of not more than $1,000, and/or as much as a year in prison.

Partner Action Items

Educating the public at large is well beyond the capability of most firms. Even the IRS Taxpayer Guide to Identify Theft and IRS Publication 4524, Security Awareness Tips for Taxpayers, fail to mention the safeguarding of a DLN at this point. Resources should be directed toward training staff to speak with clients and implementing appropriate security measures to minimize the possibility of a breach.

Train your staff: If you already have training on internal firm policies that deal with handling and storing PII, place an emphasis on DLNs. Because the costs to your firm losing an SSN and a DLN are likely the same, treat them equally. In turn, your staff should be the direct link to your clients, reinforcing the necessity for the minor inconvenience in properly handling PII.

Implement appropriate security tools: Most firms already have the tools in place to protect DLNs. Having previously implemented secure portals or encrypted email solutions to protect SSNs, it's simply a matter of educating your staff to leverage these tools they already have.

Secure portals such as Citrix ShareFile allow you to insert a request link into your email to the client. With this link, the client can send an image of their driver's license via an encrypted tunnel, protecting their DLN from nefarious characters.

Alternatively, using an encrypted email to exchange PII saves the steps required when using a portal. Solutions such as the Secure Messaging application from Mimecast allows you to send secure email messages to your client and allows them to send PII data securely.

Finally, it is easy to overlook a simple tool that has been available for years – your phone. A quick call to collect a DLN from your client is a simple and secure solution with a personal touch.

Should CPA Firms Be Worried About Data-Breach Claims?

Hurdles to Establishing Standing and Demonstrating Economic Viability

(Published March 2018 – *CPA Journal*)

Driven by unceasing news reports, CPA firms are growing increasingly concerned that data breaches are increasing in both frequency and severity. With this deluge of information, it is no surprise that partners and shareholders are increasingly concerned about the possibility of a client bringing a lawsuit following a data breach. But is this concern justified?

Although the general assumption is that one can be sued for anything, this is not necessarily true. Before a lawsuit can proceed in a federal court, and most state courts, a plaintiff must first demonstrate standing. As stated by the U.S. Supreme Court, "The question of standing is whether the litigant is entitled to have the court decide the merits of the dispute." [*Warth v. Seldin, 422 U.S. 490 (1975)*].

Establishment of standing comprises three elements. First, the plaintiff must show that an injury occurred. Second, that injury must be traceable to the defendant's (i.e., a CPA firm's) unlawful conduct. Third, there must be a request for redressability for the unlawful act, usually in terms of a monetary award. In legal parlance, a plaintiff must demonstrate injury-in-fact, traceability, and redressability.

These elements are easily understood in common claims against CPA firms. For example, suppose a firm has undeniably miscalculated a tax deduction costing the client an additional $1 million that is otherwise unrecoverable. Standing would be stated as follows:

- **Injury-in-fact**: The client suffered an injury of $1 million due to the firm's negligence.

- **Traceability**: The firm's work documented the failure to provide correct calculations, resulting in overpayment.
- **Redressability**: The client wants the firm to reimburse the $1 million, plus expenses.

When the same logic is applied to a data breach, however, how can these same principles be demonstrated? What injury could a client face? By now, it is almost certain that the information has been stolen somewhere else. Even if an individual client's identity is stolen after the firm is breached, how could it be proven to be the firm's fault? Even if all the above were true, what is the dollar value of, say, a Social Security number?

Injury-in-Fact

U.S. courts have not yet provided a definitive answer on what constitutes an injury-in-fact following a cyber breach. Some courts consider standing based upon the threat of future harm, but others refute this idea [Eric C. Surette, Liability of Businesses to Governments and Consumers for Breach of Data Security for Consumers' Information, 1 A.L.R.7th Art. 2 (2015)].

In *Krottner v. Starbucks Corp.* [628 F.3d 1139 (9th Cir. 2010)], a laptop was stolen containing the unencrypted names, addresses, and Social Security numbers of roughly 97,000 Starbucks employees. In response, Starbucks told the employees that there was "no indication that the private information has been misused."

One plaintiff alleged that she "has been extra vigilant about watching her banking and 401(k) accounts" and has spent a "substantial amount of time doing so." Another argued that he "has spent and continues to spend substantial amounts of time checking his 401(k) and bank accounts" and "has general anxiety and stress regarding the situation." A third plaintiff said that someone attempted to open a bank account in his name, but the bank promptly thwarted those efforts, and he was subsequently notified. Nowhere in the pleading did any plaintiff allege that identity theft had occurred. Nevertheless, this was enough to satisfy the court that the increased risk of future identity theft was enough to establish injury-in-fact. Specifically, the court stated, "Plaintiffs-Appellants, whose personal information has been stolen but not misused, have suffered an injury sufficient to confer standing."

While pleading the mere risk of identity theft may seem to establish injury-in-fact, not all courts are so easily persuaded. *Reilly v. Ceridian Corp.* [664 F.3d 38 (3rd Cir. 2010)] provides a useful illustration. Here, a claim was sought by the employees of a law firm after a breach at Ceridian exposed the personal and financial data of approximately 27,000 individuals at 1,900 companies. In response to the breach, Ceridian had sent letters notifying the affected parties and offered one free year of credit monitoring. Later that same year, a lawsuit was filed alleging that the plaintiffs "1) have an increased risk of identity theft, 2) incurred costs to monitor their credit activity, and 3) suffered from emotional distress."

In this case, the court stated, "We cannot...describe how Appellants will be injured in this case without beginning our explanation with the word "if": if the hacker read, copied, and understood the hacked information, and if the hacker attempts to use the information, and if he does so successfully, only then will Appellants have suffered an injury." In short, the court held that the possible risk of identity theft does not constitute an injury-in-fact without showing imminent or actual harm.

CPA firms should consider that establishing injury-in-fact is a nuanced exercise that depends on both the venue and the unique circumstances of the claim. Controlling the circumstances of a client is impossible and staying abreast of circuit court holdings is untenable. Therefore, it is advisable that firms start from the proposition that injury-in-fact will be established if even a single plaintiff alleges fraudulent activity following a breach.

Traceability

The alleged injury suffered by the plaintiffs must also be reasonably traceable to the breach suffered by the firm. While this sounds simple, the vast anonymity of the Internet provides a seemingly impossible hurdle to establishing traceability. Once again, however, the law is much more nuanced.

In *Resnick v. AvMed Inc.* [693 F.3d 1317 (11th Cir. 2012)]], two laptops containing the personal information of roughly 1.2 million individuals were stolen and subsequently sold to a person known to deal in stolen property. Of note, two of the plaintiffs showed that prior to this incident, they had never previously been the victims of identity theft but became such directly following the breach.

The question before the court was whether these facts could be reasonably linked to the breach suffered by AvMed. As held by the court, "A showing that an injury is 'fairly traceable' requires less than a showing of 'proximate cause.' Plaintiffs became the victims of identity theft after the unencrypted laptops containing their sensitive information were stolen." The judge reasoned that even though there was not incontestable proof that the identity theft resulted from the breach, there was enough of a rationally discernable link to satisfy the requirement of traceability.

Therefore, CPA firms should note that an assumption of deniability should not be considered a defense against traceability. Even an indirect link to injuries sustained by the plaintiffs may fulfill this requirement.

Redressability

Other common retorts to the impracticality of data-breach claims are the related ideas that either personal information has no value, or its value cannot be quantified. While these ideas may hold sway in casual conversation, they have no basis in the legal environment. As shown in multiple cases, the barrier to establishing standing often rests upon establishing the two prior mentioned elements, injury-in-fact and traceability.

When it comes to redressability, plaintiffs must show that a resolution in their favor will duly compensate their injuries [*Friends of the Earth Inc. v. Laidlaw Environmental Services, Inc.*, 528 U.S. 167 (2000)]. As is well known to those that have experienced a professional liability claim, plaintiffs often seek redress in terms of monetary damages. This area is no different.

Until a definitive national standard is formed, the ability of plaintiffs to establish standing in a data-breach-related case will continue to rest upon circumstances unique to the case, which are well outside the bounds of a CPA firm's control. While this sounds bleak, there is an additional factor that could provide relief: the economics of such claims.

Data-Breach Claims

Most states have specifically excluded any private right of action in their laws relating to data breaches (BakerHostetler, Data Breach Charts, July 2018, http://bit.ly/2GJZRyL). Those that have included such an action often limit the action to questions concerning the notification of, and not the alleged damages from, the breach. This effectively limits the potential award to the point where litigation may not be economically feasible (Paul G. Karlsgodt, "Key Issues in Consumer Data Breach Litigation," *Practical Law*, October/November 2014, http://bit.ly/2GVYBrr). In contrast, class-action claims are the preferred method of litigation following a data breach. Many breaches involve residents of multiple states, and class-action cases tend to focus more directly on whether a company was at fault for the data breach (Karlsgodt). This broader question allows attorneys to be more creative and expansive with the potential damages they seek.

A survey conducted by the author of 38 known class-action claims resulting from data breaches yields is encouraging for most CPA firms (see **Exhibit A – Case References** on the last page of this section). For claims where greater than 200,000 records were exposed, one anomalous defendant had $30 million in revenue, and the rest generated multi-billion-dollar annual revenues. In cases where it was alleged that fewer than 200,000 records were exposed, each company, excepting one nonprofit medical organization and one government entity, had annual revenues exceeding $600 million.

At present, the authors were unable to find a single case on file where the clients of accounting CPA firm have brought a claim following a data breach. Even the recent high-profile breach at Deloitte in September 2017 does not appear to have led to any legal action by the clients affected. Deloitte noted in its statement on the incident that "only very few clients were impacted" (Sept. 25, 2017, http://bit.ly/2TaoxWB). Though the exact number of affected clients remains unknown, it was apparently small enough to make a class-action data-breach claim unpalatable to those involved. This further supports the idea that a business must have sizeable annual revenues and lose control over vast quantities of records to face a data-breach–related class-action claim.

This is not to say that smaller firms will forever be immune to class-action data-breach claims. It does, however, point to the current reluctance of plaintiffs' attorneys to be involved in pursuing legal action against entities if relatively few records have been exposed.

Even if plaintiffs' attorneys are confident in their ability to establish standing, overcome significant legal hurdles, and win the case, the comparatively minor per capita awards make smaller class actions economically unappealing.

In short, the largest CPA firms should consider data-breach claims a possibility, remote and difficult as they may be, to end successfully for the plaintiff. For the time being, however, smaller- and mid-sized firms that do not possess vast quantities of personal information can rest a little easier.

Exhibit A - Case References

Case Reference	Alleged Records	Estimated Revenue - 2017 (Includes Parent
Bell v. Acxiom Corp., 2006 WL 2850042 (E.D. Ark. 2006)	1,600,000,000	$880 Million
In re Yahoo! Inc. Customer Data Security Breach Litig., 2018 WL 1243332 (N.D. Cal. Mar. 9, 2018)	500,000,000	$1.37 Billion
In re Target Corp. Data Sec. Breach Litigation, 2014 WL 7192478 (D. Minn. 2014)	110,000,000	$71.88 Billion
In re Sony Gaming Networks and Customer Data Security Breach Litigation, 996 F. Supp. 2d 942 (S.D. Cal. 2014)	77,000,000	$77.4 Billion
In re Adobe Systems, Inc. Privacy Litigation, 2014 WL 4379916 (N.D. Cal. 2014)	38,000,000	$7.3 Billion
In re Anthem, Inc. Data Breach Litigation, 162 F. Supp. 3d 953 (N.D. Cal. 2016)	37,500,000	$89.1 Billion
In re Zappos.com, Inc., Customer Data Sec. Breach Litigation, 893 F. Supp. 2d 1058, 95 A.L.R.6th 721 (D. Nev. 2012)	24,000,000	$3.0 Billion
Hammond v. The Bank of New York Mellon Corp., 2010 WL 2643307 (S.D. N.Y. 2010)	12,500,000	$3.9 Billion
In re Premera Blue Cross Customer Data Security Breach Litigation	11,000,000	$4.5 Billion
Fero v. Excellus Health Plain, Inc., 236 F. Supp. 3d 735, 753–54 (W.D.N.Y. 2017)	10,500,000	$5.6 Billion
In re Science Applications International Corp. (SAIC) Backup Tape Data Theft Litigation, 45 F. Supp. 3d 14 (D.D.C. 2014)	4,700,000	$4.5 Billion
In re: Community Health Systems, Inc., 2016 WL 4732630 (N.D. Al. 2016)	4,500,000	$18 Billion
Anderson v. Hannaford Bros. Co., 659 F.3d 151 (1st Cir. 2011)	4,200,000	$18.3 Billion
In re Hannaford Bros. Co. Customer Data Security Breach Litigation, 2010 ME 93, 4 A.3d 492 (Me. 2010)	4,200,000	$18.3 Billion
Moyer v. Michaels Stores, Inc., 2014 WL 3511500 (N.D. Ill. 2014)	3,000,000	$5.2 Billion
Community Bank of Trenton v. Schnuck Markets, Inc. 887 F.3d 803 (7th Cir. 2018)	2,400,000	$2.7 Billion
Key v. DSW, Inc., 454 F.Supp.2d 684 (S.D.Ohio 2006)	1,500,000	$2.8 Billion
Chambliss v. Carefirst, Inc, 189 F. Supp. 3d 564 (D. Md. 2016)	1,100,000	$8.8 Billion
Galaria v. Nationwide Mut. Ins. Co., 998 F. Supp. 2d 646 (S.D. Ohio 2014)	1,100,000	$46 Billion
Attias v. CareFirst, Inc., 865 F.3d 620 (D.C. Cir. 2017)	1,100,000	$8.8 Billion
Unchageri v. Carefirst of Maryland, Inc. 2016 WL 8255012 (C.D. Ill. 2016)	1,100,000	$8.8 Billion
Strautins v. Trustwave Holdings, Inc., 27 F. Supp. 3d 871 (N.D. Ill. 2014)	1,035,000	$12.3 Billion
Amburgy v. Express Scripts, Inc., 671 F. Supp. 2d 1046 (E.D. Mo. 2009)	700,000	$4.5 Billion
Peters v. St. Joseph Services Corp., 74 F. Supp. 3d 847 (S.D. Tex. 2015)	405,000	$6.5 Billion
In re Arby's Restaurant Group Inc. Litigation 2018 WL 3549783 (N.D. Ga. 2018)	350,000	$3.5 Billion
Storm v. Paytime, Inc., 90 F.Supp.3d 359 (M.D.Pa. 2015)	233,000	$30 Million
Kahle v. Litton Loan Servicing, LP, 486 F. Supp. 2d 705 (S.D. Ohio 2007)	229,501	$1.2 Billion
Shafran v. Harley-Davidson, Inc., 2008 WL 763177 (S.D. N.Y. 2008)	60,000	$5.6 Billion
Lewert v. P.F. Chang's China Bistro, Inc., 819 F. 3d 963 (7th Cir. 2016)	60,000	$1.2 Billion
Belle Chasse Automotive Care, Inc. v. Advanced Auto Parts, Inc., 2009 WL 799760 (E.D. La. 2009)	56,000	$9.37 Billion
Hendricks v. DSW Shoe Warehouse, Inc., 444 F. Supp. 2d 775 (W.D. Mich. 2006)	55,000	$2.8 Billion
Remijas v. Neiman Marcus Group, LLC, 794 F.3d 688 (7th Cir. 2015)	35,000	$4.71 Billion
Reilly v. Ceridian Corp. 664 F.3d 38 (3d Cir. 2011)	27,000	$600 Million
Khan v. Children's National Health System, 188 F.Supp.3d 524 (D. Md 2016)	18,000	Non-Profit
Ponder v. Pfizer, Inc., 522 F.Supp.2d 793 (M.D.La.2007)	17,000	$53 Billion
Randolph v. ING Life Ins. and Annuity Co., 486 F. Supp. 2d 1 (D.D.C. 2007)	13,000	$20.7 Billion
Beck v. McDonald, 848 F. 3d 262 (4th Cir. 2017)	2,000	Government Entity
Smith v. Triad of Alabama, LLC, 2017 WL 1044692 (M.D. Al. 2017)	1,208	$3.0 Billion

Section 11: Staying Current

Naturally, firms should remain diligent in staying current with any changes in the law, or best practices. The following are a few of the many resources that firms of all sizes may consider in this endeavor.

Staying Current

- The *Cybercrime Support Network* is a non-profit, public-private collaboration, created to assist businesses and individuals with preventing and responding to cybercrime. Their numerous thought leaders continuously update available to resources to provide the most pertinent information. They can be found at: https://fraudsupport.org/

- *Cybrary* is an IT Security education site. The majority of the site is free and contains high quality courses on the topic of cybersecurity. They can be found at: https://www.cybrary.it/

- Brian Krebs is a world-renowned security blogger that has won countless awards for his reporting. His blog, *Krebs on Security*, is constantly updated to include the latest information on high profile breaches and threats. He can be found at: https://krebsonsecurity.com/

- BakerHostetler, is a nationwide law firm with a specialty in privacy and cybersecurity law. Their newsletter, the *Data Privacy Monitor* is constantly updated with the latest goings-on in the cyber specific legal arena. They can be found at: https://www.dataprivacymonitor.com/

- The International Association of Privacy Professionals (*IAPP*) is one of the world's leaders in certifying individuals as Privacy Professionals. Numerous resources exist to assist businesses in remaining current with the latest rulings and law changes. They can be found at: https://iapp.org/

- The United States Computer Emergency Readiness Team (*US-CERT*) contains a bevy of constantly updated cybersecurity warnings and information that is generally more appropriate for cybersecurity professionals. US-CERT can be found at: https://www.us-cert.gov/

☐ *InfraGard* is a partnership between the FBI and the private sector. This provides for a timely exchange of potentially sensitive information between government officials and businesses to remain current with the latest threats. Membership is required to participate. Visit https://www.infragard.org/ for more information.

Author's Contact Information

Joseph E. Brunsman: joseph@cplbrokers.com

Daniel W. Hudson: dhudson@cplbrokers.com

References

[1] Caitlin Bronson, One In Four Insurance Agents Will Be Gone By 2018 Insurance Business (2015), https://www.insurancebusinessmag.com/us/news/marine/one-in-four-insurance-agents-will-be-gone-by-2018-17943.aspx (last visited Apr 15, 2019).

[2] Global Cyber Security Insurance Market 2018 Size, Overview, Trends, Various Insurance Types, Applications, Key Player, REUTERS (2018), https://www.reuters.com/brandfeatures/venture-capital/article?id=36676 (last visited Apr 15, 2019).

[3] Facts Statistics: Industry overview, III, https://www.iii.org/fact-statistic/facts-statistics-industry-overview (last visited Apr 15, 2019).

[4] Jeff Kosseff, Cybersecurity Law 92 Footnote 170 (2017)

[5] Estimated using Hiscox Pro Privacy Pre-Priced Application PLPPVY A0001.

[6] Laurent Heslault, Actuaries Beware: Pricing Cyber Insurance Is A Different Ballgame, LinkedIn (2017), https://www.linkedin.com/pulse/actuaries-beware-pricing-cyber-insurance-different-laurent-heslault/ (last visited Apr 15, 2019).

[7] Cybersecurity Legislation 2018, NCSL (2019), http://www.ncsl.org/research/telecommunications-and-information-technology/cybersecurity-legislation-2018.aspx (last visited Mar 13, 2019).

[8] Lydia Dishman, Why People In Finance And Insurance Are The Unhappiest Employees: Three factors contribute to the lack of job satisfaction, despite security and high wages (2015), https://www.fastcompany.com/3046257/why-finance-and-insurance-workers-among-the-unhappiest-employees (last visited Apr 04, 2019).

[9] Robert H. Jerry & Douglas R. Richmond, Understanding Insurance Law 224-225 (2018).

[10] Sarchett v. Blue Shield of California, 43 Cal. 3d 1, 14–15, 729 P.2d 267, 276 (1987)

[11] Stolen W-2 Tax Form Data Up for Grabs on the Dark Web, DARK WEB NEWS (2017), https://darkwebnews.com/dark-web/stolen-tax-form-up-for-grabs-on-dark-web/ (last visited Apr 15, 2019).

[12] Andy Greenberg, The Untold Story Of Notpetya, The Most Devastating Cyberattack In History Wired (2018),

https://www.wired.com/story/notpetya-cyberattack-ukraine-russia-code-crashed-the-world/ (last visited Apr 15, 2019).

[13] What is hacktivism?, IT PRO (2018),
https://www.itpro.co.uk/hacking/30203/what-is-hacktivism (last visited Apr 15, 2019).

[14] Timeline of events associated with Anonymous, WIKIPEDIA (2019),
https://en.wikipedia.org/wiki/Timeline_of_events_associated_with_Anonymous (last visited Apr 15, 2019).

[15] Estimating Password Cracking Times, BETTER BUYS,
https://www.betterbuys.com/estimating-password-cracking-times/ (last visited Apr 15, 2019).

[16] https://www.symantec.com/blogs/feature-stories/cryptojacking-fluctuates-along-cryptocurrency-values

[17] What is a man-in-the-middle attack?, SYMANTEC,
https://us.norton.com/Internetsecurity-wifi-what-is-a-man-in-the-middle-attack.html (last visited Apr 15, 2019).

[18] What is a man-in-the-middle attack?, SYMANTEC,
https://us.norton.com/Internetsecurity-wifi-what-is-a-man-in-the-middle-attack.html (last visited Apr 15, 2019).

[19] Amanda C. Haury, 10 Of the Most Costly Computer Viruses Of All Time Investopedia (2012),

https://www.investopedia.com/financial-edge/0512/10-of-the-most-costly-computer-viruses-of-all-time.aspx (last visited Apr 02, 2019).

[20] Kimberly Hutcherson, Six Days After A Ransomware Cyberattack, Atlanta Officials Are Filling Out Forms By Hand, CNN (2018), https://www.cnn.com/2018/03/27/us/atlanta-ransomware-computers/index.html (last visited Apr 15, 2019).

[21] Fred O'Connor, Fileless Malware 101: Understanding Non-Malware Attacks, Cybereason (2017),

https://www.cybereason.com/blog/fileless-malware (last visited Apr 15, 2019).

[22] VPNFilter: New Router Malware with Destructive Capabilities, SYMANTEC (2018), https://www.symantec.com/blogs/threat-intelligence/vpnfilter-iot-malware (last visited Apr 16, 2019).

[23] Alan Henry, The Difference Between Antivirus and Anti-Malware (and Which to use) (2013), https://lifehacker.com/the-difference-between-antivirus-and-anti-malware-and-1176942277, (last visited May 15, 2019)

[24] Michael J., Chapple M., & Gibson D., CISSP (ISC)2 Certified Information Systems Security Professional Official Study Guide 715 7th ed. (2015)

[25] Michael J., Chapple M., & Gibson D., CISSP (ISC)2 Certified Information Systems Security Professional Official Study Guide 715 7th ed. (2015)

[26] Michael J., Chapple M., & Gibson D., CISSP (ISC)2 Certified Information Systems Security Professional Official Study Guide 737 7th ed. (2015)

[27] Michael J., Chapple M., & Gibson D., CISSP (ISC)2 Certified Information Systems Security Professional Official Study Guide 572 7th ed. (2015)

[28] Michael J., Chapple M., & Gibson D., CISSP (ISC)2 Certified Information Systems Security Professional Official Study Guide 634 7th ed. (2015)

[29] Michael J., Chapple M., & Gibson D., CISSP (ISC)2 Certified Information Systems Security Professional Official Study Guide 642 7th ed. (2015)

[30] Information Resellers Consumer Privacy Framework Needs To Reflect Changes In Technology And The Marketplace (2013), https://www.gao.gov/assets/660/658151.pdf (last visited Feb 7, 2019).

[31] U.S. House Committee on Financial Services, Blaine Luetkemeyer & Carolyn B. Maloney, Data Acquisition and Technology Accountability and Security Act (Discussion Draft (115AD). Available at: https://financialservices.house.gov/uploadedfiles/03.07.2018_data_s _bill.pdf

[32] Lisa Madigan *et al*, Thoughts on The Proposed Data Acquisition And Technology Accountability And Security Act (2018), https://buckleyfirm.com/sites/default/files/Buckley Sandler InfoBytes - State AGs Data Breach Letter to Congress 2018.03.19.pdf (last visited Mar 12, 2019). Signed by 32 State Attorneys General.

[33] U.S. Const. art. VI, cl. 2

[34] Md. Code Ann., Com. Law § 14-3504 (West)

[35] D.C. Code Ann. § 28-3852 (West)

[36] Va. Code Ann. § 18.2-186.6 (West)

[37] Md. Code Ann., Com. Law § 14-3504 (West)

[38] D.C. Code Ann. § 28-3852 (West)

[39] Va. Code Ann. § 18.2-186.6 (West)

[40] State Data Breach Laws Substitute Notice Chart: Overview, Practical Law Practice Note Overview 6-601-7666

[41] Cal. Civ. Code § 1798.82 (West)

[42] Data Breach Charts, (2018), https://www.bakerlaw.com/files/uploads/documents/data breach documents/data_breach_charts.pdf (last visited Sep 2018).

[43] N.C. Gen. Stat. Ann. § 75-66

[44] Okla. Stat. Ann. tit. 24, § 162 (West)

[45] Ohio Rev. Code Ann. § 1349.19 (West)

[46] Vt. Stat. Ann. tit. 9, § 2430 (West)

[47] Data Breach Charts, (2018), https://www.bakerlaw.com/files/uploads/documents/data breach documents/data_breach_charts.pdf (last visited Sep 2018).

[48] N.C. Gen. Stat. Ann. § 75-65

[49] Wash. Rev. Code Ann. § 19.255.010 (West)

[50] CVS Caremark Settles FTC Charges: Failed to Protect Medical and Financial Privacy of Customers and Employees; CVS Pharmacy Also Pays $2.25 Million to Settle Allegations of HIPAA Violations, FEDERAL TRADE COMMISSION (2015), https://www.ftc.gov/news-events/press-releases/2009/02/cvs-caremark-settles-ftc-chargesfailed-protect-medical-financial (last visited Mar 20, 2019).

[51] CVS Caremark Settles FTC Charges: Failed to Protect Medical and Financial Privacy of Customers and Employees; CVS Pharmacy Also Pays $2.25 Million to Settle Allegations of HIPAA Violations,

FEDERAL TRADE COMMISSION (2015), https://www.ftc.gov/news-events/press-releases/2009/02/cvs-caremark-settles-ftc-chargesfailed-protect-medical-financial (last visited Mar 20, 2019).
[52] CVS Caremark Settles FTC Charges: Failed to Protect Medical and Financial Privacy of Customers and Employees; CVS Pharmacy Also Pays $2.25 Million to Settle Allegations of HIPAA Violations, FEDERAL TRADE COMMISSION (2015), https://www.ftc.gov/news-events/press-releases/2009/02/cvs-caremark-settles-ftc-chargesfailed-protect-medical-financial (last visited Mar 20, 2019).

[53] N.Y. Gen. Bus. Law § 899-aa (McKinney)

[54] N.J. Stat. Ann. § 56:8-163 (West)

[55] Fla. Stat. Ann. § 501.171 (West)

[56] Fla. Stat. Ann. § 501.171 (West)

[57] S.C. Code Ann. § 39-1-90

[58] Tenn. Code § 47-18-2107

[59] Mich. Comp. Laws Ann. § 445.72 (West)

[60] Neb. Rev. Stat. 87-801 *et seq.*

[61] Minn. Stat. Ann. § 325E.61 (West)

[62] Tex. Bus. & Com. Code Ann. § 521.053 (West)

[63] Ga. Code Ann. § 10-1-912 (West)

[64] Data Breach Charts, (2018), https://www.bakerlaw.com/files/uploads/documents/data breach documents/data_breach_charts.pdf (last visited Sep 2018).

[65] Wis. Stat. Ann. § 134.98 (West)

[66] Fla. Stat. Ann. § 501.171 (West)

[67] State Data Breach Laws Substitute Notice Chart: Overview, Practical Law Practice Note Overview 6-601-7666

[68] S.C. Code Ann. § 39-1-90

[69] State Data Breach Laws Substitute Notice Chart: Overview, Practical Law Practice Note Overview 6-601-7666

[70] State Data Breach Laws Substitute Notice Chart: Overview, Practical Law Practice Note Overview 6-601-7666

[71] R.I. Gen. Laws § 11-49.2-5.

[72] R.I. Gen. Laws § 11-49.2-5.

[73] Haw. Rev. Stat. Ann. § 487N-2 (West)

[74] Fla. Stat. Ann. § 501.171 (West)

[75] Wash. Rev. Code Ann. § 19.255.010 (West)

[76] State of Washington v. Uber Technologies, Inc., Office of the Attorney General of Washington State (2017), https://agportal-s3bucket.s3.amazonaws.com/uploadedfiles/Another/News/Press_Releases/2017_11_28Complaint.pdf (last visited Feb 28, 2019).

[77] State of Washington v. Uber Technologies, Inc., Office of the Attorney General of Washington State (2017), https://agportal-s3bucket.s3.amazonaws.com/uploadedfiles/Another/News/Press_Releases/2017_11_28Complaint.pdf (last visited Feb 28, 2019).

[78] State of Washington v. Uber Technologies, Inc., Office of the Attorney General of Washington State (2017), https://agportal-s3bucket.s3.amazonaws.com/uploadedfiles/Another/News/Press_Releases/2017_11_28Complaint.pdf (last visited Feb 28, 2019).

[79] State of Washington v. Uber Technologies, Inc., Office of the Attorney General of Washington State (2017), https://agportal-s3bucket.s3.amazonaws.com/uploadedfiles/Another/News/Press_Releases/2017_11_28Complaint.pdf (last visited Feb 28, 2019).

[80] Key Issues in Consumer Data Breach Litigation, Practical Law Practice Note 5-582-9285

[81] John M. Parker, Data Security Law- Who Can Enforce Violations of Data Security Breach Notification Statutes?-in Re Target Corp. Data Security Breach Litigation, No. 14-2522, 2014 Wl 7192478 (D. Minn. Dec. 18, 2014)., 38 Am. J. Trial Advoc. 631, 633 (2015)

[82] Jeff Kosseff, Cybersecurity Law 65 (2017)

[83] Jeff Kosseff, Cybersecurity Law 65 (2017)

[84] Jeff Kosseff, Cybersecurity Law 65 (2017)

[85] California Consumer Privacy Act, 2018 Cal. Legis. Serv. Ch. 55 (A.B. 375) (West)

[86] California Consumer Privacy Act, 2018 Cal. Legis. Serv. Ch. 55 (A.B. 375) (West)

[87] California Consumer Privacy Act, 2018 Cal. Legis. Serv. Ch. 55 (A.B. 375) (West)

[88] California Consumer Privacy Act, 2018 Cal. Legis. Serv. Ch. 55 (A.B. 375) (West)

[89] Janine Anthony Bowen *et al.*, Overview of the New California Consumer Privacy Law (2018), https://www.dataprivacymonitor.com/wp-content/uploads/sites/5/2019/01/Overview-of-the-New-California-Consumer-Privacy-Law.pdf (last visited Mar 2, 2019).

[90] Alan L. Friel, *et al.,*California Assembly Privacy Committee Votes in Favor of Advancing CCPA Amendments (2019), https://www.dataprivacymonitor.com/ccpa/california-assembly-privacy-committee-votes-in-favor-of-advancing-ccpa-amendments/?utm_source=BakerHostetler+-+Data+Privacy+Monitor&utm_campaign=a370fca0d3-RSS_EMAIL_CAMPAIGN&utm_medium=email&utm_term=0_11eb73cca1-a370fca0d3-73474273 (last visited Oct 2, 2019)

[91] 201 Mass. Code Regs. 17.01

[92] 201 Mass. Code Regs. 17.01 *et seq.*

[93] 201 Mass. Code Regs. 17.03 *et seq.*

[94] 201 Mass. Code Regs. 17.04 *et seq.*

[95] Commonwealth of Massachusetts, Plaintiff, v. Equifax, Inc., Defendant., 2017 WL 4176743 (Mass. Super.)

[96] Commonwealth of Massachusetts, Plaintiff, v. Equifax, Inc., Defendant., 2017 WL 4176743 (Mass. Super.)

[97] Commonwealth of Massachusetts, Plaintiff, v. Equifax, Inc., Defendant., 2017 WL 4176743 (Mass. Super.)

[98] N.Y. Comp. Codes R. & Regs. tit. 23, § 500.0

[99] N.Y. Comp. Codes R. & Regs. tit. 23, § 500.1

[100] FAQs: 23 NYCRR Part 500 – Cybersecurity, https://www.dfs.ny.gov/industry_guidance/cyber_faqs (Last visited Jul 4, 2019)

[101] N.Y. Comp. Codes R. & Regs. tit. 23, § 500.1

[102] N.Y. Comp. Codes R. & Regs. tit. 23, § 500.2

[103] N.Y. Comp. Codes R. & Regs. tit. 23, § 500.3

[104] N.Y. Comp. Codes R. & Regs. tit. 23, § 500.4

[105] N.Y. Comp. Codes R. & Regs. tit. 23, § 500.5

[106] N.Y. Comp. Codes R. & Regs. tit. 23, § 500.6

[107] N.Y. Comp. Codes R. & Regs. tit. 23, § 500.7

[108] N.Y. Comp. Codes R. & Regs. tit. 23, § 500.8

[109] N.Y. Comp. Codes R. & Regs. tit. 23, § 500.9

[110] N.Y. Comp. Codes R. & Regs. tit. 23, § 500.10

[111] N.Y. Comp. Codes R. & Regs. tit. 23, § 500.11

[112] N.Y. Comp. Codes R. & Regs. tit. 23, § 500.12

[113] N.Y. Comp. Codes R. & Regs. tit. 23, § 500.13

[114] N.Y. Comp. Codes R. & Regs. tit. 23, § 500.14

[115] N.Y. Comp. Codes R. & Regs. tit. 23, § 500.15

[116] N.Y. Comp. Codes R. & Regs. tit. 23, § 500.16

[117] N.Y. Comp. Codes R. & Regs. tit. 23, § 500.17

[118] N.Y. Comp. Codes R. & Regs. tit. 23, § 500.18

[119] N.Y. Comp. Codes R. & Regs. tit. 23, § 500.19

[120] N.Y. Comp. Codes R. & Regs. tit. 23, § 500.20

[121] NY Cybersecurity Regulations for Financial Services Companies: Enforcement Begins Aug. 28, McGuireWoods (2017) https://www.mcguirewoods.com/Client-Resources/Alerts/2017/8/NY-Cybersecurity-Regulations-Financial-Services-Enforcement-August.aspx (last visited Oct 2, 2019)

[122] 15 U.S.C.A. § 45 (West)

[123] FTC Policy Statement on Unfairness, FEDERAL TRADE COMMISSION (1980), https://www.ftc.gov/public-statements/1980/12/ftc-policy-statement-unfairness (last visited Mar 12, 2019).

[124] FTC Policy Statement on Unfairness, Federal Trade Commission (1980), https://www.ftc.gov/public-statements/1980/12/ftc-policy-statement-unfairness (last visited Mar 12, 2019).

[125] FTC Policy Statement on Unfairness, Federal Trade Commission (1980), https://www.ftc.gov/public-statements/1980/12/ftc-policy-statement-unfairness (last visited Mar 12, 2019).

[126] FTC Policy Statement on Deception, Federal Trade Commission (1983), https://www.ftc.gov/system/files/documents/public_statements/4105 31/831014deceptionstmt.pdf (last visited MAR 25, 2019)

[127] Jeff Kosseff, Cybersecurity Law 5-6 (2017)

[128] Internet Privacy and Data Security: Additional Federal Authority Could Enhance Consumer Protection and Provide Flexibility, 4–5 (2019). Testimony Before the Permanent Subcommittee on Investigations, Committee on Homeland Security and Governmental Affairs, U.S. Senate

[129] F.T.C. v. Wyndham Worldwide Corp., 10 F. Supp. 3d 602, 608 (D.N.J. 2014), aff'd, 799 F.3d 236 (3d Cir. 2015)

[130] F.T.C. v. Wyndham Worldwide Corp., 10 F. Supp. 3d 602, 626 (D.N.J. 2014), aff'd, 799 F.3d 236 (3d Cir. 2015)

[131] F.T.C. v. Wyndham Worldwide Corp., 10 F. Supp. 3d 602, 611 (D.N.J. 2014), aff'd, 799 F.3d 236 (3d Cir. 2015)

[132] F.T.C. v. Wyndham Worldwide Corp., 10 F. Supp. 3d 602, 611–

12 (D.N.J. 2014), aff'd, 799 F.3d 236 (3d Cir. 2015)

[133] F.T.C. v. Wyndham Worldwide Corp., 10 F. Supp. 3d 602, 613 (D.N.J. 2014), aff'd, 799 F.3d 236 (3d Cir. 2015)

[134] F.T.C. v. Wyndham Worldwide Corp., 799 F.3d 236, (3d Cir. 2015)

[135] 16 CFR § 313.3(K)(viii)

[136] Internet Privacy and Data Security: Additional Federal Authority Could Enhance Consumer Protection and Provide Flexibility, 6 (2019). Testimony Before the Permanent Subcommittee on Investigations, Committee on Homeland Security and Governmental Affairs, U.S. Senate

[137] 15 U.S.C.A. § 6809 (West)

[138] 15 U.S.C.A. § 6801 (West)

[139] Financial Institutions and Customer Information: Complying with the Safeguards Rule, FEDERAL TRADE COMMISSION (2019), https://www.ftc.gov/tips-advice/business-center/guidance/financial-institutions-customer-information-complying (last visited Mar 7, 2019).

[140] *In the Matter of Taxslayer, LLC*, FTC File No. 162 3063 (Oct. 20, 2017) (complaint); *In the Matter of Taxslayer, LLC*, FTC Docket No. C-4626 (Oct. 20, 2017) (decision and order), *available at* https://www.ftc.gov/enforcement/cases-proceedings/162-3063/taxslayer.

[141] *In the Matter of Taxslayer, LLC*, FTC File No. 162 3063 (Oct. 20, 2017) (complaint); *In the Matter of Taxslayer, LLC*, FTC Docket No. C-4626 (Oct. 20, 2017) (decision and order), *available at* https://www.ftc.gov/enforcement/cases-proceedings/162-3063/taxslayer.

[142] Operator of Online Tax Preparation Service Agrees to Settle FTC Charges That it Violated Financial Privacy and Security Rules, FEDERAL TRADE COMMISSION (2017), https://www.ftc.gov/news-events/press-releases/2017/08/operator-online-tax-preparation-service-agrees-settle-ftc-charges (last visited Apr 15, 2019).

[143] 15 U.S.C.A. § 6823 (West)

[144] FTC seeks comment on proposed amendments to safeguards and privacy rules, CONSUMER FINANCE MONITOR (2019), https://www.consumerfinancemonitor.com/2019/03/08/ftc-seeks-

comment-on-proposed-amendments-to-safeguards-and-privacy-rules/ (last visited Mar 15, 2019).

[145] 17 C.F.R. § 248.30

[146] 17 C.F.R. § 248.30

[147] 17 C.F.R. § 248.30

[148] Investment Adviser and Broker-Dealer Compliance Issues Related to Regulation S-P – Privacy Notices and Safeguard Policies, U.S. Securities and Exchange Commission - Office of Compliance Inspections and Examinations (2019), https://www.sec.gov/files/OCIE%20Risk%20Alert%20-%20Regulation%20S-P.pdf (last visited Apr 20, 2019)

[149] Investment Adviser and Broker-Dealer Compliance Issues Related to Regulation S-P – Privacy Notices and Safeguard Policies, U.S. Securities and Exchange Commission - Office of Compliance Inspections and Examinations (2019), https://www.sec.gov/files/OCIE%20Risk%20Alert%20-%20Regulation%20S-P.pdf (last visited Apr 20, 2019)

[150] Investment Adviser and Broker-Dealer Compliance Issues Related to Regulation S-P – Privacy Notices and Safeguard Policies, U.S. Securities and Exchange Commission - Office of Compliance Inspections and Examinations (2019), https://www.sec.gov/files/OCIE%20Risk%20Alert%20-%20Regulation%20S-P.pdf (last visited Apr 20, 2019)

[151] Investment Adviser and Broker-Dealer Compliance Issues Related to Regulation S-P – Privacy Notices and Safeguard Policies, U.S. Securities and Exchange Commission - Office of Compliance Inspections and Examinations (2019), https://www.sec.gov/files/OCIE%20Risk%20Alert%20-%20Regulation%20S-P.pdf (last visited Apr 20, 2019)

[152] Cyber Enforcement Actions, U.S. Securities and Exchange Commission (Continuously Updated), https://www.sec.gov/spotlight/cybersecurity-enforcement-actions (last visited Oct 01, 2019)

[153] Crystal N. Skelton, Ftc Data Security Enforcement: Analyzing the Past, Present, and Future, 25 Competition: J. Anti., UCL & Privacy Sec. St. B. Cal. 305, 319 (2016)

[154] SEC: Morgan Stanley Failed to Safeguard Customer Data, U.S. Securities and Exchange Commission (Jun 8, 2016),

https://www.sec.gov/news/pressrelease/2016-112.html (last visited Apr 20, 2019)

[155] SEC: Morgan Stanley Failed to Safeguard Customer Data, U.S. Securities and Exchange Commission (Jun 8, 2016), https://www.sec.gov/news/pressrelease/2016-112.html (last visited Apr 20, 2019)

[156] 17 C.F.R. § 275.206(4)-2 (Custody of funds or securities of clients by investment advisers.)

[157] SEC Charges Three Firms With Violating Custody Rule, U.S. Securities and Exchange Commission (Oct 28, 2013), https://www.sec.gov/news/press-release/2013-230 (last visited Apr 20, 2019)

[158] In the Matter of Gw & Wade, LLC, Respondent., Release No. 3706 (Oct. 28, 2013)

[159] In the Matter of Gw & Wade, LLC, Respondent., Release No. 3706 (Oct. 28, 2013)

[160] SEC Charges Three Firms With Violating Custody Rule, U.S. Securities and Exchange Commission (Oct 28, 2013), https://www.sec.gov/news/press-release/2013-230 (last visited Apr 20, 2019)

[161] 181 Records Retention Report NL 2, the Red Flag Program Clarification Act of 2010.

[162] 17 CFR §248.201(b)(10)

[163] SEC Case Brings Rarely Used Cyber Rules into Limelight | Publications, KIRKLAND & ELLIS, LLP (2018), https://www.kirkland.com/publications/article/2018/09/sec-case-brings-rarely-used-cyber-rules-into-lime (last visited Apr 16, 2018).

[164] SEC Charges Firm With Deficient Cybersecurity Procedures, U.S. SECURITIES AND EXCHANGE COMMISSION (2018), https://www.sec.gov/news/press-release/2018-213 (last visited Apr 7, 2019).

[165] SEC Charges Firm With Deficient Cybersecurity Procedures, U.S. SECURITAS AND EXCHANGE COMMISSION (2018), https://www.sec.gov/news/press-release/2018-213 (last visited Apr 7, 2019).

[166] SEC Charges Firm With Deficient Cybersecurity Procedures, U.S. SECURITIES AND EXCHANGE COMMISSION (2018), https://www.sec.gov/news/press-release/2018-213 (last visited Apr

7, 2019).

[167] SEC Charges Firm With Deficient Cybersecurity Procedures, U.S. SECURITAS AND EXCHANGE COMMISSION (2018), https://www.sec.gov/news/press-release/2018-213 (last visited Apr 7, 2019).

[168] SEC Charges Firm With Deficient Cybersecurity Procedures, U.S. SECURITIES AND EXCHANGE COMMISSION (2018), https://www.sec.gov/news/press-release/2018-213 (last visited Apr 7, 2019).

[169] In the Matter of Voya Fin. Advisors, Inc., Respondent., Release No. 5048 (Sept. 26, 2018)

[170] SEC Charges Firm With Deficient Cybersecurity Procedures, U.S. SECURITAS AND EXCHANGE COMMISSION (2018), https://www.sec.gov/news/press-release/2018-213 (last visited Apr 7, 2019).

[171] § 27:37. Collecting documents located in foreign countries: Privacy laws, 3 N.Y. Prac., Com. Litig. in New York State Courts § 27:37 (4th ed.)

[172] Regulation (EU)2016/679 of the European Parliament and the Council of 27 April 2016 on the Protection of Natural Persons with Regard to the Processing of Personal Data and on the Free Movement of Such Data, and Repealing Directive 95/46/EC (General Data Protection Regulation), 2016 O.J. L 119/1 [hereinafter GDPR].

[173] GDPR art. 4(1)

[174] GDPR art. 4(1)

[175] GDPR art. 6(2)

[176] GDPR art. 58

[177] GDPR art. 58(4)

[178] Nina Bryant, et al, Early GDPR Enforcement Signals Complicated Future Landscape (Mar 21, 2019), https://www.lawtechnologytoday.org/2019/03/early-gdpr-enforcement-signals-complicated-future-landscape/ (last visited Jun 12, 2019).

[179] Mostafa Al Khonaizi, Fines Under GDPR in Non-EU Jurisdictions: Enforceable or Mere Reputation Risk?, http://www.mjilonline.org/fines-under-eu-gdpr-in-non-eu-jurisdictions-enforceable-or-mere-reputation-risk/ (last visited Nov

17, 2019).
[180] Privacy Shield Framework, The International Trade
Administration (ITA), U.S. Department of Commerce,
https://www.privacyshield.gov/EU-US-Framework (last visited Oct
1, 2019).
[181] Privacy Shield Framework, The International Trade
Administration (ITA), U.S. Department of Commerce,
https://www.privacyshield.gov/EU-US-Framework (last visited Oct
1, 2019).
[182] GDPR art. 2

[183] General Data Protection Regulation (GDPR) FAQs for small
organisations, INFORMATION COMMISSIONERS OFFICE (UK),
https://ico.org.uk/for-organisations/in-your-sector/business/guide-to-
the-general-data-protection-regulation-gdpr-faqs/ (last visited Mar 7,
2019).

[184] Mission Statement, Asia-Pacific Economic Cooperation,
https://www.apec.org/About-Us/About-APEC/Mission-Statement
(last visited Oct 05, 2019).
[185] Member Economies, Asia-Pacific Economic Cooperation,
https://www.apec.org/About-Us/About-APEC/Member-Economies
(last visited Oct 05, 2019).
[186] APEC Cross-Border Privacy Rules System goes public, Asia-
Pacific Economic Cooperation, https://www.apec.org/Press/News-
Releases/2012/0731_cbpr, (last visited Oct 07, 2019).
[187] APEC Cross-Border Privacy Rules System goes public (2012),
https://iapp.org/news/a/apec-announces-schellman-company-as-
newest-us-accountability-agent-for-cbpr-certifications/, (last visited
Oct 05, 2019).
[188] Alex Wall, GDPR matchup: The APEC Privacy Framework and
Cross-Border Privacy Rules, International Association of Privacy
Professionals, https://iapp.org/news/a/gdpr-matchup-the-apec-
privacy-framework-and-cross-border-privacy-rules/, (last visited Sep
13, 2019).
[189] In the Matter of Very Incognito Techs., Inc., Corp. d/b/a
Vipvape., No. 162-3034, 2016 WL 2739343, at *1 (MSNET May 4,
2016)
[190] In the Matter of Very Incognito Techs., Inc., Corp. d/b/a
Vipvape., No. 162-3034, 2016 WL 2739343, at *1 (MSNET May 4,

2016)

[191] In the Matter of Very Incognito Techs., Inc., A Corp. d/b/a Vipvape., No. 162-3034, 2016 WL 3626839, at *1 (MSNET June 21, 2016)

[192] United States – Mexico – Canada Agreement, Executive Office of the President, Office of the United States Trade Representative, https://ustr.gov/trade-agreements/free-trade-agreements/united-states-mexico-canada-agreement, (last visited Sep 13, 2019).

[193] Commissioner Jourová's remarks on Safe Harbour EU Court of Justice judgement before the Committee on Civil Liberties, Justice and Home Affairs (Libe) (2015), European Commission, http://europa.eu/rapid/press-release_SPEECH-15-5916_en.htm, (last visited Sep 13, 2019).

[194] EU Commission and United States agree on new framework for transatlantic data flows: EU-US Privacy Shield (2016), European Commission, http://europa.eu/rapid/press-release_IP-16-216_en.htm, (last visited Sep 17, 2019).

[195] Privacy Shield, Federal Trade Commission, https://www.ftc.gov/tips-advice/business-center/privacy-and-security/privacy-shield, (last visited Sep 20, 2019).

[196] Requirements of Participation - Privacy Shield Framework, The International Trade Administration (ITA), U.S. Department of Commerce, https://www.privacyshield.gov/article?id=Requirements-of-Participation, (last visited Sep 22, 2019).

[197] Requirements of Participation - Privacy Shield Framework, The International Trade Administration (ITA), U.S. Department of Commerce, https://www.privacyshield.gov/article?id=Requirements-of-Participation, (last visited Sep 22, 2019).

[198] Daniel R. Stoller, FTC Eyes Enforcement Boost for EU-U.S. Privacy Shield Data Moves (1) (Apr 26, 2019), https://news.bloomberglaw.com/privacy-and-data-security/ftc-eyes-enforcement-boost-for-eu-u-s-privacy-shield-data-moves, (last visited Sep 22, 2019).

[199] Daniel R. Stoller, FTC Eyes Enforcement Boost for EU-U.S. Privacy Shield Data Moves (1) (Apr 26, 2019), https://news.bloomberglaw.com/privacy-and-data-security/ftc-eyes-enforcement-boost-for-eu-u-s-privacy-shield-data-moves, (last

visited Sep 22, 2019).

[200] SecurTest – Corporate Background, SecurTest, https://securtest.com/2012/index.php (last visited oct 06, 2019)

[201] In the Matter of SecurTest, Inc., a corporation., 2019 WL 2522167, at *2

[202] In the Matter of SecurTest, Inc., a corporation., 2019 WL 2522167, at *1

[203] In the Matter of SecurTest, Inc., a corporation., 2019 WL 2522167, at *1

[204] In the Matter of SecurTest, Inc., a corporation., 2019 WL 2522167, at *1

[205] In the Matter of Securtest, Inc., A Corp.., No. 182-3152, 2019 WL 4052437 (MSNET Aug. 12, 2019)

[206] Official PCI Security Standards Council Site - Verify PCI Compliance, Download Data Security and Credit Card Security Standards, PCI SECURITY STANDARDS COUNCIL, https://www.pcisecuritystandards.org/pci_security/maintaining_payment_security (last visited Mar 23, 2019).

[207] Official PCI Security Standards Council Site - Verify PCI Compliance, Download Data Security and Credit Card Security Standards, PCI SECURITY STANDARDS COUNCIL, https://www.pcisecuritystandards.org/pci_security/completing_self_assessment (last visited Mar 23, 2019).

[208] PCI DSS Compliance, Practical Law Practice Note 8-608-7192

[209] P.F. Chang's China Bistro, Inc. v. Fed. Ins. Co., No. CV-15-01322-PHX-SMM, 2016 WL 3055111, at *2 (D. Ariz. May 31, 2016)

[210] PCI DSS Compliance, Practical Law Practice Note 8-608-7192

[211] LifeLock Will Pay $12 Million to Settle Charges by the FTC and 35 States That Identity Theft Prevention and Data Security Claims Were False, FEDERAL TRADE COMMISSION (2019), https://www.ftc.gov/news-events/press-releases/2010/03/lifelock-will-pay-12-million-settle-charges-ftc-35-states (last visited Apr 7, 2019).

[212] LifeLock Will Pay $12 Million to Settle Charges by the FTC and 35 States That Identity Theft Prevention and Data Security Claims Were False, FEDERAL TRADE COMMISSION (2019), https://www.ftc.gov/news-events/press-releases/2010/03/lifelock-

will-pay-12-million-settle-charges-ftc-35-states (last visited Apr 7, 2019).

[213] LifeLock Will Pay $12 Million to Settle Charges by the FTC and 35 States That Identity Theft Prevention and Data Security Claims Were False, FEDERAL TRADE COMMISSION (2019), https://www.ftc.gov/news-events/press-releases/2010/03/lifelock-will-pay-12-million-settle-charges-ftc-35-states (last visited Apr 7, 2019).

[214] LifeLock Will Pay $12 Million to Settle Charges by the FTC and 35 States That Identity Theft Prevention and Data Security Claims Were False, FEDERAL TRADE COMMISSION (2019), https://www.ftc.gov/news-events/press-releases/2010/03/lifelock-will-pay-12-million-settle-charges-ftc-35-states (last visited Apr 7, 2019).

[215] Statement of the Federal Trade Commission FTC v. LifeLock , (2015), https://www.ftc.gov/system/files/documents/public_statements/896143/151217lifelockcommstmt.pdf (last visited Apr 7, 2019).

[216] Statement of the Federal Trade Commission FTC v. LifeLock , (2015), https://www.ftc.gov/system/files/documents/public_statements/896143/151217lifelockcommstmt.pdf (last visited Apr 7, 2019).

[217] Statement of the Federal Trade Commission FTC v. LifeLock , (2015), https://www.ftc.gov/system/files/documents/public_statements/896143/151217lifelockcommstmt.pdf (last visited Apr 7, 2019).

[218] LifeLock to Pay $100 Million to Consumers to Settle FTC Charges it Violated 2010 Order, FEDERAL TRADE COMMISSION (2015), https://www.ftc.gov/news-events/press-releases/2015/12/lifelock-pay-100-million-consumers-settle-ftc-charges-it-violated (last visited Apr 7, 2019).

[219] PCI SECURITY STANDARDS COUNCIL TESTIFIES BEFORE U.S. HOUSE FINANCIAL SERVICES COMMITTEE, PCI SECURITY STANDARDS COUNCIL (2014), https://www.pcisecuritystandards.org/pdfs/14_05_04_Congressional_Hearings_Press_Release.pdf (last visited Mar 25, 2019).

[220] Handbook for Authorized IRS e-file Providers of Individual Income Tax Returns, (2019), https://www.irs.gov/pub/irs-

pdf/p1345.pdf (last visited Jan 8, 2019). Publication 1345 (Rev 2-2019) Catalog Number 64382J

[221] 26 U.S. Code § 7216.

[222] 26 U.S. Code § 6713.

[223] Handbook for Authorized IRS e-file Providers of Individual Income Tax Returns, (2019), https://www.irs.gov/pub/irs-pdf/p1345.pdf (last visited Jan 8, 2019). Publication 1345 (Rev 2-2019) Catalog Number 64382J

[224] Tips for tax preparers on how to create a data security plan, INTERNAL REVENUE SERVICE (2018), https://www.irs.gov/newsroom/tips-for-tax-preparers-on-how-to-create-a-data-security-plan (last visited Apr 7, 2019).

[225] Internal Revenue Bulletin: 2007-26, INTERNAL REVENUE SERVICE (2007), https://www.irs.gov/irb/2007-26_IRB (last visited Apr 7, 2019). See Rev. Proc. 2007-40 synopsis.

[226] JOSEPH E. BRUNSMAN & DANIEL W. HUDSON, TRUE COURSE: THE DEFINITIVE GUIDE FOR CPA PRACTICE INSURANCE (1 ed.). See Chapter 4: Professional Liability Insurance Policy Specifics.

[227] Nicole Hong & Robin Sidel, Hackers Breach Law Firms, Including Cravath and Weil Gotshal, WALL ST. J. (Mar. 29, 2016), https://www.wsj.com/articles/hackers-breach-cravath-swaine-other-big-law-firms-1459293504.

[228] More Puckett & Faraj Lulz (Feb 4, 2012), https://pastebin.com/nD2TW0fL, (last visited Mar 29, 2019).

[229] ABA Comm. on Ethics & Prof'l Responsibility, Formal Op. 483 Lawyers' Obligations After an Electronic Data Breach or Cyberattack (2018), https://www.americanbar.org/content/dam/aba/administrative/professional_responsibility/aba_formal_op_483.pdf, (last visited Aug 20, 2019)

[230] ABA Comm. on Ethics & Prof'l Responsibility, Formal Op. 477 Securing Communication of Protected Client Information (2017), https://www.americanbar.org/content/dam/aba/administrative/professional_responsibility/aba_formal_opinion_477.pdf, (last visited Aug 20, 2019)
ABA Comm. on Ethics & Prof'l Responsibility, Formal Op. 483 Lawyers' Obligations After an Electronic Data Breach or Cyberattack (2018),

https://www.americanbar.org/content/dam/aba/administrative/profes
sional_responsibility/aba_formal_op_483.pdf, (last visited Aug 20,
2019)

[232] ABA Comm. on Ethics & Prof'l Responsibility, Formal Op. 483
Lawyers' Obligations After an Electronic Data Breach or
Cyberattack (2018),
https://www.americanbar.org/content/dam/aba/administrative/profes
sional_responsibility/aba_formal_op_483.pdf, (last visited Aug 20,
2019)

[233] ABA Comm. on Ethics & Prof'l Responsibility, Formal Op. 483
Lawyers' Obligations After an Electronic Data Breach or
Cyberattack (2018),
https://www.americanbar.org/content/dam/aba/administrative/profes
sional_responsibility/aba_formal_op_483.pdf, (last visited Aug 20,
2019)

[234] ABA Comm. on Ethics & Prof'l Responsibility, Formal Op. 483
Lawyers' Obligations After an Electronic Data Breach or
Cyberattack (2018),
https://www.americanbar.org/content/dam/aba/administrative/profes
sional_responsibility/aba_formal_op_483.pdf, (last visited Aug 20,
2019)

[235] ABA Comm. on Ethics & Prof'l Responsibility, Formal Op. 483
Lawyers' Obligations After an Electronic Data Breach or
Cyberattack (2018),
https://www.americanbar.org/content/dam/aba/administrative/profes
sional_responsibility/aba_formal_op_483.pdf, (last visited Aug 20,
2019)

[236] ABA Comm. on Ethics & Prof'l Responsibility, Formal Op. 483
Lawyers' Obligations After an Electronic Data Breach or
Cyberattack (2018),
https://www.americanbar.org/content/dam/aba/administrative/profes
sional_responsibility/aba_formal_op_483.pdf, (last visited Aug 20,
2019)

[237] ABA Comm. on Ethics & Prof'l Responsibility, Formal Op. 483
Lawyers' Obligations After an Electronic Data Breach or
Cyberattack (2018),
https://www.americanbar.org/content/dam/aba/administrative/profes
sional_responsibility/aba_formal_op_483.pdf, (last visited Aug 20,
2019)

[238] ABA Comm. on Ethics & Prof'l Responsibility, Formal Op. 483 Lawyers' Obligations After an Electronic Data Breach or Cyberattack (2018), https://www.americanbar.org/content/dam/aba/administrative/profes sional_responsibility/aba_formal_op_483.pdf, (last visited Aug 20, 2019)

[239] ABA RULE 10. SANCTIONS, Mod. Rules Law. Displ. Enforce. Rule 10

[240] Small Firm Business Continuity Plan Template, SMALL FIRM BUSINESS CONTINUITY PLAN TEMPLATE (2010), http://www.finra.org/industry/small-firm-business-continuity-plan-template (last visited Apr 7, 2019).

[241] February 2017 Disciplinary Actions, Financial Industry Regulatory Authority (2017), https://www.finra.org/sites/default/files/publication_file/February_2 017_Disciplinary_Actions.pdf (last visited Mar 20, 2019).

[242] Investor Alert: Cybersecurity and Your Brokerage Firm, Financial Industry Regulatory Authority (2015), http://www.finra.org/investors/alerts/cybersecurity-and-your-brokerage-firm, (last visited Apr 13, 2019).

[243] 48 C.F.R. § 252.204-7012

[244] Safeguarding Covered Defense Information, U.S. Department of Defense, https://business.defense.gov/Portals/57/Safeguarding%20Covered%2 0Defense%20Information%20-%20The%20Basics.pdf, (last visited Apr 15, 2019).

[245] Safeguarding Covered Defense Information, U.S. Department of Defense, https://business.defense.gov/Portals/57/Safeguarding%20Covered%2 0Defense%20Information%20-%20The%20Basics.pdf, (last visited Apr 15, 2019).

[246] Special Publication (SP) 800–171, Protecting Controlled Unclassified Information in Nonfederal Information Systems and Organizations, National Institute of Standards and Technology (NIST), http://dx.doi.org/10.6028/NIST.SP.800–171, (last visited Oct 06, 2019).

[247] Special Publication (SP) 800–171, Protecting Controlled Unclassified Information in Nonfederal Information Systems and

Organizations, National Institute of Standards and Technology (NIST), http://dx.doi.org/10.6028/NIST.SP.800–171, (last visited Oct 06, 2019).

[248] 48 C.F.R. § 252.204-7012

[249] 48 C.F.R. § 252.204-7012

[250] 48 C.F.R. § 252.204-7012

[251] 48 C.F.R. § 252.204-7012

[252] 48 C.F.R. § 252.204-7012

[253] 48 C.F.R. § 252.204-7012

[254] Safeguarding Covered Defense Information, U.S. Department of Defense, https://business.defense.gov/Portals/57/Safeguarding%20Covered%20Defense%20Information%20-%20The%20Basics.pdf, (last visited Apr 15, 2019).

[255] 48 C.F.R. § 252.204-7009

[256] In re Netcracker Technology Corporation Non-Prosecution and Security Agreement, U.S. Department of Justice – National Security Division (2017), https://www.justice.gov/opa/press-release/file/1017056/download, (last visited Apr 16, 2019)

[257] In re Netcracker Technology Corporation Non-Prosecution and Security Agreement, U.S. Department of Justice – National Security Division (2017), https://www.justice.gov/opa/press-release/file/1017056/download, (last visited Apr 16, 2019)

[258] In re Netcracker Technology Corporation Non-Prosecution and Security Agreement, U.S. Department of Justice – National Security Division (2017), https://www.justice.gov/opa/press-release/file/1017056/download, (last visited Apr 16, 2019)

[259] John S. West, Laura Anne Kuykendall, New Requirements For Protecting Sensitive Government Data Adopted For Government Contractors: Is Your Company In Compliance? (2018), Troutman Sanders, LLP, https://www.troutman.com/insights/new-requirements-for-protecting-sensitive-government-data-adopted-for-government-contractors-is-your-company-in-compliance.html, (last visited Apr 16, 2019).

[260] In re Netcracker Technology Corporation Non-Prosecution and Security Agreement, U.S. Department of Justice – National Security Division (2017), https://www.justice.gov/opa/press-

release/file/1017056/download, (last visited Apr 16, 2019).

[261] In re Netcracker Technology Corporation Non-Prosecution and Security Agreement, U.S. Department of Justice – National Security Division (2017), https://www.justice.gov/opa/press-release/file/1017056/download, (last visited Apr 16, 2019).

[262] Covered Entities and Business Associates, U.S. Department of Health and Human Services, https://www.hhs.gov/hipaa/for-professionals/covered-entities/index.html, (last visited Apr 16, 2019).

[263] HIPAA Administrative Simplification: Regulation Text; 45 CFR Parts 160, 162, and 164 (Unofficial Version, as amended through March 26, 2013) https://www.hhs.gov/sites/default/files/ocr/privacy/hipaa/administrative/combined/hipaa-simplification-201303.pdf (last visited Apr 16, 2019).

[264] CVS Pharmacy, Inc. v. Press Am., Inc., 2018 WL 318479, at *7 (S.D.N.Y. Jan. 3, 2018)

[265] HIPAA Administrative Simplification: Regulation Text; 45 CFR Parts 160, 162, and 164 (Unofficial Version, as amended through March 26, 2013) https://www.hhs.gov/sites/default/files/ocr/privacy/hipaa/administrative/combined/hipaa-simplification-201303.pdf (last visited Apr 16, 2019).

[266] 45 C.F.R. § 160.103

[267] Mark O. Dietrich, CPA/ABV, How health care data security rules may affect you: CPAs need to understand their responsibilities under HIPAA to avoid potentially severe civil and criminal penalties (2015), https://www.journalofaccountancy.com/issues/2015/jan/health-care-data-security-rules.html, (last visited Apr 20, 2019).

[268] 45 C.F.R. § 160.103

[269] 45 C.F.R. § 164.514(b)

[270] Summary of HIPAA Privacy Rules, U.S. Department of Health and Human Services, https://www.hhs.gov/hipaa/for-professionals/privacy/laws-regulations/index.html, (last visited Apr 16, 2019).

[271] Mark O. Dietrich, CPA/ABV, How health care data security rules

may affect you: CPAs need to understand their responsibilities under HIPAA to avoid potentially severe civil and criminal penalties (2015), https://www.journalofaccountancy.com/issues/2015/jan/health-care-data-security-rules.html, (last visited Apr 20, 2019).

[272] Business Associates: 45 CFR 164.502(e), 164.504(e), 164.532(d) and (e), U.S. Department of Health and Human Services, https://www.hhs.gov/hipaa/for-professionals/privacy/guidance/business-associates/index.html, (last visited Apr 16, 2019).

[273] 45 C.F.R. § 160.103

[274] 45 C.F.R. § 164.520

[275] 45 C.F.R. § 164.530(i)

[276] 45 C.F.R. § 164.530(b)

[277] 45 C.F.R. § 164.530 and 45 C.F.R. § 164.308

[278] 45 C.F.R. § 164.530

[279] HIPAA Privacy Rule, Practical Law Practice Note 4-501-7220

[280] Summary of HIPAA Privacy Rules, U.S. Department of Health and Human Services, https://www.hhs.gov/hipaa/for-professionals/privacy/laws-regulations/index.html, (last visited Apr 16, 2019).

[281] HIPAA Security Rule, Practical Law Practice Note 5-502-1269

[282] 45 C.F.R. § 164.308

[283] 45 C.F.R. § 164.316

[284] 45 C.F.R. § 164.310(a)(1)

[285] 45 C.F.R. § 164.310(b)-(c)

[286] Summary of HIPAA Privacy Rules, U.S. Department of Health and Human Services, https://www.hhs.gov/hipaa/for-professionals/privacy/laws-regulations/index.html, (last visited Apr 16, 2019).

[287] 45 C.F.R. § 164.310(d)(1)

[288] August 2018 Cyber Security Newsletter: Considerations for Securing Electronic Media and Devices, U.S. Department of Health and Human Services – Office for Civil Rights, https://www.hhs.gov/sites/default/files/cybersecurity-newsletter-august-2018-device-and-media-controls.pdf, (last visited Apr 16,

2019).

[289] 45 C.F.R. §164.312(a)(2)(iv)

[290] 45 C.F.R. § 164.312(b)

[291] 45 C.F.R. § 164.312(c)(1)

[292] 45 C.F.R. § 164.312(c)(2)

[293] 45 C.F.R. § 164.312(d)

[294] 45 C.F.R. § 164.312(e)(1)

[295] 45 C.F.R. § 164.312(e)(2)

[296] 45 C.F.R. § 164.316

[297] 45 C.F.R. § 164.402

[298] Enforcement Data, U.S. Department of Health and Human Services, https://www.hhs.gov/hipaa/for-professionals/compliance-enforcement/data/index.html, (last visited Apr 16, 2019).

[299] 2018 Cost of a Data Breach Study: Global Overview, IBM SECURITY, available at: https://www.ibm.com (last visited Mar 2019).

[300] 45 CFR §§ 164.400-414

[301] 45 C.F.R. § 164.314(a)

[302] Guidance on HIPAA & Cloud Computing, U.S. Department of Health and Human Services, https://www.hhs.gov/hipaa/for-professionals/special-topics/cloud-computing/index.html, (last visited Apr 16, 2019).

[303] Guidance on HIPAA & Cloud Computing, U.S. Department of Health and Human Services, https://www.hhs.gov/hipaa/for-professionals/special-topics/cloud-computing/index.html, (last visited Apr 16, 2019).

[304] Guidance on HIPAA & Cloud Computing, U.S. Department of Health and Human Services, https://www.hhs.gov/hipaa/for-professionals/special-topics/cloud-computing/index.html, (last visited Apr 16, 2019).

[305] In re Center for Children's Digestive Health, S.C. (2017), The United States Department of Health and Human Services – Office for Civil Rights, https://www.hhs.gov/sites/default/files/ra_cap_ccdh.pdf, (last visited Apr 20, 2019).

[306] In re Center for Children's Digestive Health, S.C. (2017), The United States Department of Health and Human Services – Office

for Civil Rights,
https://www.hhs.gov/sites/default/files/ra_cap_ccdh.pdf, (last visited
Apr 20, 2019).
[307] In re Center for Children's Digestive Health, S.C. (2017), The
United States Department of Health and Human Services – Office
for Civil Rights,
https://www.hhs.gov/sites/default/files/ra_cap_ccdh.pdf, (last visited
Apr 20, 2019).
[308] In re Center for Children's Digestive Health, S.C. Including
Appendix A Corrective Action Plan Between The United States
Department of Health and Human Services and Center for
Children's Digestive Health (2017), The United States Department
of Health and Human Services – Office for Civil Rights,
https://www.hhs.gov/sites/default/files/chcs-racap-final.pdf, (last
visited Apr 20, 2019).
[309] In re Center for Children's Digestive Health, S.C. Including
Appendix A Corrective Action Plan Between The United States
Department of Health and Human Services and Center for
Children's Digestive Health (2017), The United States Department
of Health and Human Services – Office for Civil Rights,
https://www.hhs.gov/sites/default/files/chcs-racap-final.pdf, (last
visited Apr 20, 2019).
[310] In re Center for Children's Digestive Health, S.C. Including
Appendix A Corrective Action Plan Between The United States
Department of Health and Human Services and Center for
Children's Digestive Health (2017), The United States Department
of Health and Human Services – Office for Civil Rights,
https://www.hhs.gov/sites/default/files/chcs-racap-final.pdf, (last
visited Apr 20, 2019).
[311] Guidance on HIPAA & Cloud Computing, U.S. Department of
Health and Human Services, https://www.hhs.gov/hipaa/for-
professionals/special-topics/cloud-computing/index.html, (last
visited Apr 16, 2019).
[312] In re Oregon Health & Science University (2014), The United
States Department of Health and Human Services – Office for Civil
Rights, https://www.hhs.gov/sites/default/files/ohsuracap_508.pdf,
(last visited Apr 20, 2019).
[313] In re Oregon Health & Science University (2014), The United
States Department of Health and Human Services – Office for Civil

Rights, https://www.hhs.gov/sites/default/files/ohsuracap_508.pdf, (last visited Apr 20, 2019).

[314] In re Oregon Health & Science University (2014), The United States Department of Health and Human Services – Office for Civil Rights, https://www.hhs.gov/sites/default/files/ohsuracap_508.pdf, (last visited Apr 20, 2019).

[315] In re Sandor Mark Jacobson ("Receiver"), acting on behalf of Filefax, Inc. as court appointed Receiver (2015), The United States Department of Health and Human Services – Office for Civil Rights, https://www.hhs.gov/sites/default/files/filefax-receiver-racap.pdf, (last visited Apr 23, 2019).

[316] Resolution Agreement regarding Sandor Mark Jacobson ("Receiver"), acting on behalf of Filefax, Inc. as court appointed Receiver (2015), The United States Department of Health and Human Services – Office for Civil Rights, https://www.hhs.gov/sites/default/files/filefax-receiver-racap.pdf, (last visited Apr 23, 2019).

[317] In re Anthem, Inc., (2018), The United States Department of Health and Human Services – Office for Civil Rights, https://www.hhs.gov/sites/default/files/anthem-ra-cap.pdf, (last visited Apr 23, 2019).

[318] In re Anthem, Inc., (2018), The United States Department of Health and Human Services – Office for Civil Rights, https://www.hhs.gov/sites/default/files/anthem-ra-cap.pdf, (last visited Apr 23, 2019).

[319] Anthem Pays OCR $16 Million in Record HIPAA Settlement Following Largest U.S. Health Data Breach in History (2018), The United States Department of Health and Human Services, https://www.hhs.gov/about/news/2018/10/15/anthem-pays-ocr-16-million-record-hipaa-settlement-following-largest-health-data-breach-history.html, (last visited Apr 23, 2019).

[320] State of Indiana v. Joseph Beck, Beck Family Dentistry, 49D10-1412-PL-041613

[321] Summary of 2018 HIPAA Fines and Settlements (2019), HIPAA Journal, https://www.hipaajournal.com/summary-2018-hipaa-fines-and-settlements/, (last visited May 08, 2019).

[322] Lee-Thomas v. LabCorp, 316 F. Supp. 3d 471, 472 (D.D.C. 2018)

[323] Lee-Thomas v. LabCorp, 316 F. Supp. 3d 471, 473 (D.D.C. 2018)

[324] Lee-Thomas v. LabCorp, 316 F. Supp. 3d 471, 473 (D.D.C. 2018)

[325] Lee-Thomas v. LabCorp, 316 F. Supp. 3d 471, 473 (D.D.C. 2018)

[326] Lee-Thomas v. LabCorp, 316 F. Supp. 3d 471, 474 (D.D.C. 2018)

[327] 42 U.S.C.A. § 1320d-5 through 42 U.S.C.A. § 1320d-6 (West)

[328] HIPAA Privacy, Security, and Breach Notification Audit Program, The United States Department of Health and Human Services, https://www.hhs.gov/hipaa/for-professionals/compliance-enforcement/audit/index.html#differ, (last visited May 25, 2019).

[329] HIPAA Privacy, Security, and Breach Notification Audit Program, The United States Department of Health and Human Services, https://www.hhs.gov/hipaa/for-professionals/compliance-enforcement/audit/index.html#differ, (last visited May 25, 2019).

[330] HIPAA Privacy, Security, and Breach Notification Audit Program, The United States Department of Health and Human Services, https://www.hhs.gov/hipaa/for-professionals/compliance-enforcement/audit/index.html#differ, (last visited May 25, 2019).

[331] 47 U.S.C. § 227

[332] Telephone Consumer Protection Act (TCPA): Overview, Practical Law Practice Note Overview w-000-5609

[333] Hiscox CyberClear Policy TPCCYB P0001 CW (05/16) pg. 10.

[334] Victoria FLORES, an individual, Plaintiff, v. ACE AMERICAN INSURANCE COMPANY, a Pennsylvania corporation, Defendant., 2018 WL 3525500 (S.D.N.Y.)

[335] Victoria FLORES, an individual, Plaintiff, v. ACE AMERICAN INSURANCE COMPANY, a Pennsylvania corporation, Defendant., 2018 WL 3525500 (S.D.N.Y.)

[336] Victoria FLORES, an individual, Plaintiff, v. ACE AMERICAN INSURANCE COMPANY, a Pennsylvania corporation, Defendant., 2018 WL 3525500 (S.D.N.Y.)

[337] Victoria FLORES, an individual, Plaintiff, v. ACE AMERICAN INSURANCE COMPANY, a Pennsylvania corporation, Defendant., 2018 WL 3525500 (S.D.N.Y.)

[338] 3 A.L.R.6th 625 (Originally published in 2005)

[339] Telephone Consumer Protection Act (TCPA): Overview, Practical Law Practice Note Overview w-000-5609

[340] § 13:1.Introduction, Corp Couns. Gd. to Advertising L and Agrmts. § 13:1

[341] § 13:3.CAN-SPAM Act—Preemption of state laws, Corp Couns. Gd. to Advertising L and Agrmts. § 13:3

[342] See 15 U.S.C. § 7704

[343] See 15 U.S.C. § 7706(f)

[344] See 15 U.S.C. § 7706(g)

[345] CAN-SPAM Act: A Compliance Guide for Business, Federal Trade Commission, https://www.ftc.gov/tips-advice/business-center/guidance/can-spam-act-compliance-guide-business, (last visited May 29, 2019).

[346] 15 U.S.C. § 7706(f)

[347] Controlling the Assault of Non-Solicited Pornography and Marketing (CAN-SPAM) Act of 2003, International Risk Management Institute, Inc., https://www.irmi.com/term/insurance-definitions/controlling-the-assault-of-non-solicited-pornography-and-marketing-act-of-2003, (last visited May 25, 2019).

[348] Hiscox CyberClear Policy TPCCYB P0001 CW (05/16) pg. 10.

[349] Beazley Group, Beazley Breach Response Policy F00653, 112017 ed.

[350] 42 U.S.C.A. § 12111(5)(A) (West)

[351] The Muddy Waters of ADA Website Compliance May Become Less Murky in 2019, Hunton Andrews Kurth, LLP, https://www.huntonlaborblog.com/2019/01/articles/public-accommodations/muddy-waters-ada-website-compliance-may-become-less-murky-2019/, (last visited May 25, 2019).

[352] Letter from Stephen E. Boyd, Assistant Attorney General United States Department of Justice to Rep. Ted Budd (2018), Seyfarth Shaw, LLP, https://www.adatitleiii.com/wp-content/uploads/sites/121/2018/10/DOJ-letter-to-congress.pdf, (last visited May 25, 2019).

[353] Information and Communication Technology (ICT) Standards and Guidelines, 82 FR 5790-01

[354] Web Content Accessibility Guidelines (WCAG) 2.0 (2008), W3C, https://www.w3.org/TR/WCAG20/, (last visited May 25,

2019).

[355] The Muddy Waters of ADA Website Compliance May Become Less Murky in 2019, Hunton Andrews Kurth, LLP, https://www.huntonlaborblog.com/2019/01/articles/public-accommodations/muddy-waters-ada-website-compliance-may-become-less-murky-2019/, (last visited May 25, 2019).

[356] Understanding Conformance, W3C, https://www.w3.org/TR/UNDERSTANDING-WCAG20/conformance.html#uc-levels-head, (last visited May 25, 2019).

[357] Robert H. Jerry & Douglas R. Richmond, Understanding Insurance Law 493 (2018).

[358] See *Eyeblaster*, 613 F.3d at 800-802 and *State Auto Prop. & Cas. Ins. Co. v. Midwest Computers & More*, 147 F. Supp. 2d 1113, 1116 (W.D. Okla. 2001)

[359] American Online, Inc. v. St. Paul Mercury Ins. Co., 347 F.3d 89, 95 (4th Cir. 2003)

[360] Liberty Corp. Capital Ltd. v. Security Safe Outlet, Inc., 937 F. Supp. 2d 891, 901 (E.D. Ky. 2013)

[361] Robert H. Jerry & Douglas R. Richmond, Understanding Insurance Law 497 (2018).

[362] Robert H. Jerry & Douglas R. Richmond, Understanding Insurance Law 497 (2018).

[363] *Travelers Indemnity Company of America v. Portal Healthcare Solutions, LLC*, No. 14-1944 (4th Cir. April 11, 2016)(unpublished)

[364] *Travelers Indemnity Company of America v. Portal Healthcare Solutions, LLC*, No. 14-1944 (4th Cir. April 11, 2016)(unpublished)

[365] Zurich American Insurance Co. v. Sony Corp., No 651982/2011 (N.Y. Sup. Ct. 2014)

[366] Zurich American Insurance Co. v. Sony Corp., No 651982/2011 (N.Y. Sup. Ct. 2014)

[367] Creative Hospitality Ventures, Inc. v. United States Liability Insurance Co., 444 Fed. (11th Circ. Sept. 30, 2011)

[368] Creative Hospitality Ventures, Inc. v. United States Liability Insurance Co., 444 Fed. (11th Circ. Sept. 30, 2011)

[369] ISO Comments on CGL Endorsements for Data Breach Liability Exclusions, INSURANCE JOURNAL (2014), https://www.insurancejournal.com/news/east/2014/07/18/332655.ht

m (last visited Apr 7, 2019).

[370] Travelers Crime Policy Form CRI-3001 Ed. 01-09

[371] Travelers Crime Policy Form CRI-3001 Ed. 01-09

[372] Apache Corp. v. Great Am. Ins. Co., 662 F. App'x 252, 253 (5th Cir. 2016)

[373] Apache Corp. v. Great Am. Ins. Co., 662 F. App'x 252, 254 (5th Cir. 2016)

[374] Apache Corp. v. Great Am. Ins. Co., 662 F. App'x 252, 254 (5th Cir. 2016)

[375] Apache Corp. v. Great Am. Ins. Co., 662 F. App'x 252, 254 (5th Cir. 2016)

[376] Apache Corp. v. Great Am. Ins. Co., 662 F. App'x 252, 256–57 (5th Cir. 2016)

[377] See International Communications v. Great American Ins. Co., 2018 WL 2149769 at *4 (11th Cir., May 10, 2018); Pestmaster Servs., Inc. v. Travelers Casualty & Ins. Co., 656 Fed. App'x. 332, 333 (9th Cir. 2016); Pinnacle Processing Group, Inc. v. Hartford Casualty Ins., 2011 WL, 5299557, at *5 (W.D. Wash. Nov. 4, 2011)

[378] Travelers Crime Policy Form CRI-3001 Ed. 01-09

[379] Travelers Crime Policy Form CRI-3001 Ed. 01-09

[380] Aqua Star (USA) Corp. v. Travelers Cas. & Sur. Co. of Am., No. C14-1368RSL, 2016 WL 3655265, at *1 (W.D. Wash. July 8, 2016), aff'd, 719 F. App'x 701 (9th Cir. 2018).

[381] Aqua Star (USA) Corp. v. Travelers Cas. & Sur. Co. of Am., No. C14-1368RSL, 2016 WL 3655265, at *2 (W.D. Wash. July 8, 2016), aff'd, 719 F. App'x 701 (9th Cir. 2018).

[382] Aqua Star (USA) Corp. v. Travelers Cas. & Sur. Co. of Am., No. C14-1368RSL, 2016 WL 3655265, at *3 (W.D. Wash. July 8, 2016), aff'd, 719 F. App'x 701 (9th Cir. 2018).

[383] Authors' survey of 15 well known Crime Insurance Policies.

[384] CAMICO Mutual Insurance Company Privacy and Client Network Damage Liability Coverage Endorsement Form PL-1049-A

[385] CAMICO Mutual Insurance Company Privacy and Client Network Damage Liability Coverage Endorsement Form PL-1049-A

[386] Authors' survey of 15 Professional Liability Insurance Policies.

[387] CAMICO Mut. Ins. Co. v. Heffler, Radetich & Saitta, LLP, No. CIV.A. 11-4753, 2013 WL 3481527, at *1–2 (E.D. Pa. June 28,

2013), aff'd sub nom. CAMICO Mut. Ins. Co. v. Heffler, Radetich & Saitta, L.L.P., 587 F. App'x 726 (3d Cir. 2014).

[388] CAMICO Mut. Ins. Co. v. Heffler, Radetich & Saitta, LLP, No. CIV.A. 11-4753, 2013 WL 3481527, at *2 (E.D. Pa. June 28, 2013), aff'd sub nom. CAMICO Mut. Ins. Co. v. Heffler, Radetich & Saitta, L.L.P., 587 F. App'x 726 (3d Cir. 2014).

[389] CAMICO Mut. Ins. Co. v. Heffler, Radetich & Saitta, LLP, No. CIV.A. 11-4753, 2013 WL 3481527, at *10 (E.D. Pa. June 28, 2013), aff'd sub nom. CAMICO Mut. Ins. Co. v. Heffler, Radetich & Saitta, L.L.P., 587 F. App'x 726 (3d Cir. 2014).

[390] CAMICO Mut. Ins. Co. v. Heffler, Radetich & Saitta, L.L.P., 587 F. App'x 726, 731 (3d Cir. 2014).

[391] Bryan Bros. Inc. v. Cont'l Cas. Corp., 704 F. Supp. 2d 537, 539 (E.D. Va. 2010), aff'd sub nom. Bryan Bros. Inc. v. Cont'l Cas. Co., 660 F.3d 827 (4th Cir. 2011), and aff'd sub nom. Bryan Bros. Inc. v. Cont'l Cas. Co., 419 F. App'x 422 (4th Cir. 2011).

[392] Bryan Bros. Inc. v. Cont'l Cas. Corp., 704 F. Supp. 2d 537, 539 (E.D. Va. 2010), aff'd sub nom. Bryan Bros. Inc. v. Cont'l Cas. Co., 660 F.3d 827 (4th Cir. 2011), and aff'd sub nom. Bryan Bros. Inc. v. Cont'l Cas. Co., 419 F. App'x 422 (4th Cir. 2011).

[393] Bryan Bros. Inc. v. Cont'l Cas. Corp., 704 F. Supp. 2d 537, 539 (E.D. Va. 2010).

[394] Bryan Bros. Inc. v. Cont'l Cas. Corp., 704 F. Supp. 2d 537, 539 (E.D. Va. 2010), aff'd sub nom. Bryan Bros. Inc. v. Cont'l Cas. Co., 660 F.3d 827 (4th Cir. 2011), and aff'd sub nom. Bryan Bros. Inc. v. Cont'l Cas. Co., 419 F. App'x 422 (4th Cir. 2011).

[395] Bryan Bros. Inc. v. Cont'l Cas. Corp., 704 F. Supp. 2d 537, 540 (E.D. Va. 2010), aff'd sub nom. Bryan Bros. Inc. v. Cont'l Cas. Co., 660 F.3d 827 (4th Cir. 2011), and aff'd sub nom. Bryan Bros. Inc. v. Cont'l Cas. Co., 419 F. App'x 422 (4th Cir. 2011).

[396] Bryan Bros. Inc. v. Cont'l Cas. Corp., 704 F. Supp. 2d 537, 540–41 (E.D. Va. 2010), aff'd sub nom. Bryan Bros. Inc. v. Cont'l Cas. Co., 660 F.3d 827 (4th Cir. 2011), and aff'd sub nom. Bryan Bros. Inc. v. Cont'l Cas. Co., 419 F. App'x 422 (4th Cir. 2011).

[397] Bryan Bros. Inc. v. Cont'l Cas. Corp., 704 F. Supp. 2d 537, 541 (E.D. Va. 2010), aff'd sub nom. Bryan Bros. Inc. v. Cont'l Cas. Co., 660 F.3d 827 (4th Cir. 2011), and aff'd sub nom. Bryan Bros. Inc. v. Cont'l Cas. Co., 419 F. App'x 422 (4th Cir. 2011).

[398] Bryan Bros. Inc. v. Cont'l Cas. Corp., 704 F. Supp. 2d 537, 542

(E.D. Va. 2010), aff'd sub nom. Bryan Bros. Inc. v. Cont'l Cas. Co., 660 F.3d 827 (4th Cir. 2011), and aff'd sub nom. Bryan Bros. Inc. v. Cont'l Cas. Co., 419 F. App'x 422 (4th Cir. 2011).

[399] Bryan Bros. Inc. v. Cont'l Cas. Corp., 704 F. Supp. 2d 537, 544 (E.D. Va. 2010), aff'd sub nom. Bryan Bros. Inc. v. Cont'l Cas. Co., 660 F.3d 827 (4th Cir. 2011), and aff'd sub nom. Bryan Bros. Inc. v. Cont'l Cas. Co., 419 F. App'x 422 (4th Cir. 2011).

[400] Joseph E Brunsman & Daniel W Hudson, *Should CPA Firms Be Worried about Data Breach Claims?: Hurdles to Establishing Standing and Demonstrating Economic Viability*, THE CPA JOURNAL, 2019, at 16–18.

[401] CNA Policy CAN-87510XX (11-16) CPA NetProtect Endorsement

[402] CNA Policy CAN-87510XX (11-16) CPA NetProtect Endorsement

[403] CNA Policy CAN-87510XX (11-16) CPA NetProtect Endorsement

[404] Average demanded ransom from ransomware attacks 2017 | Statistic, STATISTA (2017), https://www.statista.com/statistics/701003/average-amount-of-ransom-requested-to-msp-clients/ (last visited Apr 7, 2019).

[405] CNA Policy CAN-87510XX (11-16) CPA NetProtect Endorsement

[406] Authors' review of over 15 Accountants Professional Liability Insurance policy endorsements

[407] ROBERT H. JERRY & DOUGLAS R. RICHMOND, UNDERSTANDING INSURANCE LAW 128 (2018).

[408] Employment Practices Liability Insurance (EPLI) Policies and Coverage, Practical Law Practice Note w-006-7127

[409] Kevin LaCroix, Fifth Circuit Reverses Dismissal of Data Breach Coverage Suit Against D&O Insurer (2018), The D&O Diary, https://www.dandodiary.com/2018/07/articles/d-o-insurance/fifth-circuit-reverses-dismissal-data-breach-coverage-suit-insurer/, (last visited Jul 7, 2019).

[410] Spec's Family Partners, Ltd. v. Hanover Ins. Co., 739 F. App'x 233, 234 (5th Cir. 2018)

[411] Spec's Family Partners, Ltd. v. Hanover Ins. Co., 739 F. App'x

233, 234–35 (5th Cir. 2018)

[412] Spec's Family Partners, Ltd. v. Hanover Ins. Co., 739 F. App'x 233, 236 (5th Cir. 2018)

[413] Spec's Family Partners, Ltd. v. Hanover Ins. Co., 739 F. App'x 233, 236 (5th Cir. 2018)

[414] Spec's Family Partners, Ltd. v. Hanover Ins. Co., 739 F. App'x 233, 235–36 (5th Cir. 2018)

[415] Spec's Family Partners, Ltd. v. Hanover Ins. Co., 739 F. App'x 233, 236 (5th Cir. 2018)

[416] Spec's Family Partners, Ltd. v. Hanover Ins. Co., 739 F. App'x 233, 240 (5th Cir. 2018)

[417] Spec's Family Partners, Ltd. v. Hanover Ins. Co., 739 F. App'x 233, 239 (5th Cir. 2018)

[418] Kevin LaCroix, Fifth Circuit Reverses Dismissal of Data Breach Coverage Suit Against D&O Insurer (2018), The D&O Diary, https://www.dandodiary.com/2018/07/articles/d-o-insurance/fifth-circuit-reverses-dismissal-data-breach-coverage-suit-insurer/, (last visited Jul 7, 2019).

[419] § 14:24.Technology Errors and Omissions Liability ("Tech E&O"), 2 Data Sec. & Privacy Law § 14:24 (2018)

[420] Sasha Romanosky et al., *Content analysis of cyber insurance policies: how do carriers price cyber risk?*, 5 JOURNAL OF CYBERSECURITY 5 (2019), https://academic.oup.com/cybersecurity/article/5/1/tyz002/5366419.

[421] Lloyd's Annual Report 2017, https://www.lloyds.com/~/media/files/lloyds/investor-relations/results/2017ar/ar2017_annual-report-2017.pdf, (last visited Jul 9, 2019).

[422] See Hiscox Pro Privacy Pre-Priced Application PLPPVY A0001 (11/15) for Conditional Terms and Quotes.

[423] Sasha Romanosky et al., *Content analysis of cyber insurance policies: how do carriers price cyber risk?*, 5 JOURNAL OF CYBERSECURITY 16-18 (2019), https://academic.oup.com/cybersecurity/article/5/1/tyz002/5366419.

[424] Sasha Romanosky et al., *Content analysis of cyber insurance policies: how do carriers price cyber risk?*, 5 JOURNAL OF CYBERSECURITY 18-19 (2019), https://academic.oup.com/cybersecurity/article/5/1/tyz002/5366419.

[425] Sasha Romanosky et al., *Content analysis of cyber insurance policies: how do carriers price cyber risk?*, 5 JOURNAL OF CYBERSECURITY 19-20 (2019), https://academic.oup.com/cybersecurity/article/5/1/tyz002/5366419.

[426] Sasha Romanosky et al., *Content analysis of cyber insurance policies: how do carriers price cyber risk?*, 5 JOURNAL OF CYBERSECURITY 19-20 (2019), https://academic.oup.com/cybersecurity/article/5/1/tyz002/5366419.

[427] Sasha Romanosky et al., *Content analysis of cyber insurance policies: how do carriers price cyber risk?*, 5 JOURNAL OF CYBERSECURITY 20 (2019), https://academic.oup.com/cybersecurity/article/5/1/tyz002/5366419.

[428] Columbia Casualty Company, Plaintiff, v. Cottage Health System, Defendant., 2015 WL 2393298 (C.D.Cal.)

[429] Columbia Casualty Company, Plaintiff, v. Cottage Health System, Defendant., 2015 WL 2393298 (C.D.Cal.)

[430] Kenneth RICE, individually, and on behalf of all others similarly situated, Plaintiffs, v. INSYNC, an unknown type of corporation, Cottage Health System, a California corporation; Santa Barbara Cottage Hospital, a California corporation, Goleta Valley Cottage Hospital, a california Corporation, and Santa Ynez Valley Hospital, and Does 1-100, Inclusive, Defendants., 2014 WL 358703 (Cal.Super.)

[431] Columbia Casualty Company, Plaintiff, v. Cottage Health System, Defendant., 2015 WL 2393298 (C.D.Cal.)

[432] Columbia Casualty Company, Plaintiff, v. Cottage Health System, Defendant., 2015 WL 2393298 (C.D.Cal.)

[433] Columbia Casualty Company, Plaintiff, v. Cottage Health System, Defendant., 2015 WL 2393298 (C.D.Cal.)

[434] Columbia Casualty Company, Plaintiff, v. Cottage Health System, Defendant., 2015 WL 2393298 (C.D.Cal.)

[435] Columbia Casualty Company, Plaintiff, v. Cottage Health System, Defendant., 2015 WL 2393298 (C.D.Cal.)

[436] Columbia Casualty Company, Plaintiff, v. Cottage Health System, Defendant., 2015 WL 2393298 (C.D.Cal.)

[437] Columbia Casualty Company, Plaintiff, v. Cottage Health System, Defendant., 2015 WL 2393298 (C.D.Cal.)

[438] Columbia Casualty Company, Plaintiff, v. Cottage Health

System, Defendant., 2015 WL 2393298 (C.D.Cal.)
[439] Columbia Casualty Company, Plaintiff, v. Cottage Health System, Defendant., 2015 WL 2393298 (C.D.Cal.)
[440] Columbia Cas. Co. v. Cottage Health Sys., No. CV1503432DDPAGRX, 2015 WL 4497730, at *1 (C.D. Cal. July 17, 2015)
[441] P.F. Chang's China Bistro, Inc. v. Fed. Ins. Co., No. CV-15-01322-PHX-SMM, 2016 WL 3055111, at *1 (D. Ariz. May 31, 2016)
[442] P.F. Chang's China Bistro, Inc. v. Fed. Ins. Co., No. CV-15-01322-PHX-SMM, 2016 WL 3055111, at *1 (D. Ariz. May 31, 2016)
[443] P.F. Chang's China Bistro, Inc. v. Fed. Ins. Co., No. CV-15-01322-PHX-SMM, 2016 WL 3055111, at *2 (D. Ariz. May 31, 2016)
[444] P.F. Chang's China Bistro, Inc. v. Fed. Ins. Co., No. CV-15-01322-PHX-SMM, 2016 WL 3055111, at *2 (D. Ariz. May 31, 2016)
[445] P.F. Chang's China Bistro, Inc. v. Fed. Ins. Co., No. CV-15-01322-PHX-SMM, 2016 WL 3055111, at *4 (D. Ariz. May 31, 2016)
[446] P.F. Chang's China Bistro, Inc. v. Fed. Ins. Co., No. CV-15-01322-PHX-SMM, 2016 WL 3055111, at *9 (D. Ariz. May 31, 2016)
[447] P.F. Chang's China Bistro, Inc. v. Fed. Ins. Co., No. CV-15-01322-PHX-SMM, 2016 WL 3055111, at *9 (D. Ariz. May 31, 2016)
[448] Mondelez International, Inc., Plaintiff, v. Zurich American Insurance Company, Defendant., 2018 WL 4941760 (Ill.Cir.Ct.)
[449] Mondelez International, Inc., Plaintiff, v. Zurich American Insurance Company, Defendant., 2018 WL 4941760 (Ill.Cir.Ct.)
[450] Mondelez International, Inc., Plaintiff, v. Zurich American Insurance Company, Defendant., 2018 WL 4941760 (Ill.Cir.Ct.)
[451] Mondelez International, Inc., Plaintiff, v. Zurich American Insurance Company, Defendant., 2018 WL 4941760 (Ill.Cir.Ct.)
[452] Mondelez International, Inc., Plaintiff, v. Zurich American Insurance Company, Defendant., 2018 WL 4941760 (Ill.Cir.Ct.)
[453] Mondelez International, Inc., Plaintiff, v. Zurich American

Insurance Company, Defendant., 2018 WL 4941760 (Ill.Cir.Ct.)

[454] Mondelez International, Inc., Plaintiff, v. Zurich American Insurance Company, Defendant., 2018 WL 4941760 (Ill.Cir.Ct.)

[455] See Addison Insurance Co. v. Fay, 232 Ill.2d 446, 453–54, 328 Ill.Dec. 858, 905 N.E.2d 747 (2009)

[456] Statement from the Press Secretary, THE WHITE HOUSE (2018), https://www.whitehouse.gov/briefings-statements/statement-press-secretary-25/ (last visited Apr 8, 2019).

[457] Cybersecurity Insurance Workshop Readout Report, (2012), https://www.dhs.gov/sites/default/files/publications/November 2012 Cybersecurity Insurance Workshop.pdf (last visited Feb 2019).

[458] Hiscox Policy PLP P0004 CW (06/14)

[459] Hiscox Policy PLP P0004 CW (06/14)

[460] Axis Policy PBR-0300 (05-11)

[461] Axis Policy PBR-0300 (05-11)

[462] Thomas H. Bentz, Jr., Is Your Cyber Liability Insurance Any Good? A Guide for Banks to Evaluate Their Cyber Liability Insurance Coverage, 21 N.C. Banking Inst. 39 (2017)

[463] Thomas H. Bentz, Jr., Is Your Cyber Liability Insurance Any Good? A Guide for Banks to Evaluate Their Cyber Liability Insurance Coverage, 21 N.C. Banking Inst. 39 (2017)

[464] Beazley Policy F00654 112017 ed.

[465] Hiscox Policy PLP D0001 CW (04/14)

[466] 2018 Cost of a Data Breach Study: Global Overview, IBM SECURITY, available at: https://www.ibm.com (last visited Mar 2019).

[467] Camp's Grocery, Inc. v. State Farm Fire & Cas. Co., No. 4:16-CV-0204-JEO, 2016 WL 6217161, at *1 (N.D. Ala. Oct. 25, 2016)

[468] Camp's Grocery, Inc. v. State Farm Fire & Cas. Co., No. 4:16-CV-0204-JEO, 2016 WL 6217161, at *1 (N.D. Ala. Oct. 25, 2016)

[469] Camp's Grocery, Inc. v. State Farm Fire & Cas. Co., No. 4:16-CV-0204-JEO, 2016 WL 6217161, at *1 (N.D. Ala. Oct. 25, 2016)

[470] Camp's Grocery, Inc. v. State Farm Fire & Cas. Co., No. 4:16-CV-0204-JEO, 2016 WL 6217161, at *5 (N.D. Ala. Oct. 25, 2016)

[471] Camp's Grocery, Inc. v. State Farm Fire & Cas. Co., No. 4:16-CV-0204-JEO, 2016 WL 6217161, at *6 (N.D. Ala. Oct. 25, 2016)

[472] New Hotel Monteleone, Llc, V. Certain Underwriters at Lloyd's

Of London, Subscribing to Ascent Cyperpro Policy No.
ASC14C000944, and Eustis Insurance, Inc., 2016 WL 109835
[473] New Hotel Monteleone, Llc, V. Certain Underwriters at Lloyd's
Of London, Subscribing to Ascent Cyperpro Policy No.
ASC14C000944, and Eustis Insurance, Inc., 2016 WL 109835
[474] New Hotel Monteleone, Llc, V. Certain Underwriters at Lloyd's
Of London, Subscribing to Ascent Cyperpro Policy No.
ASC14C000944, and Eustis Insurance, Inc., 2016 WL 109835
[475] New Hotel Monteleone, Llc, V. Certain Underwriters at Lloyd's
Of London, Subscribing to Ascent Cyperpro Policy No.
ASC14C000944, and Eustis Insurance, Inc., 2016 WL 109835
[476] New Hotel Monteleone, Llc, V. Certain Underwriters at Lloyd's
Of London, Subscribing to Ascent Cyperpro Policy No.
ASC14C000944, and Eustis Insurance, Inc., 2016 WL 109835
[477] New Hotel Monteleone, Llc, V. Certain Underwriters at Lloyd's
Of London, Subscribing to Ascent Cyperpro Policy No.
ASC14C000944, and Eustis Insurance, Inc., 2016 WL 109835
[478] New Hotel Monteleone, Llc, V. Certain Underwriters at Lloyd's
Of London, Subscribing to Ascent Cyperpro Policy No.
ASC14C000944, and Eustis Insurance, Inc., 2016 WL 109835
[479] New Hotel Monteleone, Llc, V. Certain Underwriters at Lloyd's
Of London, Subscribing to Ascent Cyperpro Policy No.
ASC14C000944, and Eustis Insurance, Inc., 2016 WL 109835
(E.D.La.)
[480] See National Union Fire Ins. Co. of Pittsburgh v. Willis, 139
F.Supp.2d 827, 832 (S.D.Tex.2001), aff'd, 296 F.3d 336, 339 (5th
Cir.2002)
[481] Robert H. Jerry & Douglas R. Richmond, Understanding
Insurance Law 579-581 (2018).
[482] Cyber Insurance: Insuring for Data Breach Risk, Practical Law
Practice Note 2-588-8785
[483] 2018 Cost of a Data Breach Study: Global Overview, IBM
SECURITY, available at: https://www.ibm.com (last visited Mar
2019).
[484] *Remijas v. Neiman Marcus Grp., LLC*, 794 F.3d 688, 696 (7th
Cir. 2015)
[485] Beck v. McDonald, 848 F.3d 262, 276 (4th Cir.), cert. denied sub
nom. Beck v. Shulkin, 137 S. Ct. 2307, 198 L. Ed. 2d 728 (2017)

[486]Sasha Romanosky et al., *Content analysis of cyber insurance policies: how do carriers price cyber risk?*, 14 – Footnote 24 JOURNAL OF CYBERSECURITY 5 (2019), https://academic.oup.com/cybersecurity/article/5/1/tyz002/5366419.

[487] Robert H. Jerry & Douglas R. Richmond, Understanding Insurance Law 422-427 (2018).

[488] Hiscox Pro Policy PLP P0004 CW (06/14) at 4.

[489] Hiscox Pro Policy PLP P0004 CW (06/14) at 4.

[490] Public Statement - Network and Service Interruptions (2019), Wolters Kluwer, https://wolterskluwer.com/company/newsroom/news/2019/05/media-statement---network-and-service-interruptions.html, (last visited Oct 6, 2019).

[491] Public Statement - Network and Service Interruptions (2019), Wolters Kluwer, https://wolterskluwer.com/company/newsroom/news/2019/05/media-statement---network-and-service-interruptions.html, (last visited Oct 6, 2019).

[492] Hiscox CyberClear Policy form: TPCCYB P0001 CW (05/16)

[493] Hiscox CyberClear Policy form: TPCCYB P0001 CW (05/16)

[494] Robert H. Jerry & Douglas R. Richmond, Understanding Insurance Law 982 (2018).

[495] CFC Cyber Private enterprise policy form v2.1

[496] Hiscox Pro Policy Form, New Jersey Amendatory Endorsement, PLP E9027 NJ (07/14)

[497] Robert H. Jerry & Douglas R. Richmond, Understanding Insurance Law 738 (2018).

[498] Paul A. Grassi *et al.*, Nist Special Publication 800-63b: Digital Identity Guidelines - Authentication And Lifecycle Management Nist Special Publication 800-63b: Digital Identity Guidelines - Authentication And Lifecycle Management

(2017), https://pages.nist.gov/800-63-3/sp800-63b.html#sec3, (last visited Sep 7, 2019).

[499] Paul Cichonski, *et al.*, Special Publication 800-61 Revision 2: Computer Security Incident Handling Guide, National Institute of Standards and Technology – U.S. Department of Commerce, https://nvlpubs.nist.gov/nistpubs/SpecialPublications/NIST.SP.800-61r2.pdf, (last visited Sep 7, 2019).

[500] NIST Cybersecurity Framework Adoption Hampered By Costs, Survey Finds, DARK READING (2016), https://www.darkreading.com/attacks-breaches/nist-cybersecurity-framework-adoption-hampered-by-costs-survey-finds/d/d-id/1324901 (last visited Oct 15, 2018).

[501] The NIST Cybersecurity Framework, Practical Law Practice Note 5-599-6825 (West)

[502] The NIST Cybersecurity Framework and the FTC, FEDERAL TADE COMMISSION (2017), https://www.ftc.gov/news-events/audio-video/video/nist-cybersecurity-framework-ftc (last visited Oct 18, 2018).

[503] OHIO REV. CODE ANN. §1354.01-05 (West 2018)

[504] OHIO REV. CODE ANN. §1354.01-05 (West 2018)

[505] OHIO REV. CODE ANN. §1354.01-05 (West 2018)

[506] Exec. Order No. 13800, 82 FR 22391, 2017 WL 2062698(Pres.)

[507] The NIST Cybersecurity Framework at 8, https://nvlpubs.nist.gov/nistpubs/CSWP/NIST.CSWP.04162018.

[508] The NIST Cybersecurity Framework at 9, https://nvlpubs.nist.gov/nistpubs/CSWP/NIST.CSWP.04162018.

[509] The NIST Cybersecurity Framework at 9, https://nvlpubs.nist.gov/nistpubs/CSWP/NIST.CSWP.04162018.

[510] The NIST Cybersecurity Framework at 10, https://nvlpubs.nist.gov/nistpubs/CSWP/NIST.CSWP.04162018.

[511] The NIST Cybersecurity Framework at 10, https://nvlpubs.nist.gov/nistpubs/CSWP/NIST.CSWP.04162018.

[512] Nicole Keller, AN INTRODUCTION TO THE COMPONENTS OF THE FRAMEWORK NIST (2018), https://www.nist.gov/cyberframework/online-learning/components-framework (last visited Apr 16, 2019).

[513] The NIST Cybersecurity Framework at 7, https://nvlpubs.nist.gov/nistpubs/CSWP/NIST.CSWP.04162018.pdf

[514] The NIST Cybersecurity Framework at 8, https://nvlpubs.nist.gov/nistpubs/CSWP/NIST.CSWP.04162018.pdf

[515] The NIST Cybersecurity Framework at 7, https://nvlpubs.nist.gov/nistpubs/CSWP/NIST.CSWP.04162018.pdf

[516] The NIST Cybersecurity Framework at 38-39, https://nvlpubs.nist.gov/nistpubs/CSWP/NIST.CSWP.04162018.pdf

[517] The NIST Cybersecurity Framework at 18,

https://nvlpubs.nist.gov/nistpubs/CSWP/NIST.CSWP.04162018.pdf

[518] Managing Enterprise Risks in a Digital World: Privacy, Cybersecurity, and Compliance Collide Baker Hostetler (2019), BakerHostetler, https://f.datasrvr.com/fr1/019/33725/2019_BakerHostetler_DSIR_Final.pdf, (last visited Oct 6, 2019)

[519] Lindsey HOWARD, individually and on behalf of all others similarly situated, Plaintiff, v. CITRIX SYSTEMS, INC., Defendant., 2019 WL 2263036 (S.D.Fla.)

[520] Lindsey Howard, individually and on behalf of all others similarly situated, Plaintiff, v. Citrix Systems, Inc., Defendant., 2019 WL 2263036 (S.D.Fla.)

[521] Lindsey Howard, individually and on behalf of all others similarly situated, Plaintiff, v. Citrix Systems, Inc., Defendant., 2019 WL 2263036 (S.D.Fla.)

[522] Lindsey HOWARD, individually and on behalf of all others similarly situated, Plaintiff, v. CITRIX SYSTEMS, INC., Defendant., 2019 WL 2263036 (S.D.Fla.)

[523] U.S. Dep't of Homeland Security, Alert (TA18-086A): Brute Force Attacks Conducted by Cyber Actors (Mar. 27, 2018, last revised March 28, 2018), available at: https://www.us-cert.gov/ncas/alerts/TA18-086A (last visited June 3, 2019).

[524] Lindsey HOWARD, individually and on behalf of all others similarly situated, Plaintiff, v. CITRIX SYSTEMS, INC., Defendant., 2019 WL 2263036 (S.D.Fla.)

[525] Lindsey HOWARD, individually and on behalf of all others similarly situated, Plaintiff, v. CITRIX SYSTEMS, INC., Defendant., 2019 WL 2263036 (S.D.Fla.)

[526] Lindsey HOWARD, individually and on behalf of all others similarly situated, Plaintiff, v. CITRIX SYSTEMS, INC., Defendant., 2019 WL 2263036 (S.D.Fla.)

[527] Lindsey HOWARD, individually and on behalf of all others similarly situated, Plaintiff, v. CITRIX SYSTEMS, INC., Defendant., 2019 WL 2263036 (S.D.Fla.)

[528] Lindsey HOWARD, individually and on behalf of all others similarly situated, Plaintiff, v. CITRIX SYSTEMS, INC., Defendant., 2019 WL 2263036 (S.D.Fla.)

[529] About: Overview, Cloud Security Alliance, https://cloudsecurityalliance.org/about/, (last visited Oct 07, 2019).
[530] Working Group: Cloud Controls Matrix; Introduction, https://cloudsecurityalliance.org/working-groups/cloud-controls-matrix/#_overview, (last visited Oct 07, 2019).
[531] Security Guidance for Critical Areas of Focus in Cloud Computing V3.0 (2011), Cloud Security Alliance, https://downloads.cloudsecurityalliance.org/assets/research/security-guidance/csaguide.v3.0.pdf, (last visited Oct 07, 2019).
[532] In the Matter of Gmr Transcription Servs., Inc., A Corp., Ajay Prasad & Shreekant Srivastava, Individually & As Officers of Gmr Transcription Servs., Inc., 2015-1 Trade Cas. (CCH) 17070 (MSNET Aug. 14, 2014)
[533] In the Matter of Gmr Transcription Servs., Inc., A Corp., Ajay Prasad & Shreekant Srivastava, Individually & As Officers of Gmr Transcription Servs., Inc., 2015-1 Trade Cas. (CCH) 17070 (MSNET Aug. 14, 2014)
[534] In the Matter of Gmr Transcription Servs., Inc., A Corp., Ajay Prasad & Shreekant Srivastava, Individually & As Officers of Gmr Transcription Servs., Inc., 2015-1 Trade Cas. (CCH) 17070 (MSNET Aug. 14, 2014)
[535] In the Matter of Gmr Transcription Servs., Inc., A Corp., Ajay Prasad & Shreekant Srivastava, Individually & As Officers of Gmr Transcription Servs., Inc., 2015-1 Trade Cas. (CCH) 17070 (MSNET Aug. 14, 2014)
[536] Written Information security Program (WISP), Practical Law Standard Document w-001-0073
[537] Developing Information security Policies, Practical Law Practice Note w-001-1336
[538] Markel Cambridge Alliance, Safeguarding Client Information And Avoiding Wire Fraud. (n.d) retrieved January 2016, from Markel Cambridge Alliance Web Site: http://www.markelinsurance.com/risk-management-home/msc-articles/investment-advisors/safeguarding-client-information-and-avioiding-wire-fraud
[539] U.S. Securities and Exchange Commission, (2015, September, 22). *SEC Charges Investment Adviser With Failing to Adopt Proper Cybersecurity Policies and Procedures Prior To Breach.* retrieved

December 2015, from SEC Web Site:
http://www.sec.gov/news/pressrelease/2015-202.html

[540] Cipriani, J. (2015, June, 15). *Two-factor authentication: What you need to know (FAQ)*. retrieved December 2015, from c|net Web Site: http://www.cnet.com/news/two-factor-authentication-what-you-need-to-know-faq/

[541] Coutin, C. (2015, August, 13). *Educating Clients About Cyber Security Should Be Part of Your Role as an RIA*. retrieved September 13 2015, from Morningstar: ByAllAccounts Web Site: http://byallaccounts.morningstar.com/blog/586-educating-clients-about-cyber-security-should-be-part-of-your-role-as-an-ria.html

[542] Ameriforge Group, Inc., a Texas corporation d/b/a AFGlobal Corporation, Plaintiff, v. Federal Insurance Company, an Indiana corporation admitted to conduct insurance business in Texas, including Chubb & Son, a Division of Federal Insurance Company, Defendant., 2016 WL 1391493 (S.D.Tex.)

[543] Ameriforge Group, Inc., a Texas corporation d/b/a AFGlobal Corporation, Plaintiff, v. Federal Insurance Company, an Indiana corporation admitted to conduct insurance business in Texas, including Chubb & Son, a Division of Federal Insurance Company, Defendant., 2016 WL 1391493 (S.D.Tex.)

[544] Ameriforge Group, Inc., a Texas corporation d/b/a AFGlobal Corporation, Plaintiff, v. Federal Insurance Company, an Indiana corporation admitted to conduct insurance business in Texas, including Chubb & Son, a Division of Federal Insurance Company, Defendant., 2016 WL 1391493 (S.D.Tex.)

[545] Ameriforge Group, Inc., a Texas corporation d/b/a AFGlobal Corporation, Plaintiff, v. Federal Insurance Company, an Indiana corporation admitted to conduct insurance business in Texas, including Chubb & Son, a Division of Federal Insurance Company, Defendant., 2016 WL 1391493 (S.D.Tex.)

[546] Ameriforge Group, Inc., a Texas corporation d/b/a AFGlobal Corporation, Plaintiff, v. Federal Insurance Company, an Indiana corporation admitted to conduct insurance business in Texas, including Chubb & Son, a Division of Federal Insurance Company, Defendant., 2016 WL 1391493 (S.D.Tex.)

[547] Ameriforge Group, Inc., a Texas corporation d/b/a AFGlobal Corporation, Plaintiff, v. Federal Insurance Company, an Indiana

corporation admitted to conduct insurance business in Texas, including Chubb & Son, a Division of Federal Insurance Company, Defendant., 2016 WL 1391493 (S.D.Tex.)
[548] Ameriforge Group, Inc., a Texas corporation d/b/a AFGlobal Corporation, Plaintiff, v. Federal Insurance Company, an Indiana corporation admitted to conduct insurance business in Texas, including Chubb & Son, a Division of Federal Insurance Company, Defendant., 2016 WL 1391493 (S.D.Tex.)
[549] Ameriforge Group, Inc., a Texas corporation d/b/a AFGlobal Corporation, Plaintiff, v. Federal Insurance Company, an Indiana corporation admitted to conduct insurance business in Texas, including Chubb & Son, a Division of Federal Insurance Company, Defendant., 2016 WL 2728739 (S.D.Tex.)
[550] Ameriforge Group, Inc., a Texas corporation d/b/a AFGlobal Corporation, Plaintiff, v. Federal Insurance Company, an Indiana corporation admitted to conduct insurance business in Texas, including Chubb & Son, a Division of Federal Insurance Company, Defendant., 2016 WL 2728739 (S.D.Tex.)

Made in the USA
Columbia, SC
16 January 2020

86857260R00271